THE DIABETIC BODY

AN OWNER'S MANUAL

Timothy Gower

Consultants
Dana Armstrong, R.D., C.D.E., and
Allen Bennett King, M.D., F.A.C.P., F.A.C.E., C.D.E.

Publications International, Ltd.

Timothy Gower is a freelance writer and the author of several books. His work has appeared in many magazines and newspapers, including *Prevention, Health, Reader's Digest, Better Homes and Gardens, Men's Health, Esquire, Fortune, The New York Times,* and *The Los Angeles Times.*

Dana Armstrong, R.D., C.D.E., received her degree in nutrition and dietetics from the University of California, Davis, and completed her dietetic internship at the University of Nebraska Medical Center in Omaha. In private practice for 21 years, she has developed educational programs that have benefited more than 5,000 patients with diabetes. She is the cofounder and program director of the Diabetes Care Center in Salinas, California. She specializes in and speaks nationally on approaches to disease treatment, specifically diabetes. Having a child with diabetes, she combines her professional knowledge with personal experience and understanding.

Allen Bennett King, M.D., F.A.C.P., F.A.C.E., C.D.E., received his degrees and training at the University of California, Berkeley; Creighton University Medical School; the University of Colorado Medical Center; and Stanford University Medical Center. He is the author of more than 50 papers in medical science and speaks nationally on new advances in diabetes. During his 32 years of practice, he has seen more than 7,000 patients with diabetes, some for more than 25 years. He is an associate clinical professor at the University of California Natividad Medical Center and cofounder and medical director of the Diabetes Care Center in Salinas, California. He is the son of Earle King, who died in 1978 from the complications of diabetes.

Jeff Moores received his BFA in illustration from Parsons School of Design in New York City. In 9th grade, he started his own T-shirt business, which led to a career in illustration. He never had a boss (except for his wife, Dawn, and kids Charlie, 15, and Sam, 13). They now live happily on Honeoye Lake, NY. Please visit his Web site: www.jeffmoores.com.

Acknowledgments:

Page 263: Chart adapted from *Diabetes Care,* Vol. 27, 2004; 998–1070. Copyright © 2004 American Diabetes Association. Reprinted with permission from The American Diabetes Association.

Page 264: Chart adapted from *Diabetes Care,* Vol. 28, 2005; 186–212. Copyright © 2005 American Diabetes Association. Reprinted with permission from The American Diabetes Association.

Louis Weber, CEO
Publications International, Ltd.
7373 North Cicero Avenue
Lincolnwood, Illinois 60712

Permission is never granted for commercial purposes.

ISBN-13: 978-1-4127-1304-7

ISBN-10: 1-4127-1304-8

Manufactured in China.

8 7 6 5 4 3 2 1

Library of Congress Control Number: 2006933328

Contents

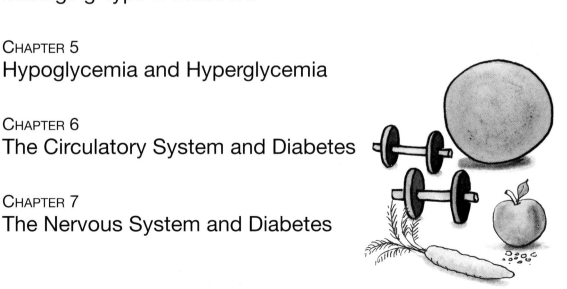

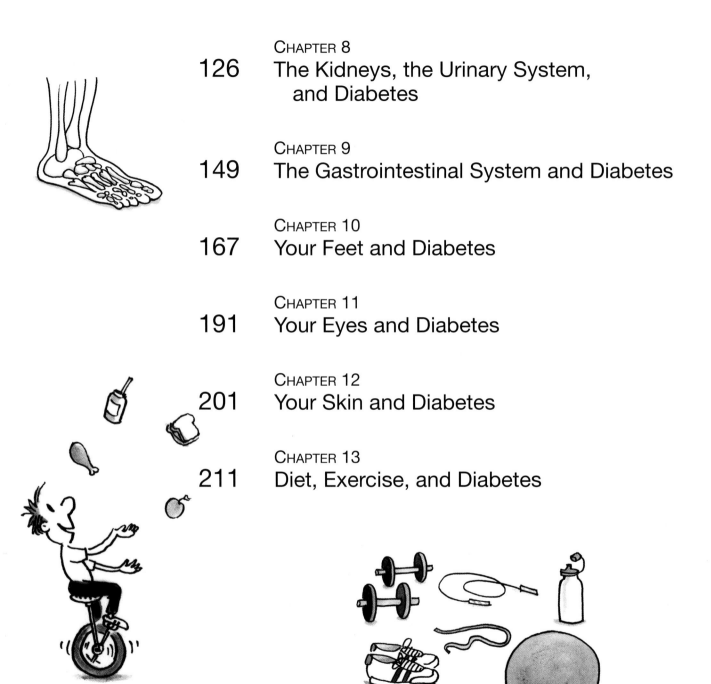

Introduction

The typical owner's manual reads as though it were written by a grammar-challenged engineer. Or worse—a lawyer. Do you really need to be warned not to use your new toaster oven while bathing? And couldn't you have figured out which end of the chainsaw to hold while operating?

But while you may feel confident enough to run your new weed whacker or electric cheese grater without reading the user's guide, coping with diabetes isn't like trimming the lawn or shredding a little parmesan for your pasta. If only that were the case! Instead, managing diabetes is a big, complex, ongoing job. Unlike most other medical conditions, the disease affects every major organ system in the body. You may already know some of the ways diabetes can damage your health, such as its potentially devastating impact on eyesight. But did you realize it can lead to skin disorders? Stomach problems? Even heart attacks?

In other words, diabetes can interfere with the structures and biological processes that allow you to live an active, independent life. As you probably know by now, the various forms of dysfunction and disability that diabetes can cause are known collectively as "complications." The purpose of this book, however, is simple: We want to *uncomplicate* diabetes and help you understand how to control the disease.

To make things *real* simple, we've organized the chapters according to these main topics:

- A diabetes primer that covers all the basics about the disease, such as what causes diabetes and how to monitor your blood sugar, along with the occasional bit of trivia. (How did a previously housetrained dog's "accident" change the course of diabetes treatment? Read on to find out.)
- Managing type 1 and type 2 diabetes with lifestyle changes and medication. You'll also learn how to sound smart around your pharmacist if you do indeed require medication.
- The major body systems and the diabetes complications that can impact them. Like any good user's guide, these chapters will introduce you to the affected body parts, show you how they're assembled, and offer tips on routine maintenance and troubleshooting.
- Lifestyle issues, examining in more detail the roles of diet and exercise, as well as sexual and psychological concerns.
- And a close-up look at some special circumstances, such as dealing with diabetes in pregnancy and caring for a child who has the disease.

Managing diabetes will always mean working closely with your doctor—and perhaps a diabetes educator, too. But, more than most other medical conditions, diabetes demands that you take charge of your own care. Since you can't call a tech support line whenever you have a question about dealing with diabetes (and who would want to wait on hold all that time, anyway?), this book will help you keep your diabetic body running smoothly for many more miles—and years—to come.

Diabetes: An Overview

Did you ever start watching a TV movie that was already half over and find yourself wondering "What the heck is going on?" Why would a hot dish like Harriet marry a chump like Hank? Who is Desiree, and why does the mention of her name make Boris twitch? What does Elmer the stable hand know about Priscilla's dark past?

Before you dip into the parts of this book that interest you most, get to know the plot and players by reading this chapter first. This overview of diabetes—what it is, how the disease develops, and other important information—will arm you with basic knowledge to help you manage the medical drama going on inside your body.

What Is Diabetes?

In the simplest terms, diabetes is an energy-production problem, also known as a metabolic disorder. If you have diabetes, your body can't efficiently use glucose, the body's main source of energy. It's not that you lack glucose. Unless you're fasting or are on the All-Beef-and-Butter diet, you've got plenty of glucose in your system from the carbohydrates that you eat. The problem is with getting the glucose into your cells, which need it to produce energy. The cells, for reasons we will explain, bar the door, preventing glucose from entering. Instead, the glucose floats around your bloodstream, slowly damaging everything in its path.

FUELING UP

Let's back up for a minute. To understand where the diabetic body goes awry, it will help to know how the body is supposed to process food and use it for energy. Humans can burn fat and protein as fuel, and in fact, muscle mass prefers fatty acids. But the body's preferred source of energy is carbohydrates, which break down into glucose. The brain prefers glucose for fuel.

Your seventh-grade teacher probably explained that carbohydrates are sugars and starches found in fruits, vegetables,

and grains, such as bread and rice. While that's true, it's hardly the whole picture, since soda pop, pizza, potato chips, cupcakes, and virtually any form of junk food you can think of are also packed with carbs. Clearly, some carbohydrate-rich foods are healthier than others. But once food has been digested, your body can't tell whether a carbohydrate came from a banana or a Baby Ruth. Carbohydrates all become glucose, regardless of their source.

SPECIFICATIONS

Quick facts about diabetes
(all numbers are estimates):

- 20.8 million Americans—7% of the population—have diabetes (diagnosed and undiagnosed cases)
- 6.2 million Americans have diabetes but don't know it
- 9.6 percent of Americans aged 20 years and older have diabetes
- 1.5 million new cases of diabetes are diagnosed each year in Americans aged 20 years and older

Insulin: the doorman

During digestion, your body converts carbohydrate into a form of sugar known as glucose, often referred to as blood sugar.

When you eat a meal that contains carbohydrate, the glucose is quickly absorbed by body cells. Some is immediately used for energy, while the rest is placed into short-term storage—in the form of glycogen—primarily in the liver and muscle mass. If you eat way more carbohydrate than you need for immediate energy and short-term reserve in the liver and muscles, your body will convert the glucose into fat, which it ships off for long-term storage, usually in the belly, butt, and thighs.

The body prefers to use alcohol for energy, then carbohydrate, and finally fat. When you eat a meal consisting of alcohol, carbohydrate, and fat, the body will first burn all the alcohol for energy, then all the carbohydrate. If the body's energy needs are met by the alcohol and carbohydrate, the fat will not be used. Instead, it will be stored.

If glucose could simply slip into your body's cells on its own, there would be no such thing as diabetes, and you could be out working in the garden or playing with the kids—or watching *Law & Order* reruns instead of reading this book. However, glucose needs assistance from a hormone called insulin, which acts like a doorman, unlocking cells so that glucose can enter and be used as fuel.

Insulin production is regulated by the pancreas, a five- or six-inch organ tucked under the stomach that looks sort of like a squished snail. The pancreas produces a pair of hormones that regulate glucose levels in the blood. Hormones are the body's expediters, zipping around from one organ to another, making things happen. When glucose levels begin to rise in the blood, the pancreas cranks out insulin to help get the glucose into the cells. When blood sugar levels drop too low, the pancreas produces glucagon, a hormone that travels to the liver with orders to convert some glycogen back into glucose, then release it into the blood. With these two hormones, the pancreas helps you maintain a stable level of blood sugar.

The Doormen Did It ... Or Didn't Do It

As mentioned earlier, people with diabetes don't lack for glucose—they have plenty of the stuff. The problem is with the doormen. In people with type 1 diabetes, these gatekeepers never show up for work. For people with type 2 diabetes, the doormen arrive for duty but can't figure out how to unlock the gate. The result is the same in both cases: Glucose can't enter cells.

Here is a closer look at the main forms of diabetes.

TYPE 1 DIABETES

If you have type 1 diabetes, the chances are pretty good that you have known it for a long time: Half of all people diagnosed with type 1 diabetes are younger than 20 years old. In fact, type 1 diabetes used to be called juvenile-onset diabetes, though doctors eventually decided that name is inaccurate since it can strike anyone, at any age. Another alternative name is insulin-dependent diabetes, since virtually all folks with type 1 require injections of the crucial hormone. Only about 5 to 10 percent of all people with diabetes have type 1 diabetes, making it far less common than type 2 diabetes.

Type 1 diabetes begins with a glitch in the immune system, the body's defense against bacteria, viruses, and other microscopic nasties that roam around inside your body, trying to make you sick. The immune system is a complex network of vessels, fluids, white blood cells, and proteins called antibodies that

TYPE 1 DIABETES: WHAT ARE THE ODDS?

A BABY BORN . . .	HAS THE FOLLOWING RISK FOR TYPE 1 DIABETES
To parents who do not have type 1 diabetes	1 in 300
To a mother 25 or older who has type 1 diabetes	1 in 100*
To a mother younger than 25 who has type 1 diabetes	1 in 25*
To a father who has type 1 diabetes	1 in 17*
To a mother and father who have type 1 diabetes	Between 1 in 10 and 1 in 4
With an identical twin who has type 1 diabetes	Between 1 in 4 and 1 in 2

If the parent developed type 1 diabetes before age 11, the risk is doubled.

patrol your innards, looking for things that don't belong. When your immune system detects a germ or anything else that is not recognized as part of the body, it fires off white blood cells and antibodies to engulf and destroy the intruder.

Unfortunately, in some people the immune system is guilty of friendly fire. It mistakes perfectly innocent and otherwise healthy body tissue for an enemy invader, attacking it with an onslaught of voracious immune cells. Depending on what part of the body your immune system attacks, the result can be one of many autoimmune diseases, which include rheumatoid arthritis, lupus, thyroiditis, and, yes, type 1 diabetes.

In the case of type 1 diabetes, your immune system unleashed an assault on the cells in your pancreas that make insulin, which are known as beta cells. As your beta cells died off, your insulin production slowed down, and it may have even stopped. Without sufficient amounts of insulin to control the amount of glucose in your blood, your blood glucose levels began to rise, causing symptoms of diabetes. The symptoms likely included

- an unquenchable thirst. You could guzzle an entire Super Big Gulp soda and still feel parched.

- a frequent need to urinate. Duh, you're probably thinking, of course I'll be racing for the bathroom if I'm drinking so much. But with type 1 diabetes your bladder may feel ready to burst whether you've been imbibing fluids or not.
- increased hunger. But don't worry about getting fat; see next item.
- sudden weight loss. Now you might

be thinking, *Do you mean I get to eat like a pig and lose a few pounds? Sign me up!* Not so fast. Type 1 diabetes causes weight loss because your body is more or less devouring itself. And you know that can't be good.

• unexplained fatigue. As in your whole body, not just your jaws from all that eating.

It's easy to see from these diverse symptoms just how important insulin is to the human body. When glucose has no way of entering your cells, the sugary substance starts to build up in the blood. Your body has to pull water out of the blood (increasing thirst) so that it can get rid of the excess glucose in the urine (which explains the frequent trips to the restroom). Your cells are screaming for fuel (triggering the "Let's order another pizza!" instinct in your brain). While they're waiting for more glucose, your cells switch to alternate sources of energy, so the body starts to run on fat. That's the reason you lose weight, but it's kind of like burning the furniture in the fireplace when you can't pay the heating bill. And the combination of high blood glucose levels and dehydration makes you feel tired.

Burning fat all day instead of glucose isn't just inefficient; it can be life threat-

ening if it goes on too long. As your body breaks down fat to use as energy, it produces leftover products called ketones. Does that word ring a bell? You may have heard of ketones and ketosis (the accumulation of ketones when fat is burned for energy) if you have tried the carbohydrate-hating Atkins diet. In his book *Dr. Atkins' Diet Revolution,* the late Robert Atkins, M.D., claimed that ketosis is "a signal for rejoicing . . . a state devoutly to be desired. . . ." Why? Because, according to Atkins, it means you're burning unsightly fat and shedding flab!

Obesity experts disagree whether intentionally triggering ketosis is a safe and effective weight-loss method, though many diet doctors insist that some people lose weight on the Atkins plan not because of metabolic trickery but because it's just another low-calorie diet. (Studies have failed to show that it's superior to other weight-loss approaches.)

What's not up for debate is whether high levels of ketones are dangerous for the person with diabetes. Normally, these compounds pass harmlessly from your system into urine to be excreted. But when carbohydrates are entirely removed from the diet—or when glu-

13

cose can't get into cells, as in advanced diabetes—ketones build up to toxic levels. At first your breath has a weird odor, like fruit-flavored paint thinner. But soon you become confused, short of breath, and nauseous. You feel dehydrated and lose your lunch. If you don't get medical attention ASAP, you slip into a coma from which you may never awaken.

Since you're taking care of your diabetes, you'll likely never have to worry about this condition, called ketoacidosis. However, monitoring ketones is part of managing diabetes, which you'll learn about later in this chapter.

TYPE 2 DIABETES

When your doctor uttered the words "You have type 2 diabetes," you were inducted into a fast-growing, nonexclusive club—a club no one wants to join. About 90 percent of all people with diabetes in the United States have type 2 diabetes. That adds up to more than 16 million Americans, or enough people to populate New York City—twice.

WELCOME TYPE 2 DIABETES 16,000,000 MEMBERS

Like type 1 diabetes, this condition used to go by other names, including non-insulin-dependent diabetes and adult-onset diabetes. How times change. Now it's clear that both of those terms are misnomers. Nearly one-third of people with type 2 diabetes require insulin injections, so a person with type 2 diabetes may indeed be insulin dependent. And type 2 isn't limited to adults, either. While most people who develop type 2 diabetes are over 35, more and more kids are turning up in doctors' offices with classic cases of type 2 diabetes, largely because more and more kids today are obese. As you read on, you'll learn why lugging around extra weight increases the risk for type 2 diabetes.

Unlike type 1 diabetes, type 2 diabetes is not an autoimmune disease. It typically begins with a phenomenon called insulin resistance, when cells throughout your body start to ignore insulin. The hormone comes knocking, but the doormen have trouble letting it in. The insulin may not be able to open the cell door, or it may require reinforcements in the form of extra-large gushes of insulin before the cells will open up. In either case, glucose builds up in the blood.

Insulin resistance causes no symptoms. It's not as though you can feel or hear

- increased hunger
- fatigue

However, type 2 diabetes often produces additional symptoms, such as
- cuts that take a long time to heal
- frequent infections (women often develop vaginitis, for example)
- blurry eyesight
- tingling or numbness in the hands and feet
- erectile dysfunction

glucose molecules crashing into your resistant, tightly closed cells. However, insulin resistance often sets the stage for type 2 diabetes. Bottom line: If you have type 2 diabetes, you almost certainly have insulin resistance.

It usually takes insulin resistance months or years to progress to type 2 diabetes, when beta cells become progressively incapable of meeting the demand for insulin. At that point, insulin levels in the blood rise, too, as the beta cells keep cranking out the hormone in an attempt to coax open stubborn cells.

People often dismiss the signs and symptoms or blame them on some other health problem. A few indicators of type 2 diabetes overlap with those experienced by type 1 patients, including
- constant thirst
- frequent need to urinate

In all likelihood, your body began to experience insulin resistance long before you were diagnosed with type 2 diabetes, especially if you have any of the latter five symptoms. Excess glucose in the blood interferes with white blood cells, which explains why cuts and sores take longer to heal. Meanwhile, germs snack on glucose, which makes them stronger, promoting more infections. Long-term exposure to glucose damages nerves, too, which can explain many other symptoms of type 2 diabetes.

While you may be able to live with these problems (some more readily than others), they should serve as a loud, clear warning that your out-of-control blood sugar is slowly trashing your body like a rowdy rock band wrecks a hotel room. Left untreated, type 2 diabetes—or any type of diabetes, for that matter—can lead to medical catastrophe. Later chapters examine the various ways diabetes can damage the body and what you can do about it.

GESTATIONAL DIABETES

You're stuck wearing maternity clothes. You miss having a glass of wine with dinner. You can't see your feet when you stand up. And now you find out that your pregnancy is causing diabetes? That's the frustrating news for an estimated three to seven percent of expectant mothers who learn they have developed gestational diabetes.

Gestational diabetes accounts for about three percent of all cases of diabetes. However, it usually doesn't arise until after 20 weeks of pregnancy. Any pregnant woman can develop gestational

DIABETES: A BRIEF (AND ONLY SLIGHTLY DISGUSTING) HISTORY

Papyrus documents unearthed in Egypt that appear to be medical records, dating back to 1552 B.C., mention patients with symptoms that sound like diabetes. In the first century A.D., a doctor named Aretaeus in Asia Minor (now part of Turkey) noticed that some of his patients were weak and constantly thirsty, and they needed to urinate a lot. It seemed to him that something

was causing fluids to be drawn out of their bodies, so he called the condition *diabetes,* which is the Greek word for "siphon."

An 11th century Arab physician, Avicenna, fine-tuned the diagnosis when he discovered that people with diabetes produced what he called—and we're not making this up—"wonderfully sweet" urine. Which raises the inevitable question: How did he scientifically verify *that*? He did it the same way wine lovers detect hints of blackberry and plum in a glass of cabernet sauvignon: He tasted it. (We're hoping he gargled before going home and kissing Mrs. Avicenna.)

Centuries later, a similarly brave and selfless British physician detected notes of clover in the urine of his diabetic patients and coined the phrase *diabetes mellitus,* adding the Latin word for "honey sweet." Mind you, all this taste testing served a purpose. Doctors eventually learned diabetes, but it's definitely more common if you

- are older than 25
- have a parent or sibling with diabetes
- are African-American, American Indian, Asian-American, Hispanic-American, or Pacific Islander
- are overweight
- have already had gestational diabetes or have given birth to an infant who weighed more than nine pounds
- have ever been told by a doctor that you have prediabetes, impaired glucose tolerance, or impaired fasting glucose. (You'll read more about these almost-diabetic conditions later in the chapter.)

So what's the harm in having high blood sugar for a few months? For starters, that the sweetness of diabetics' urine came from sugar. A theory developed that the diabetic body produces too much of the sweet stuff, in the form of glucose, which is flushed out in the urine.

Doctors eventually began to suspect that the culprit was a malfunctioning organ. But which one? The kidneys came under scrutiny first, then the liver. However, in 1889 a pair of enterprising scientists found the truth when they removed a dog's pancreas, only to return the next day and discover that the previously house-trained pooch had peed all over his cage. Noting that people with diabetes have a hard time holding their water, the doctors suspected that the pancreas might play some role in controlling blood sugar. Testing the dog's urine confirmed their suspicion: It was loaded with glucose.

Until then, scientists thought that the pancreas manufactured digestive enzymes and not much else. It soon became clear, however, that when the pancreas was missing or malfunctioning, glucose built up in the blood, resulting in diabetes. So maybe the problem wasn't that the body made too much glucose. Maybe the pancreas made too little of something else.

At last, scientists figured out the role played by cells in the pancreas called islets of Langerhans (named for the man who discovered them). In the early 1920s, other researchers showed that these pancreatic cells make a substance that "unlocks" cells throughout the rest of the body, allowing glucose to enter so it can be used as a source of energy. Since doctors have a peculiar need to show off their knowledge of dead languages, they named the substance "insuline," after the Latin word *insula,* which means "island," which is a synonym of "islet." Today, the all-important hormone is known simply as insulin.

women with gestational diabetes often develop high blood pressure, which brings its own risks for both mother and baby. What's more, they frequently give birth to very large—okay, fat—babies who weigh more than nine pounds. Not only do fat babies often require a caesarean-section delivery, but they're also more likely to be fat children and to develop diabetes by their teen years or young adulthood (because of their genetic inheritance, not the intrauterine environment).

The news about gestational diabetes isn't all bad. After all, there's a reliable cure for the problem: having your baby, after which most women's blood sugar levels return to normal. However, the condition lingers in a small number of women, who are then diagnosed with either type 1 or type 2 diabetes. Regardless, if you have gestational diabetes once, the odds are two out of three that you'll develop it again with a subsequent pregnancy. More concerning, women who have gestational diabetes stand a 20 to 50 percent risk of developing type 2 diabetes within a decade.

OTHER TYPES OF DIABETES

Type 1, type 2, and gestational diabetes are the main types of the disease, but they're not the only ones. The following are other diabetes permutations.

"Double" Diabetes

Although it's not a term you will find in most medical text books, many doctors today say they are treating a growing number of type 1 diabetes patients who have developed insulin resistance, the classic symptom of type 2 diabetes. Some doctors are treating these hybrid patients with drugs that make their bodies more sensitive to insulin. The term "double diabetes" may also be used to describe a person with type 2 diabetes who develops antibodies that destroy the pancreas's beta cells (the ones that produce insulin); in most cases, these patients will require insulin injections. Just to make matters more confusing, double diabetes is sometimes called type 3 diabetes.

Prediabetes

Think of it as "diabetes lite" or the diabetic gray zone. Your blood sugar is higher than it should be but not high enough for you to be diagnosed with type 2 diabetes. (We'll explain the values doctors use to measure blood sugar later in this chapter.) One survey estimated that 40 percent of Americans aged 40 to 74 have prediabetes. Most people who have prediabetes develop full-blown type 2 diabetes within 10 years. However, making certain changes, such as losing weight, can prevent that from happening.

Latent Autoimmune Diabetes of Adulthood (LADA)

LADA is also known as slow-onset type 1 diabetes. Call them late bloomers: About 5 to 10 percent of people with diabetes are adults who develop the type 1 variety of the condition, which is typically first diagnosed in children and teens. Doctors often mistake the condition for plain old type 2 diabetes, basing their diagnosis solely on a patient's age and high blood sugar. But people with LADA don't have insulin resistance and aren't necessarily overweight. Those are important distinctions, since they influence which treatments work for LADA.

Maturity-Onset Diabetes of the Young (MODY)

MODY is something like the flipside of LADA. It usually turns up in young adults,

INSULIN AND YOUR HEART

The oldest rule in the book is that too much of a good thing can make you sick, and that applies to insulin in a big way. While you need insulin to survive, sending gushers of the hormone into your blood can eventually damage arteries, which makes insulin resistance a cause of heart disease.

Insulin resistance is one part of a spectrum of conditions that make up the medical threat originally known as Syndrome X but now more commonly called metabolic syndrome or insulin resistance syndrome (probably because Syndrome X sounds like something out of a science fiction movie). The National Cholesterol Education Program defines metabolic syndrome as the presence of any three of the following conditions:

* Excess weight around the waist (that is, a waist measurement of more than 40 inches for men and more than 35 inches for women)
* High levels of blood fats called triglycerides (150 mg/dl or higher)
* Low levels of HDL ("good") cholesterol (below 40 mg/dlr for men and below 50 mg/dl for women)
* High blood pressure (130/85 or higher)
* High fasting blood glucose levels (110 mg/dl or higher)

Other medical organizations use slightly different criteria for defining metabolic syndrome. And some doctors don't think metabolic syndrome exists at all, since it has no single cause; in addition to the cluster of factors mentioned above, other culprits include high levels of inflammation in the blood vessels and disorders that damage the endothelium, or lining of blood vessels. In fact, in recent years scientists have debated whether there's any point in using metabolic syndrome as a medical diagnosis. However, there is little argument about the fact that insulin resistance—the hallmark of type 2 diabetes—raises the risk of heart disease. (You'll read more about the link between high blood sugar and cardiovascular disease in Chapter 6.)

though it occurs in teens and children, too. Because patients are youngish, doctors often misdiagnose the condition as type 1 diabetes. However, MODY is a genetic disorder that interferes with insulin production. Unlike people with type 2 diabetes, those with MODY don't have insulin resistance and are usually slender. Again, getting the right diagnosis is critical in order to choose the proper treatment approach for MODY.

Secondary Diabetes

Certain diseases and drug therapies pack a diabetic double whammy by making people more vulnerable to blood sugar problems, either by directly interfering with insulin or by producing physical changes that increase insulin resistance (such as weight gain) and can lead to diabetes. When another identifiable medical problem or medication precipitates the development of diabetes, it is called secondary diabetes. A brief list of conditions that may cause secondary diabetes includes

depression, HIV, pancreatitis, certain hormonal disorders (such as Cushing's syndrome and hyperthyroidism), and some genetic disorders (such as cystic fibrosis). Drugs linked to secondary diabetes include diuretics and other drugs used to treat high blood pressure, hormones, antidepressants, anticonvulsants, and some forms of cancer chemotherapy, among others.

What Causes Diabetes? (or, "What did I do to deserve this?")

Ask a doctor this question and you may get a long, complicated answer that leaves you wishing you hadn't opened your big mouth. Or you may get a shrug and this unsatisfying response: "Nobody knows."

In a sense, both answers are accurate. Scientists have pinpointed a number of genes that seem to be involved in creating your body's blood sugar problems. Yet they also know that some trigger in the environment is probably necessary, too. But what are those triggers? And how do they keep insulin from doing its job? Researchers are still sorting out these questions. Here's a look at what they know so far.

TYPE 1 DIABETES

Some people inherit their mother's freckles or father's bald spot. If you have type 1 diabetes, there's a good chance one of your parents passed along to you an abnormal gene or cluster of genes that puts you at greater-than-average risk for developing the condition. (For those of you who were busy dozing or passing notes during high school biology class, everyone inherits a blend of genes from both parents that not only determines what you look like but also greaty influences your health.)

Being born with these genes doesn't guarantee that you will develop type 1 diabetes, however. These inherited genes only make you *susceptible* to developing diabetes. Something else has to trigger changes in your body to create your blood sugar problem. But what?

Scientists aren't sure, but they have a short list of suspects. According to one theory, a virus or some environmental toxin worms its way into the body and confuses the immune system because it resembles proteins found on beta cells. The immune system tends to shoot first and ask questions later, so it destroys anything that looks like it could be a threat—including insulin-producing beta cells in the pancreas. Type 1 diabetes occurs more often in people who have had a viral illness, as these can trigger

the onset of type 1 diabetes in a susceptible individual.

Other scientists have speculated that switching a baby from breast milk to cow's milk too early is the culprit. However, the dairy-diabetes connection remains controversial. In fact, in 2003 a pair of studies in the *Journal of the American Medical Association* found no connection between consuming cow's milk and diabetes. Some causes are more clear-cut. For example, certain prescription medications can trigger type 1 diabetes (see "Secondary Diabetes," page 20.)

Mr. Pancreas

TYPE 2 DIABETES

If you have type 2 diabetes, you may have begun by now to regret every can of cola and candy bar you ever consumed. After all, if high blood glucose is your problem, didn't gobbling and guzzling all that sugar cause you to develop diabetes?

The precise answer to that question is "Not exactly," though having a sweet

THE OBESITY-DIABETES CONNECTION DOWN SOUTH

Most doctors believe that obesity is an important cause of diabetes. Mississippi is the state with the highest rate of obesity: 25.9 percent of the state's population (and 28 percent of adults). It also has the highest rate of diabetes (11 percent). Coincidence? What do you think?

tooth probably didn't help matters. Despite the common misconception, consuming sugary foods doesn't cause diabetes. However, eating too much of any kind of food— whether it's bonbons or bacon cheeseburgers—can make you gain weight. And getting fat worsens insulin resistance, a problem that's at the core of type 2 diabetes.

Insulin resistance is the medical term for the concept described earlier: Cells throughout your body have begun to ignore insulin, so your pancreas keeps cranking out more of the hormone to move glucose past those stubborn cell membranes. According to the Centers for Disease Control and Prevention, 41 million Americans have insulin resistance. That's about 14 percent of the U.S. population.

Now, if you have been paying attention and taking notes, you are probably scratching your head about a few things, namely: If more than 40 million Americans have insulin resistance, why

do only about 21 million people have diabetes? And another thing: If obesity makes insulin resistance worse, and insulin resistance can lead to type 2 diabetes, why do some skinny people develop the disease?

The answer to the first question contains both good news and bad news for people who have insulin resistance but never develop type 2 diabetes. Even though the pancreas has to work overtime to meet demand, it still is eventually able to produce enough insulin to "unlock" cells throughout the body. That means glucose is burned as energy instead of building up in the blood, where it can damage organs. People with insulin resistance require much more insulin to use glucose than normal, but the pancreas manages to meet the demand. However, having all that insulin flooding the bloodstream may increase the risk of heart attack. (See "Insulin and Your Heart," page 19.)

Meanwhile, about 5 to 10 percent of people with insulin resistance can't make enough insulin to usher blood sugar into cells, so they eventually develop type 2 diabetes. People with type 2 diabetes seem to be born with genes that make them susceptible to the condition. In fact, the odds of a parent handing down the risk of type 2 diabetes is even greater than with type 1 diabetes: More than two-thirds of kids with type 2 diabetes have at least one parent who has the same blood-sugar problem. (See "Type 1 Diabetes: What Are the Odds?," page 12, for more details about type 1 diabetes and inheritance.) Scientists are zeroing in on genes that control how the pancreas releases insulin when glucose hits the bloodstream. People with type 2 diabetes appear to inherit glitches on these genes that make their insulin lose effectiveness over time.

But if bad genes alone caused type 2 diabetes, then rates of the condition would probably remain relatively stable over the years. That's not the case in the United States, where public health experts say that the incidence of diabetes has risen to epidemic proportions. In fact, according to one prediction, one out of three kids born today will end up with type 2 diabetes—not exactly a shining legacy.

So what's going on? What's causing the diabetes boom? Part of the answer is another boom—the baby boom, that is. Type 2 diabetes becomes more common with age, and that huge population of people born between 1946 and 1964 has started getting their AARP cards and pricing retirement property. (Heck, Mick Jagger—*Mick Jagger!*—is a grandfather.) As more boomers begin to have blood sugar woes, the number of people with diabetes in this country will continue to swell.

But doctors say other rising numbers have contributed even more to the current diabetes boom: those soaring digits on our bathroom scales. Studies show that obese people, particularly those whose excess belly fat gives their bodies an "apple" shape, are far more likely to be insulin resistant than those

ARE YOU OVERWEIGHT?

Stepping on the scale doesn't tell the whole story. Doctors use body mass index (BMI) to determine whether a person's weight is proportionate to their height. If your BMI falls between 25 and 29, you're overweight. If it's 30 or higher, you are considered obese.

Here's how to calculate your BMI:
1) Weigh yourself first thing in the morning, without clothes.
2) Confirm your height, in inches.
3) Multiply your weight in pounds by 700.
4) Divide the result in step 3 by your height in inches.
5) Divide the result in step 4 by your height in inches again.

The resulting number is your BMI.

who are slender. That's because internal fat, which is found inside the abdomen, muscle, liver, and beta cells, affects insulin resistance. Apple-shaped people, it turns out, have stockpiles of fat in the inner body. For apple-shaped people especially, weight loss tends to improve insulin resistance—shedding pounds makes their cells more sensitive to insulin. That is less true for people with so-called "pear shapes," who tend to have fat on the thighs and hips. That kind of fat lies just beneath the skin, instead of deep in the body. Unfortunately, you have no say in where you store your fat. That's controlled by your genes.

Just how tubby have we become? About 65 percent of Americans are overweight, and 30 percent of them are considered obese. (For perspective, the Centers for Disease Control and Prevention defines a person who is 5 feet 4 inches tall and weighs more than 145 pounds as overweight; someone who is the same height and weighs more than 174 pounds is considered obese.) Compare those statistics to the late 1970s, when fewer than half of Americans were overweight and just 15 percent were obese. What's more, the number of Americans who are more than 100 pounds overweight quadrupled between 1986 and 2000.

It's no mystery why Americans have packed on the pounds. The human body evolved with a handy survival mechanism—that is, a super-efficient fat-packing capacity. Prehistoric populations often suffered through long periods when there wasn't much food on the dinner table, either because the hunt failed or the fish weren't biting. The cave people who survived were those who had a little fat tucked away on their hips or in the belly to provide a reserve of energy during lean times.

Unfortunately, our brains remain hard-wired to instruct our bodies to pack on extra fat even though food shortages are rarely a problem in our super-sizing, fast-food nation. What's more, our bodies are built for the hard work of hunting and gathering. Yet today, too many of us simply gather fat as we hunt for something good on cable while waiting for the pizza delivery guy. Most Americans don't get enough physical activity, and more than one-quarter say they don't exercise at all.

If you're overweight and don't exercise, don't beat yourself up. Your upbringing probably had a huge influence on the foods you choose and whether or not the only time you break out in a sweat is when you become consumed with panic because your local grocer ran out of Dove Bars. Fortunately, small changes can have a big impact on diabetes management. You'll read more about the role of diet and exercise later on.

How Does My Doctor Know I Have Diabetes?

Your blood sugar gave you away, of course. Doctors do look for other clues when diagnosing diabetes, though. For instance, if a patient walks in complaining that he or she is always parched and dashing for the restroom, a physician may suspect diabetes, especially the type 1 variety. However, the diagnosis of diabetes isn't confirmed until

blood sugar has been measured. If a patient has obvious diabeteslike symptoms, a doctor may perform a *random blood glucose* test. This test can be performed any time and doesn't require preparation. If your blood sugar level is more than 200 milligrams per deciliter (mg/dl), you have diabetes.

The *fasting blood glucose* test is the more definitive diagnostic method, however. This test is often included in the routine blood analyses conducted as part of annual physical examinations. Doctors also use the test if a patient is overweight, has a family history of diabetes, or offers any other reason to

BLOOD GLUCOSE: WHAT THE TESTS TELL

	FASTING BLOOD GLUCOSE (FBG) TEST	RANDOM BLOOD GLUCOSE (RBG) TEST	ORAL GLUCOSE TOLERANCE (OGT) TEST
You have **diabetes** if:	Your FBG > 125 mg/dl on two consecutive blood tests	RBG ≥ 200 mg/dl, plus you have symptoms of diabetes	Your OGT is ≥ 200 mg/dl
You have **impaired fasting glucose** if:	Your FBG ≥ 100 mg/dl < 126 mg/dl		
You have **impaired glucose tolerance** if:			Your OGT ≥ 140 mg/dl and < 200 mg/dl
You're in the clear if:	Your FBG < 100 mg/dl		Your OGT < 140 mg/dl

suspect that the condition may be silently at work.

If you have had a fasting blood glucose test, you probably haven't forgotten it, especially if you love breakfast. As the name implies, the test measures how much blood sugar is in your system when your stomach is empty. Everyone's glucose spikes after eating a meal, but sugar levels drop within a few hours in people who do not have diabetes. In those with diabetes, blood sugar remains relatively high long after the dishes have been cleared and washed.

Typically, patients receive instructions not to eat after midnight on the day before the test, then arrive at a lab bright and early to have a blood sample taken. After the blood has been drawn, as the hungry patient bolts for the nearest coffee shop, the lab analyzes the blood. If the test produces a reading lower than 100 mg/dl, you can breathe a little easier: You don't have diabetes. However, a reading of 126 mg/dl or higher is a red flag. But since other influences, such as stress and certain illnesses, can raise blood sugar, doctors usually order a retest to

ONE REASON TO BE A MORNING PERSON?

If you had your blood sugar tested in the morning, being an early bird may have helped you get a proper diagnosis. The reason? Doctors diagnose diabetes when a patient's blood sugar level measures 126 mg/dl or higher on two consecutive fasting plasma glucose tests. Scientists established the threshold of 126 mg/dl based on studies of blood sugar levels measured in the morning after an 8-hour fast. But sometimes patients undergo glucose tests in the afternoon. That's a problem, because many people—including all people with diabetes—experience a spike in blood sugar, known as the "dawn phenomenon," between 4 A.M. and 8 A.M. Blood sugar naturally dips by afternoon. A study in 2000 compared two groups of more than 6,000 people who underwent blood-sugar testing. One group went to the lab in the morning, the other in the afternoon. The study found that people tested in the morning were twice as likely to be diagnosed with diabetes. Since people in both groups were similar ages and had comparable health status, the researchers estimated that using current standards for blood-sugar testing in the afternoon may miss up to half of all cases of undiagnosed diabetes.

confirm the diagnosis. (See "One Reason to Be A Morning Person?," page 26, to learn why it may be better to test in the morning.)

Inquiring minds may wonder: What if my blood sugar is above 100 mg/dl but below 126 mg/dl? If that's the case, you have a form of prediabetes (which we discussed earlier) called impaired fasting glucose. In short, you don't have diabetes, but you may be joining the club one day. A reading in this middle zone offers a strong clue that you have had insulin resistance for some time.

If one of these two tests determine that a patient's blood sugar is close to normal but the doctor has some reason to suspect diabetes (for instance, if the patient has classic symptoms of the condition), a third test may be ordered to clarify matters. An oral glucose tolerance test measures how well your body processes sugar that surges into your bloodstream after a meal.

This test is more sensitive than the fasting blood glucose test, since it does a better job of detecting prediabetes. However, the oral glucose tolerance test takes longer to perform and involves more hassle for the patient. As with the fasting glucose test, you can only drink water and can't eat for eight hours prior to your visit to the lab. Bring a good book, because you'll be there for the better part of the morning. After your blood sugar is measured once, you're given a drink containing 75 grams of glucose. After you toss back the sweet beverage, you have a seat and wait.

Two hours later, a lab technician measures your blood sugar a second time. The number you want to hear is 139 mg/dl or lower; that means you don't have diabetes. A blood sugar level between 140 and 199 mg/dl is called impaired glucose tolerance, a second type of prediabetes. Again, this isn't the worst news you could receive, but it should get your attention because it means you're a diabetic in the making.

If the reading on an oral glucose test is 200 mg/dl or higher, you receive an invitation to return for a repeat test. A second score over 200 mg/dl means you have diabetes.

But which kind? Your doctor may have performed other tests to determine whether you have type 1 or type 2 diabetes. High levels of islet-cell antibodies in the blood, low levels of a substance called C-peptide in the blood (which indicates how much insulin you're making), and high level of ketones in the urine all indicate type 1 diabetes.

Tools for Monitoring Diabetes

If you ever dreamed of becoming a physician when you grew up, congratulations: Now's your chance to play doctor. The only catch is that you have to play patient, too. Diabetes requires that you assume a great deal of responsibility for monitoring your health status and maintaining your well-being. In fact, by one estimate, diabetes patients provide 95 percent of their own care. (Good luck billing your HMO, though.)

The goal, of course, is to maintain safe and healthy blood sugar levels—what doctors like to call "tight control." Since diabetes is often symptomless, that makes monitoring your glucose levels essential. This chapter describes the tools you need to do just that.

Monitoring Blood Sugar: Getting to Know Your Tools

Knowing if your blood sugar is high, low, or just right will guide decisions about what and how much you should eat, whether you need medication, and how active you can be. For example, if a reading shows that your blood sugar is too low, you'll know it's time to munch on a carbohydrate-rich food (or pop a glucose pill, which you can store with your meter) to give your levels a boost. A high blood sugar reading signals that you need to bring glucose levels back down to normal. How you do that will depend on your personal diabetes treatment plan. Some medications, such as sulfonylureas, decrease glucose levels by increasing insulin production. Other medications, such as TZDs and metformin, decrease glucose levels by decreasing insulin resistance or decreasing liver glucose production.

What's more, keeping close tabs on your blood sugar levels can provide your physician with critical information that he or she can use to make decisions about what treatments will work best for you. Finally, knowing that you are maintaining healthy, safe blood sugar levels provides some reassurance that you will avoid the complications

diabetes can cause. We'll discuss those complications later in the book.

TO MONITOR OR NOT TO MONITOR

Should you monitor your glucose? If you're reading this book, then the answer is probably yes. Most experts agree that glucose monitoring is most important—make that essential, mandatory, no ifs, ands, or buts—for people with type 1 diabetes and anyone with diabetes who takes insulin or drugs to increase insulin levels.

To be more specific, the American Diabetes Association recommends glucose monitoring for anyone who
- takes insulin or diabetes pills
- is receiving intensive insulin therapy
- is pregnant
- is having a hard time controlling blood glucose levels
- is having severe low blood glucose levels or is producing ketones due to high blood glucose levels
- is experiencing low blood glucose levels without the usual warning signs

But even if none of these criteria applies to you, wouldn't you want to know right away if your blood sugar is silently rising? By checking your glucose once a day—it takes just three minutes—you could spot a problem before it gets out of control. Record keeping—another essential part of tracking your glucose levels—adds about another five minutes, tops.

To be on the safe side, ask your doctor (or diabetes educator, if you're working with one) when and how often you should test your glucose. While there are no established rules for type 2 patients who take oral medications, insulin users are generally advised to test their blood at least four times a day, preferably before each meal and at bedtime. Although the frequency of testing isn't standardized, it's particularly recommended to obtain information for evaluating potential treatment changes. For instance, you can test before a meal to evaluate your basal glucose; two hours after a meal to evaluate the effect of food; before, during, or after exercise to determine the effect of exercise on glucose; and in the middle of the night if you have concerns about hypoglycemia (low blood sugar). Pregnant women who take insulin or have gestational diabetes should test their blood frequently, too. And there are specific

Mr. Glucose

circumstances when monitoring blood sugar is a good idea, such as when your doctor prescribes a new drug or changes a dosage.

Required Tools for Diabetes Management

Monitoring your blood glucose is simple once you've assembled your diabetes-management tool kit. You have lots of options, so take some time to learn about their advantages and disadvantages. It's also a good idea to consult your physician or diabetes-care team for purchasing advice.

MEET YOUR GLUCOSE METER

This nifty little electronic device is the basic tool you need for self-monitoring blood glucose (which you will sometimes see abbreviated as SMBG). It's about the size of an MP3 player (or a small Walkman... or a transistor radio, depending on which decade you were born in). Most glucose meters run on batteries and some come with slick-looking carrying cases, which can also store the other tools you will need to test your blood sugar. (More on those tools in a moment.)

There are several dozen types of glucose meters available, but most operate on one of two principles. Reflectance photometers blast a tiny light beam at the blood sample and measure changes in the light that bounces back. Newer-style devices called electrochemical meters measure electrical current produced by glucose in the blood sample.

Both varieties of glucose meters produce a number that indicates the glucose level in your blood.

Here's some good news about glucose meters: They usually don't cost much. In fact, if you ask around, you can

THE WHOLE TRUTH ABOUT GLUCOSE METERS

Warning: The following information will only apply to a small number of readers. If you know for a fact that your glucose meter delivers plasma-calibrated or plasma-equivalent readings, you are free to skip this section and go do something else. (Why not check your glucose? You can't do it too often, after all.) However, if you have your doubts, read on.

Home glucose monitors analyze blood in a different way than technicians at labs measure glucose. Home devices assess how much glucose is present in the entire blood sample. Labs, on the other hand, measure the amount of glucose in the blood's plasma, which is the watery part of blood that's left over after red blood cells are removed. These two methods of measuring glucose produce slightly different results.

Got it? Good, because things get just a little more complicated. Most home glucose meters are plasma-calibrated or plasma-equivalent devices. That means they measure the whole blood sample, but—like a cheap tipper in a restaurant—they automatically add 12 percent to the total. This handy feature translates the reading into a number roughly equivalent to what a lab would produce when measuring plasma glucose. That makes it easier for you to compare your readings at home with the lab tests your doctor has ordered.

Almost all meters sold today are plasma-calibrated. However, two models on the market (the One Touch Basic and One Touch Profile) deliver whole-blood readings, meaning they don't automatically adjust the results to match lab-style tests. (Though if you can recall some middle-school mathematics, you can do so yourself.) Some older meters also produce whole-blood readings. Readings from a whole-blood meter are just as valid as those from a plasma-calibrated meter. However, it's critical for you and your doctor to know which type of meter you're using, so bring yours along to your next office visit to find out for sure.

probably get one for free. Your health insurance may cover the cost of diabetes supplies. But even if it doesn't, or you don't have insurance, pharmacies and clinics often hand out glucose meters at no charge. What kind of crazy, kind-hearted companies give away their products for free, you ask? That's easy: Companies that want to sell you their test strips, which are an essential part of monitoring glucose. Test strips are not interchangeable—you need to use the kind that are made to fit in your meter, and you'll go through them by the dozens.

Glucose-testing Components

Here's a look at test strips as well as the other critical pieces of your glucose-testing kit:

Lancing device. These are also known as a lancet device or finger-prick device. The latter name says it all. You use this palm-size tool to poke a very small hole in your skin—usually a finger—to produce a drop of blood for the glucose meter to analyze. Your glucose meter may come with a lancing device, but if you don't like the way it works, shop around—there may be another model you find easier to use. Because some of us are more thick-skinned than others,

lancing devices are adjustable, so you can control how deeply they plunge in. Obviously, the shallower the puncture, the lower the "ouch factor."

Lancet. This thin, disposable needle is the business end of the lancing device. The needle is encased in a cylinder, which you insert into the lancing device. The skinnier the lancet, the less painful the prick. Doctors usually tell patients to dispose of a lancet after one use, but many patients with diabetes ignore that advice and use the same lancet several times. This is not a good idea, however, because you can't clean it. If you clean the tip with alcohol, you'll rub off the coating that makes it easier for the lancet to slide into the skin. Using a lancet more than once, then, puts you at risk for infection. Besides, repeated use dulls the lancet, making for a more painful puncture. For obvious reasons, never share a lancet with another person. You may be sharing more than the lancet—an infection, perhaps.

Test strips. These strips hold blood samples for a glucose meter to analyze. Test strips are sold in bunches by the vial or in individual foil wrappers. You don't have a choice, though, about which way to purchase them. Whether you buy strips in vials or individual foil wrappers will depend on the meter you've selected, as each meter company determines which way its strips are sold. If you test less often, you may want to purchase a meter that uses foil-wrapped strips, because those packed in vials can spoil over time, especially if exposed to light and moisture. Test strips are coated with a chemical that allows the meter to analyze the glucose level in your blood sample. Unfortunately, the amount of chemical on strips varies from one batch to the next. To account for these small differences, you must recalibrate your meter every time you buy a new box or vial of strips. Don't worry, your strips will come with instructions for calibrating the meter. Some meters even recalibrate themselves. Recalibrating is usually as easy as changing a code number on your meter or inserting a chip code into your meter.

INSTRUCTIONS FOR GLUCOSE TESTING

There are several dozen different types of glucose meters available, but most work in a similar fashion. The following are some generic instructions for using a glucose meter:

- Wash your hands with soap and water, or rub them clean with alcohol.

FINGER PRICKING A PAIN?

According to one study, nearly two-thirds of people with diabetes say they have skipped glucose testing at one time or another because they don't like pricking themselves.

If playing pincushion with your fingers makes you dread glucose-testing time, then you may want to talk to your doctor about alternative-site testing.

Some glucose monitors let you take blood samples from other parts of the body, such as the upper arm, forearm, base of the thumb, or thigh. Beware, however, that these sites may not be appropriate for all patients or circumstances. Fingertips are commonly used for glucose testing not only because they're—warning, pun alert—handy but because blood sugar changes turn up sooner in the fingers than in other parts of the body. In other words, you may not be getting the latest available news about your glucose status if you're mining for blood in your legs or arms.

The Food and Drug Administration recommends *always* using finger pricks for glucose testing when

- you think your blood sugar is low.
- you don't feel any symptoms but an alternative-site test shows that you're hypoglycemic.
- an alternative-site test produces results that don't match how you feel.

Another alternative for finger-prick phobes are lancing devices that swap needles for lasers, which use light to poke tiny holes in the skin. The FDA approved at-home laser devices in 1998. But be prepared to dig deep into your pockets with those sensitive fingers of yours, since these high-tech tools cost in the low four figures.

Be sure to dry your hands well; moisture or traces of alcohol can affect your reading.

- Touch the lancing device against your skin—usually the fingertip—and press a button, which releases a spring that injects the lancet. The prick will hurt less if you lance the side of your fingertip, where there are fewer nerve endings. Also, it may help to squeeze the finger you're testing first to bring blood to the surface before lancing.
- Hold your hand down until a bead of blood forms on the finger.
- Dab the blood onto the test strip.
- Insert the test strip into the glucose meter and take a reading.

And what number should you hope to see—that is, what should your glucose goals be? That depends on a lot of things, including your age, what form of diabetes you have (and how long you have had it), and other factors. Your doctor will likely give you a range of pre- and post-meal blood-sugar levels to aim for. However, the American Diabetes Association has established standard goals for people with diabetes:

- Before a meal: 90 to 130 mg/dl
- After a meal: Less than 180 mg/dl

NUMBER CRUNCHING: USING A LOGBOOK

Your glucose meter provides a snapshot of your blood glucose level at any given moment. But your doctor wants to see the big picture: How is your body handling glucose over a period of weeks and months? That's where your logbook comes in.

Think of a logbook as a blood-sugar diary. You use it to record your glucose meter reading every time you test your blood. A page in a typical logbook features a large chart, with columns for breakfast, lunch, dinner, bedtime, and other/snack. The rows list the days of the week, with an "average" row at the bottom. When you fill all the days of the week, use a calculator to figure out your average glucose level for each period of the day.

Some logbooks have space where you can log in other information, such as how many grams of carbohydrates you consumed during a meal (you'll see why that's important later on) and how much insulin you took if you're an insulin user. The chart may also include a column for "comments," in which you can note any activities (such as exercise) or events (like eating a pound of Godiva chocolates) that may have affected your glucose levels.

This information is a gold mine for your physician. A logbook can help determine whether your medication is adequate to keep your blood glucose within a healthy range, suggesting whether you may be taking too much or too little. It also reveals patterns in blood-sugar fluctuations that may offer clues about how you can avoid peaks and valleys.

If writing things down on a piece of paper sounds hopelessly low-tech, fear not: Techno-geeks have discovered diabetes. For starters, your physician may ask you to use a specific type of

TROUBLESHOOTING CHECKLIST: GLUCOSE-READING PROBLEMS

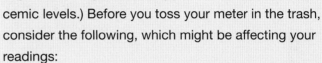

If your glucose meter consistently produces readings that seem inaccurate, it's important to make sure it's working properly. (For instance, say you feel fine, but the meter keeps insisting that your blood sugar has plunged to hypoglycemic levels.) Before you toss your meter in the trash, consider the following, which might be affecting your readings:

☐ Is your glucose meter properly calibrated?

☐ Do you know whether your glucose meter measures whole blood or plasma?

☐ Have you recently performed a quality-control check on your glucose meter as recommended by the manufacturer ?

☐ Are the test strips spoiled? (Strips wrapped in aluminum foil are less prone to spoilage.)

☐ Are you using the right test strips for your glucose meter model? If you're using "third-party" strips made by other manufacturers, are they appropriate for your meter?

☐ Could some other influence or substance, such as another medical condition or high doses of vitamins, be interfering with your test results?

☐ Do you live at a high altitude? Has the meter been stored in an unusually cold, hot, or humid place? Climate can affect how glucose meters function.

meter that allows him or her to download your data onto a computer. Then, special software can create charts and graphs that indicate trends in your glucose levels. What's more, the technologically inclined can use personal computers, personal desk assistants, Web sites, and even their cell phones to record glucose data.

The closer you look at glucose meters, the more you may be overwhelmed by bells and whistles; each year brings new models that do more for you. If you are having trouble choosing one, check *Diabetes Forecast,* the American Diabetes Association's magazine, which publishes an annual review of glucose meters on its Web site (find it at www.diabetes.org). The ADA doesn't endorse products, but the comprehensive review it publishes allows you to compare the features of different meters.

GETTING UNDER YOUR SKIN: CONTINUOUS GLUCOSE MONITORING SYSTEMS

If testing your blood sugar three or four times a day can help you manage diabetes, why not do it even more often? How about, say, 288 times a day? You can do just that while exercising, cleaning the gutters, or eating dinner, thanks to a device called the CGMS System Gold made by Medtronic MiniMed. (Another manufacturer, Abbott Laboratories, plans to introduce a similar device, called the Navigator.)

The CGMS System Gold is made up of two parts: a pager-size monitor and a needlelike sensor. The sensor is inserted into a part of the body the manufacturer refers to as "subcutaneous tissue," which you know better as your belly (though sometimes the sensor is inserted into the hip). The sensor measures glucose levels in the fluid just beneath the skin. Every five minutes, the CGMS System Gold takes a reading, which it stores in its memory. After three days, when you remove the device, it has taken up to 864 glucose readings. Your doctor downloads the information onto a computer and presto, he or she has a detailed history of your blood sugar levels for the past three days, which may allow for super–fine-tuning of your insulin treatment regimen.

Unfortunately, you can't peek at your glucose readings during board meetings or bus rides, since the CGMS System

Gold model on the market in 2005 does not have a readout screen. That also means that you can't rely on the device to monitor your daily glucose status, so you still have to take your usual blood-sugar readings with a meter. However, a new continuous glucose monitoring system product, called the Guardian RT System (also manufactured by Medtronic MiniMed), was approved by the U.S. Food and Drug Administration in August 2005 and debuted in a controlled market release in seven U.S. cities, including Austin, Texas; Boston, Massachusetts; Chicago, Illinois; Houston, Texas; Minneapolis/St. Paul, Minnesota; San Antonio, Texas; Tampa, Florida; and Salinas, California. The Guardian RT is a patient-owned continuous glucose-monitoring system that displays an updated real-time glucose value every five minutes and alerts patients when glucose levels become too high or too low. This device gives you access to readings and alarms 24 hours a day, 7 days a week, allowing for better and more precise management of blood glucose levels. Once the company has analyzed feedback from the limited release and fine-tuned its product training and education, the system will become more broadly available.

INTERPRETING A1c READINGS

In general, every 1 percent increase in A1c equals a 35 mg/dl rise in glucose.

A1c %	Average Blood Glucose (mg/dl)
5	100
6	135
7	170
8	205
9	240
10	275
11	310
12	345
13	380

THE LONG VIEW: A1c TESTING

You may be getting to know the folks at the local lab on a first-name basis, since your doctor will likely want you to come in every few months for a procedure called an A1c test. (At-home versions of the test are now available, too.)

As you know, when you breathe, your lungs take in oxygen. The lungs, in turn, hand over oxygen molecules to red blood cells. Like tiny FedEx trucks, red blood cells deliver oxygen to cells in every tissue in your body, which need the Big O to produce energy. Each of those little couriers has a special compartment for carrying oxygen, a protein called *hemoglobin.*

Glucose molecules love attaching themselves to proteins (a process called *glycation*), and hemoglobin is no exception. When glucose and hemoglobin hook up, the result is *glycated hemoglobin* or *glycohemoglobin*. The more glucose you have in your blood, the more glycated hemoglobin you will have. The A1c test measures glycated hemoglobin. This test is sometimes called a hemoglobin A1c or HbA1c test. There are several different types of glycated hemoglobin; the type named A1c just happens to be the easiest to measure and least likely to be influenced by what you ate the night before.

But why measure this little sugar-protein package at all when it's easy enough just to measure blood sugar, period? As we have already seen, the blood-sugar testing you do at home offers a snapshot of how well you are controlling glucose at that very moment. The A1c test, meanwhile, is more like a chronicle or history, giving your doctor a look at how well you have been controlling glucose on average in recent months.

Neat trick, no? But how the heck does it do that? Red blood cells have a shelf life of about two or three months, so your body is constantly churning out new ones, while others are dying off. At any given time, you have red blood cells on the job that are brand new, others that have been around for a few days or weeks, and still others that are ready to call it quits. Once the hemoglobin in a red blood cell links to a glucose molecule, it stays that way. The A1c test measures young, middle-aged, and old hemoglobin, indicating what percent has been carrying sugar over the last few months.

Most experts suggest having an A1c test at least twice a year. It's also a good idea to have the test before starting on a new medication, then following up in a few months to see how well it's controlling blood sugar. Don't toss out your glucose meter and logbook, though. You still need to take daily readings for status updates on your blood sugar. And your logbook not only provides information about daily fluctuations in your glucose levels, but comparing the results of an A1c test with the averages you compile on your own over time can tell you whether or not your glucose meter is providing accurate readings.

People who don't have diabetes usually have about five percent of hemoglobin that's glycated. In a person with runaway, out-of-control diabetes, the figure can rise to more than 20 percent. You want to keep yours as close to normal as possible, of course, in order to avoid the complications that high blood sugar can cause over the long term. The American Diabetes Association recommends an A1c goal of less than seven percent, though your doctor owes you a high-five if you can keep it even lower.

KETONE ALERT: USING URINE TEST STRIPS

When some critical function goes haywire in your body, the kidneys are often the first to know. These organs act like toxic-waste sites, filtering bad stuff from the blood and eliminating it through the urinary tract. If you run low on insulin and can't use glucose for energy—which, as you know by now, can make you sick—your body has to burn other sources of fuel. This alternative strategy produces high levels of waste products, so the fastest way to find out if your insulin has dropped perilously low is to test your urine for metabolic garbage known as ketones.

Don't worry: It's not a taste test, though in the old days physicians often made their assistants sample patients' urine to see if it was sweet. (Doctors who treated a lot of people with diabetes must have had a heck of a time hanging on to good help.) In fact, while you can tell whether your body isn't burning blood sugar by measuring glucose in the urine with special kits, the tests

TWO-FOR-ONE KETONE TESTING

Since ketones float around in the blood before the kidneys filter them, and since people with diabetes become experts at poking their skin with needles, it's worth asking: Why not just measure ketone levels in the blood at the same time you check blood-sugar levels? A company called Abbott Diabetes Care wondered the same thing and produced a meter called the Precision Xtra, which measures both glucose and ketone levels with just a drop of blood. Whichever method you choose, if a test result shows that your ketone levels are too high, call your doctor right away.

aren't terribly accurate. Instead, your doctor may ask you to test your urine periodically for the presence of ketones, harmful substances that your body produces in the absence of insulin.

Remember, when insulin levels drop and your cells can't get the glucose needed for fuel, they resort to burning fat for energy. Sounds like a swell slimming strategy, but relying on this fall-back energy source for too long can be bad news for the body. Burning fat makes ketones, which spill into the blood and urine. When ketone levels rise too high, you can become sick and possibly slip into a coma.

That's why you may need to disappear into the bathroom now and then to find out whether your urine is brimming with ketones. If the idea of obtaining a urine sample from yourself sounds unappealing at first, don't worry: It will soon seem routine. Besides, it could save your life. Doctors typically recommend testing your urine for ketones if

- you have type 1 diabetes and your blood sugar rises above 240 mg/dl.
- you have any form of diabetes and your blood sugar rises above 300 mg/dl.
- you have any form of diabetes and you become seriously ill or are under severe psychological stress.
- you have any form of diabetes and become pregnant. (Your doctor will advise how often you should test yourself.)
- you are experiencing ketoacidosis for any reason.

You can buy ketone strips for urine testing at any pharmacy. Follow label instructions and discuss how to use the test with your doctor or diabetes educator. In general, you will use a clean, dry container to "catch" a small amount of urine (and if you "drop" it, you better clean it up or you risk becoming very unpopular with other members of the household). Then you dip the strip into the urine and wait a few moments. Ketones in your urine will cause a chemical reaction on the test strip, prompting a color change. The degree of color change will indicate your ketone levels when you compare the strip to the chart provided by the manufacturer.

Managing Type 1 Diabetes

Remember the old days, when gas stations had attendants in spiffy uniforms who cheerfully pumped fuel into your car? Today, you usually have to fill your own tank.

Remember the old days, when your pancreas pumped insulin? If you have type 1 diabetes, your body has turned into a self-service station. Since your pancreas no longer makes insulin, you are responsible for keeping your blood levels topped off with this important hormone. This chapter tells you how.

If you have had type 1 diabetes since you were a kid and think you already know the drill, read on anyway. You'll learn about alternative methods for injecting insulin, pitfalls to avoid, and experimental treatments that may one day make your daily date with the needle a thing of the past.

Insulin: A Brief History

The modern age has been full of amazing technological advances—high-speed travel, the Internet, blue M&M's. . . However, if you have type 1 diabetes, you are no doubt a big fan of one particular 20th century innovation: insulin therapy. Before there was insulin therapy, people whose bodies stopped producing the hormone didn't hang around for long; there wasn't much doctors could do for them.

In the 19th century, after researchers figured out that the body needs this critical hormone to burn glucose as energy, doctors tried different ways to restart production of insulin in people with type 1 diabetes. Some physicians even tried feeding fresh pancreas to patients. The experiment failed (and probably left more than a few patients begging for a palate-cleansing sorbet), as did the other attempts to replace missing insulin.

Finally, in 1922 a former divinity student named Dr. Frederick Banting figured out how to extract insulin from a dog's pancreas. Skeptical colleagues said the stuff looked like "thick brown muck." Banting injected the insulin into the keister of a 14-year-old boy named Leonard Thompson, whose body was so ravaged by diabetes that he weighed only 65 pounds. Little Leonard developed abscesses on his bottom and still felt lousy, though his blood sugar improved slightly. Encouraged, Banting refined the formula for insulin and tried again six weeks later. This time Leonard's condition improved rapidly. His blood sugar dropped from 520 mg/dl to a more manageable 120 mg/dl. He gained weight, and his strength returned. (Poor Lenny—although his diabetes remained in control for years, he died of pneumonia when he was just 27.)

Banting and a colleague, Dr. John Macleod, won the Nobel Prize for their work. Commercial production of insulin for treating diabetes began soon after. For many years, drug companies derived the hormone using pancreases that came primarily from stockyards, taken from slaughtered cows and pigs, which didn't need the organs anymore.

Animal insulin has saved millions of lives, but it has a problem: It causes

DIABETES MEDICATIONS, BY THE NUMBERS

Among adults in the United States who have been diagnosed with diabetes:

- 16 percent take insulin only.
- 12 percent take both insulin and oral diabetes medications.
- 57 percent take oral diabetes medications only.
- 15 percent do not take insulin or oral diabetes medications.

allergic reactions in some users. Since the early 1980s, most people with diabetes have used human-derived insulin. You'll be relieved to know that human-derived insulin is harvested by an entirely different method than that used to obtain animal insulin. Using genetic engineering techniques, scientists figured out how to insert the gene for human insulin into bacteria, which in turn churns out pure, high-grade hormone—insulin that your body can't tell from the homemade variety.

Insulin: What Kind Should You Use?

In the early days of insulin therapy, there was only one variety. After injecting the hormone, it started lowering glucose levels in 60 minutes or less, reached its peak performance within a few hours, then fizzled out, lasting no longer than 8 hours.

Doctors still prescribe this early version of diabetes medicine, known simply as regular insulin. But scientists eventually figured out that tweaking the amino acids in insulin made it behave differently. In particular, they were able to alter the speed at which insulin is absorbed by the body. The longer it takes your body to absorb a drug, the longer it remains active.

INSULIN: THE LONG AND SHORT OF IT

Today, there are several types of insulin available. Some are like greyhounds, sprinting into your bloodstream but wearing themselves out quickly. Other varieties are more like Siberian huskies, trotting along at a steady pace for long stretches. Still other forms of insulin are like Airedale terriers. . . okay, not really, but you get the idea.

Molecular manipulation allows scientists to alter insulin's speed and durability in three ways:

- Onset: how long it takes the insulin to enter your bloodstream and get to work lowering your blood glucose
- Peak Time: how long it takes insulin to reach maximum strength, when it works hardest
- Duration: how long the insulin works before it quits

THE FACTS OF (SHELF) LIFE

Would Martha Stewart make a crème brûlée with stale, old eggs? Don't bet your spice spoons! You should apply the same devotion to freshness when it comes to insulin by following these simple rules:

- Store unopened vials of insulin in the refrigerator.
- Check the expiration date before opening a new vial; if it has passed, don't use the insulin.
- Contrary to common belief, an in-use vial does not need to be refrigerated; room temperature is fine. But if the mercury rises above 85 degrees, store the opened vial in the fridge.
- Toss out an in-use vial after 28 days.

INSULIN: DECISIONS, DECISIONS

TYPE OF INSULIN	EXAMPLES	ONSET OF ACTION*	PEAK OF ACTION*	DURATION OF ACTION
Rapid-acting	Humalog (lispro)	5 to 15 minutes	60 minutes	3 to 5 hours
	NovoLog (aspart)	5 to 15 minutes	30 to 90 minutes	3 to 5 hours
	Glulisine (Apidra)	5 to 15 minutes	30 to 90 minutes	3 to 5 hours
Short-acting (Regular)	Humulin R			
	Novolin R	30 to 60 minutes	2 to 3 hours	5 to 8 hours
Intermediate-acting (NPH)	Humulin N			
	Novolin N	1 to 3 hours	4 to 10 hours	10 to 16 hours
	Humulin L			
	Novolin L	1 to 2.5 hours	7 to 15 hours	18 to 24 hours
Intermediate- and short-acting mixtures	Humulin 50/50	Depends on composition of mixture	Depends on composition of mixture	Depends on composition of mixture
	Humulin 70/30			
	Humalog Mix 75/25			
	Humalog Mix 50/50			
	Novolin 70/30			
	Novolog Mix 70/30			
Long-acting	Ultralente	6 to 10 hours	10 to 16 hours	18 to 24 hours
	Lantus (glargine)	2 to 4 hours	peakless	20 to 24 hours
	Detemir (Levimir)	2 to 4 hours	6 to 14 hours	16 to 20 hours

All figures are estimates; each user has a unique response to insulin, so the actual time of onset, peak, and duration varies. (The part of the body you use for injection affects times, too.)

All this variety adds up to several benefits for you. For starters, longer-acting insulin can reduce the number of injections you need in a day. What's more, combining two different types of insulin may help improve glucose control. For example, your doctor might prescribe a long-acting form of insulin called glargine, which has no peak but stays active for 24 hours, dripping insulin into your system to maintain daily business. However, to accommodate the spike of glucose that hits your system after eating, you may also take a premeal blast of short-acting insulin. Ultimately, the goal is to create a hormonal environment in your body that mimics what your pancreas would do, if only it could.

Premixed insulin represents an option for patients who take two different types of insulin. There are a number of pre-measured preparations available, which typically blend short- and long-acting forms of insulin, or intermediate- and short-acting forms. The goal of using premixed insulin is to reduce the number of injections the patient must make in a day. Premixed insulin has some benefits and downsides, so it isn't for everyone. For example, the convenience of premixed insulin makes it the best choice for

- older patients who lack the dexterity to inject themselves or whose memories are too foggy to remember to take insulin on schedule.
- patients who have some trouble mixing two types of insulin in one syringe.
- patients who find it difficult to make adjustments to their insulin dosages based on changes in their glucose readings.
- patients who still can't find the motivation to inject insulin several times a day despite their doctors' cautions, warnings, and threats that chronically high blood sugar corrodes arteries and nerves, leaving patients with devastating damage to organs and limbs.

Some studies have found that patients (especially senior citizens) make fewer dosing errors when they use premixed insulin instead of mixing two types of insulin on their own. However, while using premixed insulin may seem more convenient, it requires some discipline. For instance, to accommodate the onset, peak, and duration of the two different insulins, you must stick to a strict eating schedule and avoid consuming more or less food than planned. Also, some doctors feel that it's very difficult to achieve tight glucose control while using premixed insulin. At best, these blended hormone treatments prevent very high or very low swings in blood sugar.

Advantages of premixed insulin:
- No need to play chemist, since the insulin is mixed for you
- Fewer daily injections

Disadvantages of premixed insulin:

- So long, spontaneity: Premixed solutions require you to eat a specific amount of food at set times and to strictly adhere to a regular schedule of physical activity
- Harder to maintain normal glucose control

Getting to the Point: Tools for Injecting Insulin

Wouldn't it be swell if insulin came in an easy-to-swallow pill or maybe a tasty beverage? Unfortunately, tiny, sensitive insulin molecules wouldn't stand a chance in the hostile environs of your stomach, where digestive enzymes would rip them to shreds. (How's that for irony? The pancreas has two jobs, producing insulin and, yes, digestive enzymes.) That means you have to bypass your gut and deliver this must-have hormone directly into your bloodstream. Tradition-ally, that has required an injection through the skin.

Before you conjure images of daggerlike syringes, though, there's good news. If you need to inject insulin, the size of the needles you'll be using may surprise

you, because they're relatively tiny. What's more, you can choose from several newfangled alternatives to traditional syringes that may better suit your needs. In fact, recent develop-ments in insulin-delivery technology may allow you to skip the needles altogether, in some cases. (See Insulin Inhalers, page 49.)

HYPODERMIC SYRINGES

Just reading those words can make you wince. Your doctor has been jabbing you with these sharp objects since you were a tiny tot. Syringes are cylinders with plungers on one end and hollow needles fitted into the other. Fortunately, the needles used to inject insulin have gone on a crash diet in recent years. They're sharper than ever, too. Slender gauges and finer points mean they hurt less. Some have special slick coatings, too, which let the needle slide under your skin more easily. Anyone who takes insulin will tell you that it's a bigger deal to test your blood glucose than to give your-self a shot. Your doctor or diabetes educator will help you select a syringe that's appropriate for the dose of insulin you'll be taking.

THE NOT-SO-GOOD OLD DAYS

Before modern, disposable needles became available, people with diabetes injected insulin with thick glass needles that had to be sterilized in boiling water every day and sharp-ened with a pumice stone or razor strap.

INSULIN "PENS"

Warning: These insulin tools really do look like writing instruments, so don't accidentally take out your fountain pen and give yourself a dose of India ink. (The stains will never come out of your arteries.) Like pens you use for writing, some insulin pens use replaceable cartridges and are designed to be permanent; others are disposable (you toss them out after the prefilled cartridge is empty). Insulin pens allow you to "dial" the dose of insulin you need. You simply place the tip to your skin and press the plunger to inject. Speaking of tips, here's a good one: When injecting insulin with a pen, count to six slowly before pulling out the needle in order to keep insulin from leaking out of the injection site. (The same advice applies to short syringe needles.) Some people find insulin pens more convenient, especially if they have to inject frequently. What's more, people who use other methods for injecting insulin (such as syringes or pumps) often carry an insulin pen as an emergency backup.

JET INJECTORS

Got a bad case of belonephobia? That's the medical term for fear of needles and sharp objects. You're in good company; about one person in ten is needle-phobic. An insulin jet injector may be just what you need. These clever tools use high pressure to force a jet stream of insulin through the skin. There is a possible downside, though: Jet injectors can cause bruising.

INSULIN PUMPS

Short of having an organ transplant (which is an option you will read about later in this chapter), an insulin pump is the closest thing to a full-time replacement for your pooped-out pancreas. An insulin pump is a small battery-operated computer, about the size of a pager. (This is a big improvement over the original models introduced in the 1970s, which were strapped onto the back like a jet pack George Jetson might wear to buzz around in space.) The computer is attached to a flexible tube with a catheter on the tip. The computer contains an insulin reservoir and clips onto a belt, waistband, or some other article of clothing. Using an insertion needle, you place the catheter just under the skin, usually on the abdomen. The process is similar to giving yourself a standard insulin injection, with a big exception: Once you have inserted the

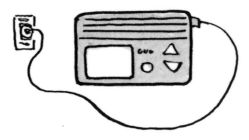

catheter, it can remain in place for two or three days before it needs to be replaced and the injection site changed. And you know what that means—fewer needle jabs.

Based on how much insulin you need and the type you use, you program the computer to deliver an even dose of the hormone (known as basal insulin) throughout the day. However, you can override the computer program with the press of a button and give yourself little pick-me-up doses (called bolus insulin) when necessary—before eating, for instance. And maybe after eating, too, if you had not planned to have dessert but your willpower crumbled when the waiter uttered the words "chocolate cheesecake." It's easy enough to compensate for the occasional splurge. However, hypoglycemia caused by excessive insulin leads to weight gain. The more exact control provided by the pump helps to avoid hypoglycemia.

Studies suggest that people with diabetes who use insulin pumps are better able to manage their blood sugar levels than those who use other methods. However, pumps have a few potential disadvantages. Infection is a risk if you don't change the insertion site frequently and get sloppy with your technique. Also, mechanical problems can cause a pump to malfunction and tubes may become jammed. Or you could simply run out of insulin and not realize it. Any one of these problems could cause glucose levels to soar, resulting in a life-threatening condition called ketoacidosis. However, improvements in pump technology make these problems rare.

Insulin pumps are pricey, too—typically in the four figures; however, most health insurers (including Medicare and Medicaid) cover the cost.

Perhaps the most obvious problem with insulin pumps is figuring out what to do with the tiny computer when you exercise, sleep, go skinny-dipping, or engage in any other activity where you might find it inconvenient to have an electronic appliance attached to your belly. However, it's pretty clear that people with diabetes find these minor hassles worth tolerating and like the convenience of a device that frees them from making scheduled injections. After all, the insulin pump's popularity rises every year. According to the journal *Postgraduate Medicine,* the number of users in the United States rose from just 6,000 in 1990 to 162,000 by 2001. By 2004, the number of users was estimated at 200,000, according to an August 2006 update in *Diabetes Self-Management.*

INSULIN INHALERS

How's this for a breath of fresh air? In mid 2006, the drugmaker Pfizer received Food and Drug Administration (FDA) approval to introduce the first major alternative to needle injections since the discovery of insulin. Exubera is a form of powdered insulin that patients inhale through a plastic hand-held device similar to inhalers used by people with asthma and allergies. Diabetes patients can use Exubera instead of injecting rapid-acting insulin before meals. However, the drug does not replace longer-acting insulin, so hang on to those syringes and pens if you require basal insulin (that is, the injections you give yourself in the morning and at bedtime). Patients must have their lung function tested before receiving a prescription for Exubera; if you have asthma or lung disease, or if you

smoke, the drug is off-limits. Some users may develop a cough or experience a slight loss of lung capacity.

Flesh Trade, or Why You Need to Rotate Injection Sites

If you inject yourself with a needle in the same spot day after day, a funny thing happens: The pierce of the needle hurts less. Even so, you should resist the temptation to establish a permanent pricking point.

Here's why: Insulin causes fat to build up. If you plug the same spot with insulin over and over, eventually the surrounding skin can become swollen and lumpy. This problem is so common that doctors gave it a name: Lipohypertrophy, which basically means "lots of fat that formed a growth." By one estimate, up to 30 percent of people with type 1 diabetes develop lipohypertrophy. It's not just a cosmetic problem, either, though you probably won't be wearing a swimsuit to the beach if you get it. Since fat lacks a good supply of blood vessels, it does a poor job of absorbing insulin, so over time your usual dose won't adequately lower blood sugar. Doctors often discover that when long-time diabetes patients who inject insulin

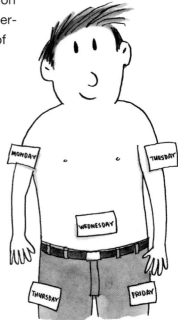

develop problems with glucose control, lipohypertrophy is the culprit.

HOW ABOUT A LITTLE PANCREAS WITH THAT KIDNEY?

The vast majority of pancreas transplants in this country are performed in conjunction with kidney transplants. The organs are usually implanted at the same time (known as simultaneous pancreas-kidney, or SPK). However, in some cases a successful kidney transplant is followed by a pancreas implant (called a pancreas-after-kidney transplant). Research shows that the organs function better when they are both replaced.

Pancreas transplants in the United States:

- 85 percent are simultaneous pancreas-kidney transplants.
- 10 percent are pancreas-after-kidney transplants.
- 5 percent are pancreas-alone transplants.

Taking a few simple measures will prevent these unsightly and disruptive lumps. Farmers rotate crops to give their land a rest. Do the same thing with your injection sites. There are four spots on your body that are optimal for injecting insulin: Your belly is best—it absorbs insulin fastest. The upper part of your outer arms is the next best choice, followed by your outer thighs. Finally, at the bottom of the list, is your bottom. These sites make good targets for your needle because they have relatively few nerves and major arteries, which you don't want to puncture.

But don't alternate injection sites willy-nilly. Remember, different types of insulin are absorbed by the body at different speeds, so the site you choose will further influence how fast an injection enters the bloodstream. In general, you may find it best to inject premeal boluses of insulin into the abdomen so they can get right to work, while using your backside for long-acting insulin. Best bet: Work with your doctor or diabetes educator to create a site-rotation plan.

Here's another good rule of thumb—make that two thumbs—to keep in mind: Every time you return to a site, make your injection one inch (or about two finger widths) from the previous injection.

Harvest Time: Pancreas and Islet Transplants

As everyone knows by now, when you see a guy in a white coat dashing through a hospital carrying a picnic cooler, he's probably not heading out to a tailgate party at a football game. More likely, he's carrying an organ that has been surgically removed, or "harvested," from a recently deceased donor. Organ transplantation, which once seemed like science fiction, has become common. So why not replace your insulin-poor pancreas with one that's still pumping out plenty of the hormone?

A pancreas transplant can eliminate or reduce the need for daily insulin injections and may prevent (and even reverse) some of the complications diabetes can cause (which you'll be reading about later in this book). But unless you're in pretty bad shape, your doctor probably won't recommend a transplant.

A doctor may recommend a pancreas transplant if a diabetes patient's life is threatened by elevated glucose levels. However, the typical candidate for a new pancreas (new to *you,* that is) is a person with type 1 diabetes who needs a kidney transplant, too. As you'll read later on, this combination is hardly unusual, since high, uncontrolled blood sugar can damage the kidneys. So doctors often figure that if they're replacing a diabetes patient's kidney, they may as well throw in a pancreas while they're at it. Having a healthy pancreas may help prevent damage to the implanted kidney. Furthermore, studies show that patients who have a pancreas implanted with a kidney survive longer than patients who only receive a pancreas.

A transplanted pancreas is not a replacement organ, per se, since the surgeon will leave your own pancreas in place; after all, it may not make insulin, but it still produces digestive juices. The transplant is sewn into place in the lower abdomen and attached to blood vessels and the small intestines (or, in some cases, the bladder).

Following surgery, the patient's ever-alert immune system will notice that a foreign object has turned up inside the body, so it will naturally want to attack the new pancreas. To help prevent this internal insurrection from destroying or "rejecting" a new organ, all transplant patients must take immunosuppressive drugs for the rest of their lives. As you might imagine, suppressing the immune system can come at a cost. A weakened defense allows infections to flourish, so patients have to be vigilant about fevers, sores, and other unexplained symptoms. Drugs that suppress immunity also increase the risk for some cancers. Organ transplants seem to raise cholesterol and blood pressure, too.

Since organ transplants are a major ordeal and carry some risks, and since there are effective treatments for diabetes, pancreas-only transplants aren't very common. Surgeons in the United States perform fewer than 200 of the surgeries each year. Combination kidney-pancreas transplants are more common but still account for fewer than 1,500 surgeries annually. To put the number in perspective, about 15,000 kidney transplants are performed each year in the United States.

A Beta Way? Islet Transplants

You developed type 1 diabetes because your immune system attacked your pancreas, having confused it for an intruder. However, those marauding immune cells didn't wipe out your entire pancreas. Instead, they targeted just one type of cell, known as beta cells.

Think about it. When the oil filter in a car gets old and clogged, you don't replace the entire engine. So instead of replacing the entire pancreas in a person with diabetes, why not just restore the cells that make insulin?

Scientists have been tinkering with this idea since the late 1960s. Beta cells live on *islets* (pronounced EYE-lets, like the little holes you thread shoelaces through), which are clusters of cells that cover the pancreas. Islet transplantation is a much simpler, less traumatic procedure than a full pancreas transplant, requiring only local anesthesia in most cases. After islet cells have been removed from the pancreas of a donor cadaver, the surgeon uses ultrasound to guide a catheter into the upper abdomen, where the cells are injected into the liver.

Huh? Why not inject these pancreatic cells into...*the pancreas*? Access is the problem. The pancreas is hard for surgeons to reach, even with today's tiny medical instruments. But the liver can provide a happy home for transplanted islet cells, which—if all goes as planned—will eventually attach to blood vessels and start producing insulin.

Although islet transplantation is still considered experimental, studies suggest it could one day become a widely used therapy for type 1 diabetes. A group of researchers at the University of Alberta, in Edmonton, Canada, reported in 2003 that about half of the patients they have injected with islet cells were insulin-free a year later. Another small study by scientists at the University of Minnesota published in the *Journal of the American Medical Association* in 2005 reported that five out of eight patients injected with islets were able to stay off insulin therapy for more than a year. The U.S. government is sponsoring a large study of islet transplantation.

Intrigued? Keep your eyes on the medical news to monitor how research on islet transplantation is faring.

Managing Type 2 Diabetes

It has become medical boilerplate: After just about every office visit, doctors give patients strict orders to eat right and exercise. We hear these cautions so often that it's easy to zone out and think, Right, doc, whatever you say.... I wonder if I have time to stop for a cheeseburger on the way back to work....

It's time to listen up if you have type 2 diabetes, because physical activity and careful meal planning aren't just good ideas—they are proven therapies that can control your blood sugar. Follow the right regimen in the gym and dining room and you can postpone, and maybe even eliminate, the need for diabetes drugs.

However, even if you do everything right, you may eventually need an insulin boost to keep your blood sugar in check. Fortunately, adding one or more medications described in this chapter to a daily regimen of fitness and food smarts will get your glucose under control.

Hormone Helpers:
Three Ways to Make More Insulin and Make It Work Better

Pity your poor pancreas if you have type 2 diabetes. That odd-shaped organ in your midsection still makes insulin, trying mightily to meet your body's growing demand. But as eager insulin molecules try to persuade your fat and muscle cells to accept shipments of sweet, fuel-efficient glucose, they're getting more doors slammed in their face than the Fuller Brush man. That is, you have insulin resistance, which forces your pancreas to make more and more of the key hormone. Unfortunately, your pancreas may be getting very tired. If you don't take proper steps, it could poop out altogether.

Fortunately, there is plenty you can do to help keep your pancreas pumping and your organs safe from overexposure to blood sugar. In the following pages, you'll learn about the three tools you can use to keep type 2 diabetes under control. Because the first two—diet and exercise—are so important and dependent on one another, we'll only offer an overview here. Later in the book, you'll find a chapter devoted entirely to the importance of designing—and sticking to—a healthy meal plan, along with a close look at the role regular physical activity should play in your self-care regimen. (Besides, while diet and exercise form the core of your initial treatment, both are important for people with type 1 diabetes, too.)

You may never need the third tool, which is the medications doctors can prescribe to lower blood sugar. But if you do, the pharmaceutical industry has come up with an arsenal of drugs that attack the problem from several different angles. Some medications boost insulin production; other medications reduce the amount of glucose circulating in your body. Still others lower insulin resistance by making your cells more responsive, or "sensitive," to the hormone. (As an added bonus, many of these medications have desirable side effects, such as lowering your risk for heart disease. Some will even help you lose weight.)

How will your doctor decide whether you need medication? At least twice a year you'll have blood drawn for an A1c test, which measures levels of sugar-protein packages called glycated hemoglobin to give an overall picture of how well you're managing glucose levels. (See pages 37–38 for an explanation of the A1c test.) Your goal will be to score seven percent or less on the A1c analysis; that is, your blood levels of glycated hemoglobin should be seven percent or lower.

Want to ace the test? Read on.

The Big Myth: The "Diabetic Diet"

Take a deep breath and repeat: *I don't have to give up sugar... I don't have to give up sugar... I don't have to give up sugar...*

Maybe you grew up with a schoolmate who had diabetes whose parents wouldn't let her eat candy. Maybe you've found yourself in the bakery section of the supermarket and stared with horror and distaste at the specially marked "sugar-free" cakes and brownies. Or perhaps you have simply made the logical deduction that, because high blood sugar is your problem, filling up on the sweet stuff probably isn't going to help matters.

But eliminating sugar from your diet isn't fun—and it's impractical, too. In fact, nutritionists say there is no need—make that no way—to follow a "diabetes diet," since there is no such thing. Instead, you can help control your glucose levels by following a balanced meal plan consisting of nutritious foods and occasional indulgences, made up of enough calories to keep your engine running and maintain a healthy weight (or few enough to shed pounds if you're lugging around too many).

That's not to say that the amount of sugar you consume doesn't matter. If you subsist on lollipops and Mountain Dew, chances are you will have pretty lousy glucose control. But remember: Sugars are carbohydrates, and as Gertrude Stein never wrote, a carb is a carb is a carb once it hits your gut. To your body they are all sources of glucose. Studies in the 1990s determined that the dietary key to controlling blood sugar is to avoid consuming too many carbohydrates, period.

So while most of the carbohydrates in your diet should come from healthy sources, such as fruits, vegetables, and whole grains, you can make room for a treasured sweet treat now and then. Your doctor or diabetes educator will

help you determine what daily total is healthy for you. Bottom line: You can have your cake and eat it, too, as long as you curb your carbs for the rest of the day.

(Strictly speaking, the carbohydrate story is a little more complex, since some sources of this nutrient—complex carbs, for instance—are less likely to cause blood sugar spikes. The finer points of meal planning are covered in Chapter 13.)

DIABETES BY THE POUND

How much does being overweight increase the risk of type 2 diabetes? Imagine two men, both 5 feet 10 inches tall. The first weighs 167 pounds, while the other tips the scales at 209 pounds. The latter man is five times more likely to develop type 2 diabetes, according to a 2005 Harvard University study.

GIRTH CONTROL

Although counting carbs is important, controlling girth is just as important if you have type 2 diabetes. After all, people who develop the disease tend to have one thing in common: a silhouette that could

use some reshaping. Perhaps your belts are showing signs of serious strain. One might say that you've become a bit of an endomorph.

Okay, let's just spit it out: You could probably stand to lose a few pounds. Maybe a few dozen pounds or more, but who's counting? Join the club. About two-thirds of Americans are overweight, according to the Centers for Disease Control and Prevention (CDC). The folks at the CDC have a keen interest in the current obesity epidemic in the United States, since packing excess baggage puts you at risk for a long list of diseases. Type 2 diabetes is high on that list.

Scientists are kind of cagey when it comes to discussing obesity and insulin resistance. There is no question that the two go hand in hand, but which comes first?

No one is really sure, although a few things are not in doubt. Insulin resistance seems to run in families, so it's pretty clear that a gene or set of genes that you inherited from your parents made you susceptible to it. And increasing fat, especially intra-abdominal fat, also leads to increased insulin resistance.

However, there's a happy flip side to that equation: Shedding fat makes cells more sensitive to insulin, which leads to better glucose control. Whether you decrease fat via general weight loss or specifically decrease intra-abdominal fat, you will lower your resistance to insulin. In fact, losing just 5 to 10 percent of body weight produces meaningful improvements in insulin sensitivity, according to a 2001 review in *Obesity Research.* In Chapter 13, you'll read up on ways to keep your weight under control while eating a balanced diet that helps maintain healthy blood sugar levels and reduces risk factors for other conditions, especially heart disease. Exercise, as you'll see soon, also lowers insulin resistance.

Exercise: Sweat Therapy

If your idea of exercise is the 50-yard dash from your car to the takeout window of the local burrito joint, the following news may come as a mild shock. Frequent and regular doses of physical activity are an integral part of your plan for managing type 2 diabetes. Your doctor may as well have gotten out a prescription pad and scrawled:

- Take 30-minute exercise break once daily.
- May cause perspiration and loss of hairdo.

- If you miss a dose, do not panic. But don't slack off tomorrow.

Some experts believe that one of the main reasons obese people develop insulin resistance is that they simply don't get enough exercise. When you work out, your muscle cells need to make more energy than usual, so they seem to forget all about insulin resistance and suck up glucose, causing blood sugar to plummet. One analysis of several studies on the effect of exercise on insulin resistance found that patients with type 2 diabetes who work up a sweat regularly can lower their A1c test results by 0.5 to 1.0 percent. That's a significant drop that could forestall or prevent loss of eyesight, kidney damage, limb pain, and other common complications.

Now that sounds worth a little huffing and puffing, doesn't it? And that's the beauty of exercise: Small doses reap big benefits. It's true that exercise therapy is what doctors call "dose dependent"—that is, the more you do, the better your health. But you don't have to run the Boston Marathon to improve your glucose

CAN EXERCISE PREVENT DIABETES?

A study known as the Diabetes Prevention Program (or DPP for short) gathered more than 3,200 people with the form of prediabetes known as impaired glucose tolerance (defined as a blood sugar level between 140 and 199 mg/dl following an oral glucose test). Half were instructed to get off their duffs and start exercising regularly. Nothing too grueling— just 30 minutes of walking or some other moderate physical activity at least five days a week. After three years, researchers compared this group to another group of patients with prediabetes who were not required to work out and found that the exercisers were half as likely to develop full-blown diabetes.

control. Studies show that small spurts of physical activity throughout the day add up and can help do the trick.

Of course, regular exercise does more than lower blood sugar. It also improves cholesterol, blood pressure, and other risk factors for heart disease. People who exercise regularly are less likely to develop colon and breast cancers or to become depressed, and they take fewer medications and require fewer visits to the hospital or doctor's office.

Before you jump on the treadmill, keep in mind that having diabetes may affect your choice of activities and require you to take certain precautions. Depending on how advanced your condition is, your physician may steer you away from forms of exercise that would do more harm than good. If high blood sugar has damaged nerves in your feet, for instance, the pounding of jogging or even long-distance walking probably won't help matters. But if the treadmill is out, you can swim, cycle, or find some other exercise that takes the load off your feet.

If you have been on the sidelines for years, research hints that you're more likely to stick with an exercise plan and avoid injury if you start out with some form of supervised regimen. You could sign up for an aerobics class, for instance, or hire a fitness trainer for a few sessions. What matters most, however, is that you make exercise as much a part of your day as brushing your teeth or monitoring your glucose. (You *are* monitoring your glucose, right?)

Drugs: Better Glucose Control Through Chemistry

Okay, so it turns out that jumping on the treadmill for 45 minutes a day, eating salad for lunch, and switching to low-carb pasta wasn't enough. You took a blood test, and your doctor delivered the news: An A1c test shows that your blood sugar is still too high. Or maybe you were able to lower it into the safe range for a few months or even years, but your glucose has begun to creep upward. If you don't take additional steps, you may soon begin to feel the effects of your raging blood sugar from head to toe.

Don't sweat it—your doctor has at his or her disposal a long list of medications that can help. (But keep up the sweating and the salads; antidiabetes drugs are an addition to exercise and a healthy diet, not a replacement.)

Most of the medications used to treat type 2 diabetes fall into one of several categories:
- Drugs that decrease insulin resistance
- Drugs that work inside your pancreas to increase the body's supply of insulin
- Drugs that retrain your existing supply of insulin to work more effectively
- Drugs that reduce the rate at which your body absorbs sugar
- Drugs that control appetite and blunt huge glucose spikes following meals

The good news: Most of these drugs come in the form of a pill. The not-as-good news: Many of these medications can cause side effects ranging from bothersome to debilitating, though in many cases lowering your dosage brings relief or the effects fade over time. You will probably have to take whatever drug or combination of drugs your doctor prescribes for the rest of your life. But research shows that controlling blood sugar can delay the onset of the complications you'll be reading about later on.

Here's a closer look at each type of drug your doctor may prescribe to help control your blood sugar. (Caution: Many of the medication names you are about to read are difficult to pronounce. We've eased your way by providing a phonetic translation of each name. Italics indicate the syllable that's stressed. Still, be prepared for some tongue-twisters.)

ORAL DRUGS FOR TYPE 2 DIABETES

The following medications are a bit like superheroes. Each one has a unique power. But instead of saving the world with their superhuman strength and speed, these drugs simply act in different parts of the body to ensure that you are able to maintain stable blood sugar.

ORAL DRUGS FOR DIABETES

Type of Drug	Name(s)	How They Work
Sulfonylureas	*First Generation* Chlorpropamide (Diabinese) Tolazamide (Tolinase) Tolbutamide (Orinase) *Second Generation* Glipizide (Glucotrol) Glyburide (DiaBeta, Micronase, Glynase) Glimepride (Amaryl)	They make your pancreas produce more insulin.
Meglitinides	Repaglinide (Prandin) Nateglinide (Starlix)	Like sulfonylureas, they make your pancreas produce more insulin, only faster, making them ideal for controlling post-meal blood sugar. Less risk of hypoglycemia.
Biguanides	Metformin (Glucophage) Metformin ER (Glucophage XR)	They slow the release of glucose from the liver. Less risk of hypoglycemia. May produce weight loss.
Thiazolidinediones (also called glitazones)	Rosiglitazone (Avandia) Pioglitazone (Actos)	They lower insulin resistance and risk factors for heart disease. May repair damaged kidneys.
Alpha-glucose Inhibitors	Acarbose (Precose) Miglitol (Glyset)	Prevent breakdown of starches and some other sugars, which lowers blood sugar. They don't cause hypoglycemia.

Note: Women on oral diabetes medications who become pregnant are usually switched to insulin therapy.

What to Keep in Mind

May cause hypoglycemia and weight gain. Other possible effects include upset stomach and heartburn.

May cause back pain, headaches, gastrointestinal problems, and other symptoms.

May cause gastrointestinal problems ER/XR may increase triglycerides. Should not be used by heavy drinkers, people with kidney or liver problems, lung disease, and certain other conditions.

Must have liver function monitored regularly. May cause weight gain, increase fertility, and reduce effects of contraceptive pills.

May cause flatulence and other gastrointestinal problems. Starch blocking limits carbohydrate options for treating hypoglycemic episodes.

Sulfonylureas

Insulin was the only treatment available for people with diabetes until this class of drugs (pronounced sul fuh nil *yoor* ee uhz... see what we mean?) was introduced in the 1950s. Sulfonylureas work by stimulating the pancreas to perk up and make more insulin. If you work in an office or factory, your boss may have hired an efficiency expert to find ways to make the staff more productive. Sulfonylureas do the same thing for your pancreas. But instead of recommending more overtime and shorter lunch breaks, sulfonylureas get inside the pancreas's beta cells and cause them to release more insulin.

The sulfonylureas are usually broken down into older "first generation" pills and newer "second generation" pills (see "Oral Drugs for Diabetes"). First generation sulfonylureas are falling out of favor because, in general, the second generation versions are more potent and have fewer side effects. Over time, some of your pancreas's insulin makers will simply die off or slow down production. Here's a good reason for people with type 2 diabetes to perform daily glucose readings: As beta cell function decreases over time, the same amount of your sulfonylurea medication will be less effective at reducing glucose. Your doctor may prescribe another version of the drug, or he or she may tell you to stop taking it altogether and switch to one of the other drugs described here.

What You Should Know About Sulfonylureas. A healthy pancreas is acutely sensitive to glucose levels in the blood, so it only produces as much insulin as the body needs. Sulfonylureas keep your beta cells working all the time, so a steady stream of insulin pours into the blood whether it's needed or not. As a result, blood sugar levels can drop too low, causing hypoglycemia. (This problem is especially common in the elderly and people who have liver or kidney disease.) On the other hand, if your dose is too low, blood sugar can remain too high. Adjusting your dose can help relieve these problems.

Sulfonylureas may cause you to put on a few pounds or develop heartburn and other stomach problems. If you become pregnant, your doctor may switch you to another drug. Finally, drinking alcohol while taking certain sulfonylurea drugs may cause nausea, vomiting, and flushed skin. In other words, you won't exactly be the life of the party, so talk to your doctor about mixing booze and any diabetes drug.

Meglitinides

These drugs act like sulfonylureas that have had too much caffeine. Like sulfonylureas, they trigger beta cells to release insulin. The difference is that meglitinides are impatient: They want insulin *now*. What's more, while sulfonylureas linger in your system all day, meglitinides rush in and out quickly. Because of their hyperactive nature, meglitinides play a specific role in managing type 2 diabetes: You take these drugs before meals to boost insulin production in order to lower the predictable post-meal rise in blood sugar.

By the way, you may also see these drugs referred to as nonsulfonylurea secretagogues. The scary second word simply refers to something that stimulates secretion, or the act of making and discharging a substance. But don't worry, you will not be tested on this material.

What You Should Know About Meglitinides. Meglitinides appear to cause hypoglycemia less often than sulfonylureas, but it's still a possibility, especially if your dose is too high. Other side effects are uncommon but can include backaches, headaches, cold and flu symptoms, chest pain, gastrointestinal problems, joint pain, tingling skin, certain infections, and vomiting.

Biguanides

Unlike sulfonylureas and meglitinides, these drugs ignore the pancreas and don't increase insulin levels. Instead, they take some of the burden off the pancreas by fixing a problem with another organ, the liver. The liver stockpiles glucose and makes glucose out of fragments of other molecules, which it releases when blood sugar levels dip too low, such as between meals, especially overnight. After all, even though you're in la-la land, your body still needs glucose; if your glucose dried up, your organs would shut down and even the loudest alarm clock could not wake you.

When it works as it should, the liver slows the release of glucose when there's a lot of insulin in the blood, a sure signal that there's already plenty of sugar to go around. However, if you have type 2 diabetes, your liver never gets the memo instructing it to stop releasing glucose. It just keeps unloading the sweet stuff into the blood, making insulin's job that much harder.

Biguanides are multitalented drugs, but their main role is to put a clamp on the liver so that it releases less glucose into

IS METFORMIN SAFE?

In a word, yes, though you may have heard that it causes a rare but deadly complication called lactic acidosis. Here's the real deal: A predecessor of metformin, known as phenformin, was introduced in the 1950s. Phenformin worked like a charm, but it was banned in the United States in 1977 because some patients who took the drug developed lactic acidosis. Lactic acid is a waste product produced by cells when they burn glucose during hard exercise or other times when oxygen levels in the body are low. When too much lactic acid builds up, muscle pain, erratic heartbeat, rapid breathing, and other problems can result. Lactic acidosis is fatal about 40 percent of the time.

Scientists reconfigured the drug to eliminate the lactic acidosis threat, and Bristol-Myers Squibb introduced the new version, known as metformin, in 1995. Not surprisingly, doubts about the drug linger, and occasional reports arise of lactic acidosis in patients who take metformin. However, according to a commentary published in the July 2004 edition of *Diabetes Care,* an American Diabetes Association journal, virtually all cases of lactic acidosis linked to metformin have been in patients who took overdoses or shouldn't have been taking it in the first place, such as people with kidney disease or excessive alcohol intake. According to the commentary, when metformin is used as labeled, the increased risk of lactic acidosis is either zero or very close to zero.

the blood. With less glucose floating around in the blood, insulin demand drops.

Biguanides have several key advantages over sulfonylureas and meglitinides, because they do not cause hypoglycemia and are less likely to make you pack on pounds. Some users even lose weight. They increase your IQ 50 points and leave your breath smelling minty fresh... well, maybe not, but as you can see, biguanides have a lot going for them.

What You Should Know About Biguanides. These valuable drugs are not without potential problems. About one-third of patients who take biguanides develop gastrointestinal problems, including upset stomach, gas, diarrhea, and vomiting. (The reason some users lose weight could be that they feel too lousy to eat.) Headaches and fatigue may occur, too. The good news is that these side effects usually fade within a few weeks. It may also help to start with small doses, gradually building up. Taking biguanides with meals can reduce stomach distress, as well.

Biguanides are among the most widely prescribed diabetes drugs, but they're not for everyone. Your doctor will choose another therapy for you if

- you're a heavy drinker. Of course, you already know darn well that you should either be a teetotaler or light sipper, since having more than one to two drinks increases lactate and may increase the risk of lactic acidosis if you take biguanides and drink. (If you didn't know that, now you do.)
- you have kidney or liver disease
- you are over 80, unless tests show that your liver and kidneys are still working hard
- you have congestive heart failure or any other condition that interferes with circulation
- you have serious asthma or lung disease
- you are pregnant
- you are a child. (And if you are a child, isn't it past your bedtime?)

One last word about biguanides: They lower levels of vitamin B_{12} in 10 to 30 percent of patients. However, taking calcium supplements may offset the drop, since your body needs the mineral to absorb vitamin B_{12}. Ask your doctor if you should be taking extra calcium.

Thiazolidinediones

Try saying *that* three times fast. Thankfully, these drugs (thigh uh zo li deen *die ohnz*) are often collectively referred to by other names, including glitazones, TZDs, and insulin sensitizers. The last name offers a clue about the role of thiazoli…let's just call them the glitazones. For a person with type 2 diabetes, problems begin with the condition known as insulin resistance. Your pancreas makes insulin, which tries mightily to usher glucose into muscle and fat cells, but too often it fails. So your pancreas has to make more insulin so your cells can get their fuel. It's as though your cells can't hear insulin molecules knocking until there's a mob of them outside.

The glitazones make cells more sensitive to insulin so that they respond to a light tap on the door and allow glucose to enter. Actually, the way the glitazones work is a bit more complex, but the bottom line is this: These drugs reduce insulin resistance, which will help keep your blood sugar levels under control. In turn, the insulin-making beta cells in your pancreas don't have to work so hard. That means they're less likely to conk out altogether, meaning you would require insulin injections.

SPLITSVILLE: CAN DIVIDING PILLS SAVE YOU MONEY?

Maybe. Drugmakers often charge the same price for different dosages of the same medication. Patients who pay for their own drugs sometimes ask their doctors to prescribe double doses, which they split in half to save cash. The practice is perfectly safe with certain pills, according to the *Medical Letter on Drugs and Therapeutics,* an independent nonprofit publications for physicians that reviews and evaluates drugs. That includes several widely used diabetes drugs. If your doctor agrees to prescribe a double dose, follow these simple rules:

- Use a pill cutter (available in drugstores) instead of a razor or old butter knife to avoid cutting yourself or ruining part of the pill.
- To maintain even dosing, always take the two halves of a split pill consecutively. Some patients chop a month's worth of pills all at once, then dump the fragments back in the bottle. But studies show that it's just about impossible to produce evenly cut pill fragments. Pop small fragments for several days in a row, and your blood levels of the drug could drop too low—or vice versa.
- Never split pills without your doctor's consent. Some pills (such as capsules) should not be divided.

Pill splitting may not only be for self-payers, since some insurers have begun to offer lower co-payments to customers who agree to divide their oral medications. Ask your provider about cutting yourself a deal.

Wait, there's more! The glitazones may also reduce your risk for heart disease, which is higher than normal because you have diabetes. Like biguanides, the glitazones lower triglycerides and raise HDL ("good") cholesterol. Their impact on LDL cholesterol is more complex. The glitazones actually cause a small rise in levels of the "bad" kind of cholesterol. However, these drugs also make LDL particles bigger and puffier. Cardiologists believe that small, dense LDL cholesterol particles do the most damage in your arteries. Speaking of your arteries, glitazones also seem to protect the lining of blood vessels, which makes them less likely to clog up. Last but not least, as you will read later on in this book, diabetes makes you more vulnerable to kidney disease. However, the glitazones seem to repair damaged kidneys.

What You Should Know About Glitazones. The glitazones have something else in common with metformin—an ancestor they would like to forget. The Food and Drug Administration (FDA) ordered an early version of these drugs, called troglitazone (brand name: Rezulin), taken off the market in the United States in 2000. The problem: While troglitazone did a spiffy job of controlling blood sugar, in rare cases it caused serious—sometimes fatal—liver damage. The FDA declared that two other similar drugs, rosiglitazone and pioglitazone, were safer to use. Still, if your doctor prescribes one of these two drugs, he or she will undoubtedly insist on monitoring your liver function through occasional blood tests.

As with many diabetes drugs, the glitazones may cause you to gain a few pounds. (See "Diabetes by the Pound," page 56.) Your doctor will probably switch you to another drug if you become pregnant, as this class of drug is not recommended in pregnancy. And if you're a woman and don't want to become pregnant, beware: The glitazones can lower blood levels of oral contraceptives, which makes them less effective. They also appear to increase ovulation in some women, which makes them more fertile.

Alpha-Glucosidase Inhibitors

If high blood sugar is the problem, why not cut back on how much of the stuff you let into your system in the first place? Alpha-glucosidase (al pha glu *cos* i dase) is a type of enzyme that lines the small intestine. Its job is to break down certain forms of sugar, especially starch, so they can pass through the intestine and into the bloodstream. Alpha-glucosidase inhibitors (AGIs) interfere with these enzymes so they don't work as well. As a result, a small amount of glucose trickles into your blood, but starch molecules are denied entry. They remain stuck in the intestines, where they wend their way along the tube's torturous route until being excreted.

You take an AGI with your first bite of food, which helps prevent post-meal sugar spikes. To a lesser extent, they lower blood glucose levels between meals, too.

What You Should Know About Alpha-Glucosidase Inhibitors. Have you ever eaten a big, steaming bowl of baked beans, then experienced certain uncomfortable and socially embarrassing side effects the next day? The same thing can happen with AGIs. Beans are packed with fiber, which your body can't digest. Like fiber, all that starch you're not digesting when you take an AGI eventually makes it to the large intestine, where it is attacked by bacteria. The process of breaking down fiber, starch, or any other undigested sugar produces gas. Lots of it. The resulting flatulence, abdominal pain, and diarrhea can be bad enough that some patients plead with their

doctors to give them a prescription for some other drug. Some patients find that these problems with the body's food-processing apparatus aren't as severe if they start with a small dose.

AGIs don't cause hypoglycemia, though taking them with certain other diabetic drugs can produce low blood sugar. Keep in mind that if you do develop hypoglycemia while using these drugs, you have to be choosy about what you eat to remedy the problem since AGIs block certain sugars. (Glucose tablets, honey, or fruit juice will do the trick.)

If you have had any serious intestinal condition in the past, your doctor probably won't recommend these drugs. Likewise, AGIs are usually considered off-limits for pregnant women.

INJECTED DRUGS
Popping a pill is painless, but some diabetes medications must bypass your belly and be sent directly into the bloodstream. The potential payoff—better glucose control—is worth the tiny prick in the skin, however.

Exenatide
The Gila monster is a brawny, two-foot lizard with a brutal, venomous bite that

BETTER TOGETHER: COMBINING DRUGS

Each of the medications you just read about has something to offer the patient with type 2 diabetes. But, like a hot dog and mustard, some things work better in combination than they do alone. If you are taking an oral diabetes drug, chances are you will eventually need a second and possibly a third medication to keep your glucose under control. In fact, for every 100 patients with type 2 diabetes who begin taking oral drugs today, 50 will need a second drug to keep their blood sugar under control within three years. In nine years, 75 of those patients will require a combination of pills, according to the August 2005 issue of *Treatment Guidelines from the Medical Letter,* an independently published newsletter for physicians.

One of the most common drug pairings for treating type 2 diabetes is a sulfonylurea with metformin. The rationale for this combination is simple: They complement one another. The sulfonylurea increases insulin production by stimulating the pancreas, while metformin reduces the amount of glucose released by the liver. Combination pills are available, too. One, Glucovance, combines the sulfonylurea glyburide with metformin. Another, Avandamet, is a one-two punch of the glitazone rosiglitazone and metformin.

lives in the desert of the southwestern United States. Why the zoology lesson? Because these scaly critters produce a hormone that may be the key to better glucose control for some people with type 2 diabetes.

Here's why: Gila monsters only eat four times a year—mostly small animals, eggs, and whatever else they can find. The rest of the year, the big lizards survive off fat packed away in their chunky tails and bellies. Since it would be pointless, and probably not too healthy, to keep cranking out insulin during those long months between meals, Gila monsters developed the ability to turn off their pancreases. That led researchers to wonder: When Gila monsters finally do sit down to dinner, they need insulin to process food. How do they turn their pancreases back on?

Scientists eventually discovered a hormone called exendin-4 in the Gila monster's saliva, of all places. (Collecting Gila spit is probably not the highlight of a lab assistant's day.) To be more precise, exendin-4 is an incretin hormone that's produced in the intestines. Humans make incretins, too. When you eat, your gut senses glucose and immediately sends incretins to the pancreas with orders to produce insulin. But in people with type 2 diabetes, the signal from incretins is too weak to stimulate insulin production.

Exendin-4, on the other hand, has to be potent enough to arouse a pancreas that's been snoozing for months. Exenatide (brand name: Byetta) is a synthetic version of exendin-4. Because exenatide imitates exendin-4, it's called an incretin *mimetic*. ("Mimetic" comes from the word "mime," of course.)

Studies show that exenatide keeps blood sugar low not only by stimulating insulin production but also by instructing the pancreas to make less of that other critical hormone, glucagon. As glucagon is suppressed, the liver in turn puts out less glucose. That means less strain on the pancreas. In fact, some research suggests that exenatide even causes the pancreas to make new beta cells.

Exenatide also causes food to pass through your stomach at a more leisurely rate, which slows the rapid rise in glucose after a meal. It also means your belly feels full longer, so you eat less. In fact, while most diabetes drugs cause weight gain, exenatide seems to have the opposite effect. In one study, people with type 2 diabetes who took the drug for 30 weeks lost more than six pounds, on average.

So what's the catch? Although it's a powerful drug, exenatide is rather delicate in one sense: It can't tolerate the rough trip through your gastrointestinal system, so it has to be injected just like insulin. Exenatide doses come in prepackaged "pens," similar to the ones used by many diabetes patients who require insulin injections. Exenatide users give themselves two injections per day, before breakfast and dinner. Because most people would rather toss back a pill with a glass of water than poke a needle in their belly or backside, your doctor probably won't prescribe exenatide unless other oral diabetes pills fail to keep your glucose under control.

What You Should Know About Exenatide. Exenatide can cause nausea, though it often fades over time. Some other side effects that users have reported include vomiting, diarrhea, the jitters, dizziness, headaches, and upset stomach. Taken alone exenatide doesn't cause hypoglycemia, but blood sugar may drop too low if the drug is paired with one of the sulfonylureas. People who have kidney disease or serious gastrointestinal problems shouldn't use exenatide. Animal studies show that exenatide may harm fetuses, so women who use the drug and become pregnant may be switched to another medication.

Pramlintide

Let's get the unwelcome news out of the way first: Like exenatide, pramlintide is an injected drug. Then again, if your doctor prescribes pramlintide, you are probably already accustomed to pricking and poking yourself, since the medication is used in conjunction with insulin injections. That means it's designed for people with type 1 *and* type 2 diabetes.

Pramlintide (brand name: Symlin) is a synthetic version of yet another hormone that plays an important role in controlling blood sugar. It turns out that beta cells hold down two jobs. Not only do they produce insulin, but they also make the hormone amylin. Beta cells churn out amylin at the same time as insulin when you eat. Like those gut incretins you read about earlier, amylin lowers glucagon levels, so your liver doesn't release unneeded glucose. It also makes the stomach empty into the intestines more slowly after a meal, which prevents glucose spikes.

Unfortunately, if you have type 2 diabetes, your beta cells may be so beat up that you're not producing enough amylin. If you have type 1 diabetes, you probably aren't making the hormone at all. By replacing amylin, pramlintide helps keeps blood sugar levels stable after meals. Some users even lose a few pounds. Your doctor will only add pramlintide to your daily regimen if insulin injections have failed to lower your glucose levels into the safe zone.

Pramlintide is injected just like insulin at mealtimes. But the two hormones don't blend well, so you can't combine the two drugs into one syringe. If you need to take both drugs, you'll still have to inject twice.

What You Should Know About Pramlintide. Monitoring your blood sugar is a must if you're using pramlintide (as it is if you're injecting insulin); if your blood sugar is a bit on the low side, a dose of the drug could send it into a freefall and you'll develop severe hypoglycemia. The most common side effect of pramlintide is nausea, followed by loss of appetite, headache, vomiting, stomach pain, fatigue, dizziness, and upset stomach. You might also develop redness, pain, or minor bruising at the spot where you inject pramlintide.

Be sure to talk to your doctor about any other medications you may be taking if he or she prescribes pramlintide. Because it slows down activity in your stomach, it could alter the effectiveness of some drugs.

INSULIN THERAPY

When doctors abandoned the old name "non-insulin dependent diabetes mellitus" in favor of the sleeker "type 2 diabetes," they weren't merely opting for a more minimalist, time-saving moniker. Instead, they were acknowledging that, for at least one-quarter of their patients with the condition, the old name is just plain wrong. Although most people with type 2 diabetes have functioning pancreases when they are diagnosed, over time a patient's beta cells may not be able to keep up with demand for insulin, even if taking oral diabetes drugs.

Research shows that oral medications are frequently not enough for patients to maintain healthy blood sugar. For instance, a 1998 British study of nearly 600 people with type 2 diabetes found that within three years of starting on metformin and a sulfonylurea, just one-third of patients had A1c readings below seven percent. This is critical, as over the long term, levels higher than seven percent can lead to organ damage. On the other hand, properly executed insulin therapy is just about foolproof, with a stellar track record for lowering blood sugar.

When blood tests reveal glucose levels that remain stubbornly high, doctors will usually tell the patient that he or she needs a shot in the arm—literally (but the abdomen, thigh, or rear will also do). Although many physicians once considered insulin injections to be the treatment of last resort for their patients with type 2 diabetes, many now see this form of hormone replacement therapy as a way to manage the disease at earlier stages in order to prevent the serious, debilitating complications that can result from chronically elevated blood sugar.

If your doctor recommends insulin therapy, you're in good company. According to a 2004 survey published in the journal *Diabetes Care,* 27 percent of Americans with type 2 diabetes inject insulin. Within that group, about 60 percent use only insulin, while the remainder take a combination of insulin and one or more oral drugs.

If you are currently taking oral diabetes drugs and your doctor wants you to add insulin to your regimen, chances are you will only have to inject the drug once a day, probably in the evening or just before going to bed. Unlike the early days of insulin therapy, when there was only one type to choose from, today you and your doctor can select from several different varieties in order to fine-tune your treatment. Some hit your bloodstream and start working right away, while others take their time and last all day. For a comprehensive look at insulin therapy, see Chapter 3.

Some patients bring a whole new meaning to the phrase "insulin resistance" when their physicians bring up the therapy. In other words, they refuse the treatments because they want

HERBS YOUR ENTHUSIASM?
THINK TWICE BEFORE TAKING DIETARY SUPPLEMENTS FOR DIABETES

Walk into any vitamin shop or health food store and you'll find plenty of pills and other products bearing label claims like "maintains healthy sugar" or "boosts insulin." Surf the Internet and you'll find even more "natural" products that sure sound like they would benefit someone with diabetes. These herbs, vitamins, minerals, and other dietary supplements are often (though not always) cheap, and you can take them without a prescription. Should you?

Only if you meet two conditions: 1) Your doctor says it's okay, and 2) You're a gambler. Dietary supplements are not closely regulated by the Food and Drug Administration (FDA). While new drugs have to undergo extensive testing before hitting the market, dietary supplements are regulated more like food; that is, any company can sell them without having to prove that the products do much of anything.

And that's just the problem. None of the herbs and supplements marketed to people with diabetes has been adequately studied, so you have no way of knowing whether any of them help control blood sugar. For instance, some supplement sellers claim that high doses of the mineral chromium can reduce insulin resistance. However, the authors of a review in the journal *Diabetes Care* called the evidence for that claim "inconclusive." In fact, the authors examined every study they could find in which natural pills and potions were used to control glucose levels and found that "there is insufficient evidence to actively recommend or discourage use of any particular supplement...."

Ginseng, cinnamon, vitamin E, or any of the other natural pills touted as blood sugar saviors might actually work. But until more evidence is available, such claims are hard to swallow.

nothing to do with needles. Or maybe they associate insulin treatments with their old Aunt Mabel who needed to inject the drug and, heck, she was blind and always complained about her aching feet.

In fact, doctors sometimes say that patients who are hesitant or unwilling to take this important therapy have "psychological insulin resistance." A 2005 survey of more than 3,800 people with diabetes conducted by the Behavioral Diabetes Institute in San Diego found that more than one-quarter refused insulin therapy. Patients give a variety of reasons for not wanting to take insulin; we'll take a closer look at these fears and concerns in Chapter 15, which discusses psychological aspects of diabetes—that is, how the disease can mess with your head and what to do when that happens.

Despite this common aversion to insulin therapy among people with type 2 diabetes, doctors seem to be doing a pretty good job of persuading patients that the treatments are worth the trouble. While the number of type 2-ers who take only insulin has dropped since 1994, the portion using insulin *and* an oral diabetes drug has tripled and then some.

SOME DRUGS TO WATCH FOR

Worldwide, there are about 200 million people with diabetes, so it's not surprising that the pharmaceutical industry is hard at work developing new drugs to treat the condition. (What company wouldn't want to discover a cure for diabetes? Can you spell "ka-ching"?) A new class of drugs called DPP-IV inhibitors designed for people with type 2 diabetes may be closest to reaching the market. Earlier, you read about incretins, hormones produced by the intestines that instruct the pancreas to make insulin when you eat. An enzyme called DPP-IV turns off incretin; DPP-IV inhibitors block the enzyme, which in theory should allow for greater insulin production. Early studies show that people with type 2 diabetes who take the drug experience impressive dips in blood sugar. Several companies are developing their own versions of the drug.

Another drug that could benefit people with diabetes and may become available by 2007 has a curious history. Scientists have long known that smoking marijuana makes people ravenously hungry for pizza, potato chips, cookies, and other high-calorie foods. (Yes, this phenomenon has actually been proven in lab studies, even though the same scientists could have amassed equally convincing evidence by walking into practically any college dorm in the country.)

Some buzz-kill researchers came up with an idea: Would turning off cell receptors in the brain that are stimulated by chemicals in marijuana eliminate "the munchies"? And if so, could doing so help people who battle the bulge control appetite? A French pharmaceutical company developed a drug called rimonabant that does just that. A 2005 study found that overweight people who took rimonabant for a year sustained an average weight loss of 15 pounds, while a similar group of people who took empty placebo pills lost just 4 pounds.

This news alone should be of interest to people with type 2 diabetes who struggle with weight problems. However, rimonabant also seems to produce a modest but significant drop in blood sugar, beyond the glucose improvement that might be expected from simply losing weight. The drug also raises HDL ("good") cholesterol and lowers unhealthy blood fats called triglycerides, which decrease the risk for heart disease. If the drug is approved by the FDA, some doctors who treat people with diabetes have already said they plan to prescribe it to patients with mildly elevated blood sugar.

Hypoglycemia and Hyperglycemia

In many aspects of life, success depends on finding the right balance. If you forget the sugar when you bake a birthday cake, for example, it will taste like Styrofoam. But if you accidentally double the sugar portion, you'll have a treacly torte that's just as inedible. Either way, you won't get many requests for seconds.

Likewise, the key challenge in managing diabetes is keeping your blood sugar in a happy state of equilibrium. Yet, there are many ways to disrupt this balance, including—ironically—taking the very medications you may use to control diabetes. Knowing how to recognize and respond to the symptoms of high and low blood sugar will help keep you blowing out the candles for many years to come.

Hypoglycemia: The Basics

Keeping blood sugar from rising too high is the goal for anyone with any variety of diabetes. But hypoglycemia (high po gly *see* me uh) is, in a sense, the result of too much success. This term for very low blood sugar is a combination of three Greek words: *Hypo* = under, *glykys* = sweet, and *haima* = blood. Anyone can become hypoglycemic, but for people with diabetes, curbing the threat of nose-diving blood sugar is part of daily life.

When glucose levels drop off, cells throughout much of the body can adjust by living off fat and protein, at least temporarily. But one very important organ—the one located between your ears—can't use fat and protein for energy. Since the brain needs glucose to survive, it regards a sugar shortage as a crisis. Early symptoms are no big deal. You feel hungry and a little shaky and nervous, like you had too much coffee. But soon you begin to feel woozy and need to sit down. Your heart thumps, and you break into a cold sweat. Unless you take the proper steps, you may become confused and talk incoherently. Your vision blurs and your head

feels ready to burst. In a sense, it is: In extreme cases, hypoglycemia causes convulsions and even comas.

What causes a plunge in blood sugar? In a person who does not have diabetes, hypoglycemia is fairly uncommon, since the body comes equipped with an efficient system that keeps blood sugar levels balanced. When blood sugar begins to drop, the pancreas senses trouble and slows down insulin production, so the body doesn't use up glucose so quickly. For an added boost, the pancreas makes the hormone glucagon, which signals the liver to convert some glycogen to glucose, then release the sugary stuff into the blood. It all happens so quickly that a dip in blood sugar is brief and goes unnoticed.

This system can get out of whack if you have diabetes, making it tricky to maintain balanced blood sugar. That's especially true if you inject insulin or take sulfonylureas or meglitinides, two widely used medications that perk up insulin production in the pancreas. Getting the proper dose of these therapies exactly right is something of an art. To avoid frequent bouts of hypoglycemia, you must become expert at tweaking your dosage when necessary and knowledgeable about the steps you can take to help keep your blood sugar from plummeting.

Preventing Hypoglycemia

Chances are, you are going to experience at least a touch of hypoglycemia now and then. Accepting that these occasional spells are part of coping with diabetes can make them less upsetting or disruptive. Better yet, take the following advice and limit your bouts with low blood sugar.

MEDICATIONS

Insulin therapy and insulin-stimulating drugs are lifesavers. But these treatments know how to do one thing—lower blood sugar—and even when glucose levels reach perilously low levels, they keep doing just that, ignoring cues from the body to knock it off. One common cause of hypoglycemia is medication overkill: Even though you took the recommended dose, it was more medicine than your body needed, like extinguishing a lit match with a fire hose.

In other words, you artificially increased insulin levels beyond the amount you needed to control blood sugar. This can occur because you goofed up and took too much medicine, of course. But often

TROUBLESHOOTING CHECKLIST

Hypoglycemia, or low blood sugar, is a risk for anyone who has diabetes. However, it's most common among patients who inject insulin or take insulin-stimulating drugs, including sulfonylureas and meglitinides. Consider hypoglycemia when you begin to feel any of these symptoms in the extreme:

- ☐ Excessive hunger
- ☐ Nervousness
- ☐ The jitters or shakiness
- ☐ Sweating for no apparent reason
- ☐ Anxiety
- ☐ Weakness, loss of coordination
- ☐ Dizziness or feeling light-headed
- ☐ Sleepiness
- ☐ Confusion
- ☐ Difficulty speaking
- ☐ Blurred vision

If any of the following occurs while you're in bed, low blood sugar is a possibility:

- ☐ You have a nightmare or cry out in your sleep
- ☐ You awaken with pajamas or bed sheets that are wet with perspiration. (Check your blood glucose if the sweats might be associated with perimenopause.)
- ☐ In the morning you feel tired, confused, or irritable or you awaken with a headache
- ☐ If you still have symptoms after eating a sugary snack or taking a glucose pill or supplement, go to an emergency room immediately or call 911 (or local emergency number)

SO YOU THINK YOU'RE HYPOGLYCEMIC

Here's what to do:

1. Confirm your hunch by checking your blood sugar. If it's over 70 mg/dl, your blood sugar is okay, but consider what else might be making you feel weird. If your blood sugar is 70 mg/dl or lower, assume you have hypoglycemia. If you can't check your blood sugar but suspect it may be too low, play it safe and take further steps.

2. Eat, drink, or swallow 15 grams of simple sugar.

3. Wait 15 minutes, then check your blood sugar again. If it's above 70 mg/dl, the crisis is averted. If it's still lower than 70 mg/dl, consume another 15 grams of sugar.

4. Wait another 15 minutes, then check your blood sugar. If it's above 70 mg/dl and more than 30 minutes (some experts say 60 minutes) until your next planned meal, have a snack that contains carbohydrates, protein, and fat.

5. If your blood sugar doesn't rise above 70 mg/dl, repeat the process until it does. If it remains stubbornly low, call your doctor or go to an emergency room.

Be sure that family, friends, and coworkers can recognize symptoms of hypoglycemia; if you fail to notice and act on them in time, your condition may worsen to the point that you are unable to help yourself. Make sure they know what to do—and what not to do—if you can't swallow or become unconscious, or if you are unable to treat your hypoglycemia for any reason.

- They *should* give you a glucagon injection immediately, even if it's not clear you have low blood sugar.
- They *should* call 911 or the local emergency number if the glucagon doesn't relieve your symptoms.
- They *shouldn't* attempt to give you insulin or other diabetes medicine.
- They *shouldn't* attempt to feed you.

this problem is unavoidable and happens even if you do everything right. Your quirky corpus can change its mind about how much insulin it needs from day to day. You can even monitor your glucose levels with the vigilance of a hawk and still end up having a hypoglycemic episode. (In fact, experts say that people with type 1 diabetes can count on having at least one per week.) However, various lifestyle decisions and choices you make every day will affect how well insulin therapies work, as you'll learn when you read on.

Tip:

- Discuss with your doctor or diabetes educator how much insulin or insulin-stimulating medication you need and how your lifestyle will affect the dose you should take.

MEALS

Say you are about to head down to the cafeteria for lunch when the boss asks if you faxed that 50-page document to Los Angeles—the one that was supposed to be there an hour ago. Or you're halfway through dinner when your long-lost twin sister Mildred shows up at the door. You are probably not going to say, "Great to see you, Millie, but give me five minutes while I finish this tuna sandwich."

Because you have diabetes, you must be sure that your body has enough insulin to process the food you eat, especially if you inject insulin or take sulfonylureas or meglitinides. But when you skip or put off a meal—or eat less than you planned—you can end up with more insulin than you need.

Tips:
- Try to eat meals and snacks at the same time every day.
- Avoid skipping meals.
- Clean your plate—eat as much as you planned. However, if you need to overeat to prevent low blood glucose, discuss this with your doctor.
- Talk to your doctor or diabetes educator about what to do on days when interruptions to your meal routine are unavoidable.

EXERCISE AND OTHER PHYSICAL ACTIVITY

Keeping fit has unquestionable benefits for anyone with diabetes. But if you have diabetes, especially the type 1 variety, exercise requires a bit more planning than simply deciding whether you'll use the stair-climber or elliptical trainer when you get to the gym.

The problem begins with your muscles. During exertion, their fuel demand skyrockets. In a person who does not have diabetes, insulin levels drop and glucagon rises, causing the liver to release glucose so cells can burn it as energy. As a result, blood sugar levels remain fairly constant.

Unfortunately, if you have type 1 diabetes, your pancreas doesn't respond to exercise and the greater demand for glucose by reducing insulin levels because, well, you don't have any insulin to cut back on. Instead, you add insulin to your blood by injecting it. But the dose you need while sitting around the house staring at the fish tank is much higher than what you need while playing full-court basketball. If you don't adjust the dose accordingly, high insulin levels in the blood prevent the liver from releasing stored glucose and blood sugar levels will fall. The result: Game over.

Exercise-induced hypoglycemia is also a concern for people with type 2 diabetes who take a sulfonylurea or meglitinide. Although your pancreas may want to slow insulin production during exercise, both drugs make sure it keeps busy making the hormone.

THE ROAD TO RUIN?
DRIVING AND HYPOGLYCEMIA

Shaky hands and rattled nerves. Dizziness and blurred vision. Confusion and loss of coordination. A serious episode of hypoglycemia is guaranteed to spoil a leisurely Sunday drive in the country. Although people with diabetes who take the proper precautions can be excellent drivers, studies show that patients who have the disease (especially type 1) can pose a risk on the road.

A 2003 study in *Diabetes Care* found that about one in three people with type 1 diabetes had become hypoglycemic while driving. Not surprisingly, they had more than twice as many accidents as their nondiabetic spouses. The type 1 patients had significantly more traffic violations, too.

Other studies offer clues about how diabetes patients can ensure that when they set off for work in the morning, they don't end up in the emergency room. A 1999 survey in the *Journal of the American Medical Association* found that 45 percent of people with type 1 diabetes said they would be willing to get behind the wheel even if they knew their blood sugar was too low. Another study of 202 motorists with insulin-treated diabetes found that 59 percent said they never test blood sugar before driving.

If you are at risk for hypoglycemia, these simple measures can keep you out of accidents and traffic court:
- Always test your blood sugar before driving. If it's too low, don't drive until you have taken the steps outlined in "So You Think You're Hypoglycemic" on page 78.
- Keep a carbohydrate snack in the car at all times. If you feel the symptoms of hypoglycemia coming on while driving, pull over and attempt to correct your blood sugar.

Beware of another postworkout phenomenon known as delayed hypoglycemia. After exercising, your tired muscles restock themselves with glucose and your liver takes its sweet time (sorry!) rebuilding its inventory of glycogen (the stored form of glucose). While all this is going on, blood sugar can remain low. If you don't eat enough food after strenuous exercise, delayed hypoglycemia can strike—usually between 6 and 15 hours later. But delayed hypoglycemia can actually occur as many as 28 hours after a workout. One study found that over a two-year period, 48 out of approximately 300 young type 1 diabetes patients had a bout with delayed hypoglycemia. The problem may be more likely to occur if you increase the intensity or duration of your exercise regimen.

Tips:
- Talk with your doctor or diabetes educator about adjusting your insulin dose or snack intake before working out, playing a sport, or participating in any other activity that will make you huff and puff.
- Inject insulin in the abdomen before exercise; research shows that flexing, stretching, pumping limb muscles absorb injected insulin too quickly during exercise.

- Plan on having a snack during very long bouts of exercise, such as long-distance running or cross-country skiing.
- Monitor, monitor, monitor. Check your blood sugar levels before and after exercising—even during, if you're in the gym or on the track for a long time.
- Eating a snack after a long workout helps reduce the risk for delayed hypoglycemia.

ALCOHOL

If you know a little about the chemistry of alcoholic beverages, it may seem odd to learn that drinking booze can cause low blood sugar. After all, many forms of alcohol contain carbohydrates, which break down into glucose in the body. (A can of beer, for example, contains roughly the same amount of carbs as a piece of taffy.) In fact, if you are well fed, drinking a lot of alcohol can have the opposite effect, causing blood sugar to soar too high. (Hyperglycemia is discussed later in this chapter.)

However, drinking alcohol on an empty stomach can cause your blood sugar to plummet. If you haven't eaten in a while, your blood sugar levels may already be on the low side. Without food to break down into glucose, your liver converts stored glycogen into simple sugar, which it releases into the blood to keep your organs functioning, especially the one between your ears. Don't forget, brain cells are fussy eaters and will only consume glucose for energy.

But tossing back a few cocktails or glasses of wine when your body is relying on the liver for its supply of glucose can turn happy hour into a horror show. Alcohol interferes with the liver's ability to produce glucose molecules, which can leave the body bereft of its most efficient energy source.

Tips:

If you want to enjoy an adult beverage or two without sending your blood sugar into a tailspin, follow these rules:

- Check your blood sugar before the first sip. If it's low, either don't have any alcohol or teetotal until you have had something to eat and given your glucose a boost.
- Always drink with a meal or shortly after eating.
- Become a moderate: One drink for women and two for men is the daily max. And the 24-ounce super schooner of ale at your favorite pub counts as two drinks, not one. (A "drink" usually means 12 ounces of beer, 5 ounces of wine, or 1.5 ounces

of liquor.) Don't hit the sauce more than one or two days a week.

- Take a break between drinks. If you're at a party and feel funny walking around without a drink, have a tall glass of seltzer with lemon.
- Stick to light beers, dry wine, and cocktails mixed with diet sodas—they contain fewer carbohydrates. Avoid sugary drinks.

ROUTINE MAINTENANCE

Careful planning, with the aid of your doctor or diabetes educator, can help prevent hypoglycemia and make the condition easier to manage when it does arise.

- Know the symptoms of hypoglycemia.
- Try to stick to a regular meal schedule and eat as much food as planned.
- Don't overdo exercise.
- Discuss with your doctor or educator how to adjust insulin or medication doses on occasions when you may eat more or less than planned or may be more active than normal.
- Don't abuse alcohol.
- Have a fast-acting carbohydrate snack, such as a small box of raisins, handy at all times.
- Educate family members, friends, and coworkers about hypoglycemia and what to do if you need their help correcting your blood sugar.
- If you have a glucagon emergency kit, make sure the medicine hasn't expired.

- If you become hypoglycemic and start stumbling around or acting confused, your bar mates or fellow partygoers may assume you have had a drink or three too many. Far from wanting to help you, they may try to avoid you. Tell someone in advance that you have diabetes and may need assistance.
- Alcohol can keep blood sugar suppressed for up to 12 hours, so check your glucose before going to bed. If it's below 100 mg/dl, have a snack.
- Wear a MedicAlert identification or any other type of bracelet or necklace that identifies you as someone who has diabetes.

Sweet Salvation: Treating Hypoglycemia

If you have diabetes and suddenly notice that you feel light-headed and jittery, especially if you use insulin therapy, there's an excellent chance you have developed hypoglycemia. But confirming your suspicion is a good idea, since low blood sugar can occur for other reasons. (See "Other Causes of Hypoglycemia," page 84.) Here's yet another good reason to keep your glucose meter handy. If a spot check reveals a glucose reading that's 70 mg/dl or lower, low blood sugar is the culprit.

The solution is surprisingly straightforward. You don't have to take a special drug that triggers your pancreas to produce hormones or that knocks out enzymes responsible for modulating some complex biochemical reaction. Your blood sugar is low, so the goal is to put more into circulation, ASAP. The fastest way to boost glucose is by consuming 15 grams of simple sugars, which break down rapidly in the body. You might have to give yourself another dose if your symptoms don't fade within 15 minutes or so. (See "So You Think You're Hypoglycemic—Here's What to Do," page 78.)

Your medicine chest, nightstand, glove compartment, desk, briefcase, purse, and gym bag are all good places to keep a stash of quick fixes for hypoglycemia. Some good choices include:

- 2 or 3 glucose tablets
- ½ cup of fruit juice
- ½ cup of a regular soft drink (not a diet beverage, which contains no sugar)
- 1 cup of milk
- Small boxes of raisins
- 5 or 6 pieces of hard candy
- 1 or 2 teaspoons of honey or sugar
- A tube of glucose gel or other anti-hypoglycemia product (more about those later)

You might read this list and have a question or two, such as:

Since when is milk a sugar powerhouse? Surprise! Milk contains a form of simple sugar called lactose. Some people can't digest lactose, however, which can cause unpleasant gastrointestinal problems. However, if milk isn't a bother, it can be a healthy source of hypoglycemia-fighting sugars, since it also contains calcium, protein, and other good things.

Mmm, cheese—that's made from milk, right...? Nice try, but most cheeses (especially aged varieties, such as cheddar and Swiss) are relatively low in lactose, so they won't raise your blood sugar much.

Then how about candy bars? They contain a lot of sugar. They sure do, along with a lot of fat from chocolate, nuts, peanut butter, and other ingredients. Fat slows sugar from being absorbed in the gut. Besides, fat is an ultradense source of calories, so

restocking your blood with glucose by chowing on chocolate bars will contribute to ultradense hips and thighs.

Aren't those special hypoglycemia products a rip-off? Maybe not. Hard candy, raisins, and soft drinks can relieve hypoglycemia effectively. But snack-type foods and beverages can lure you into nonemergency noshing. That is, if your will is weak, you may gobble or gulp them just because you're hungry or thirsty. Not only could you find yourself empty-handed if your blood sugar dips, but the unneeded sugar could cause glucose to soar, along with your weight. On the other hand, while glucose tablets and gels won't make you gag, you probably won't be tempted to break them out for your mid-afternoon snack. (The American Diabetes Association Web site at www.diabetes.org offers a comprehensive list of products for preventing and treating hypoglycemia.)

Other Causes of Hypoglycemia

Using insulin or insulin-stimulating medications increases the risk for low blood sugar, but the problem can be triggered by other conditions and circumstances. If you develop symptoms but your glucose levels appear to be safe (and you know your glucose meter is working properly), talk to your doctor. Hypoglycemia can also be caused by

- other medications, including aspirin, sulfa drugs (for treating infections), pentamidine (for serious pneumonia), and quinine (for malaria)
- alcohol, especially if you go on a bender. Heavy doses of booze interfere with the liver's ability to release glucose.
- other illnesses, including diseases of the heart, kidneys, and liver. Also, rare tumors called insulinomas produce insulin, which would raise levels

WHAT YOU DON'T KNOW...

...can hurt you, a lot, if you have diabetes. People who have had the disease for a long time can develop a condition called "hypoglycemia unawareness." As the name suggests, people who have hypoglycemia unawareness have a hard time recognizing familiar symptoms of low blood sugar in themselves. Anyone who takes insulin should have a glucagon emergency kit, but if you feel that you may miss the early clues of hypoglycemia, it's particularly important to have one. Be sure to talk to your doctor about getting a glucagon emergency kit. Glucagon, as you already know, is a hormone that causes the liver to release glucose into the bloodstream. These kits contain a vial of glucagon and a syringe. Be sure to familiarize friends, coworkers, and family members with the symptoms of hypoglycemia, and teach them how to use the syringe in case you experience an episode of severe hypoglycemia.

of the hormone too high, causing blood sugar to drop.

- hormonal deficiencies. More common in children, a shortage of glucagon, as well as other hormones (including cortisol, growth hormone, and epinephrine) can cause hypoglycemia.

Hypoglycemia is rare in children, but it can happen. Refer to Chapter 16 for descriptions of several conditions that can mimic low blood sugar in infants and kids.

Hyperglycemia

Astute readers have probably already figured out that if *hypo*glycemia means too little glucose in the blood, then *hyper*glycemia must mean too much blood sugar. But isn't that the topic of this entire book? Isn't the basic problem of diabetes that you have too much sugar in your blood?

Yes, but—you guessed it!—the story is a bit more complex. Technically speaking, a doctor could say you have hyperglycemia if a blood test shows that your glucose is higher than it should be (usually defined as more than 100 mg/dl between meals and 140 mg/dl or higher after eating). It's no big deal if your glucose creeps up a little now and then,

but chronically elevated blood sugar can be debilitating and potentially fatal. If you don't take the steps discussed in previous chapters for controlling diabetes, you will probably *at minimum* develop one or more of the complications explained in chapters to come.

But the term hyperglycemia can also refer to an acute case of very high blood sugar, which you definitely want to avoid, too. Hyperglycemia can lead to two serious conditions. One occurs primarily (though not exclusively) in people with type 1 diabetes, while the other is mostly a concern for type 2 patients.

DIABETIC KETOACIDOSIS

In Chapter 1, you learned about ketones, which are leftover products your body makes when it burns fat instead of glucose for energy. Any time you shed flab on a weight-loss diet, your body cranks out ketones. You produce a whole lot of ketones on some diets, such as the famous (or infamous, depending on your viewpoint) Atkins plan. Atkins allows only small servings of carbohydrates, dramatically reducing your body's main source of glucose. Still, your cells get some glucose on low-carb diets. In a person who does not have type 1 diabetes—whose pancreas still makes insulin—the concentration of ketones in your body while eating a low-carb diet never poses a serious health threat, other than to drive away friends and loved ones (ketones can make your breath smell like you brush your teeth with paint thinner).

However, trouble starts if your blood becomes flooded with ketones, which can happen if your body runs very low on insulin. That risk is always a possibility with type 1 diabetes. At first you may simply need to urinate a lot to unload all the glucose you're not burning. Since you're losing so much water in the urine, you'll become thirsty, too. As your blood becomes more saturated with ketones, you will probably begin to feel lousy in all ways—tired, nauseated, feverish. Your heart will race, and you'll pant like a big dog on a hot day. If you don't receive medical attention, you could slip into a coma and die.

Some common causes of diabetic ketoacidosis include:

- Infections. As your body fights bacteria, it produces hormones that interfere with insulin and trigger the liver

---

TROUBLESHOOTING CHECKLIST

Maintaining tight control of blood sugar will help prevent diabetes complications. But preventing super-high spikes can avert disaster. Knowing the early symptoms of hyperglycemia will allow you to seek medical attention before the condition becomes life threatening. They include

☐ a frequent need to urinate

☐ excessive thirst

☐ breath that smells like paint thinner (some people say the odor is "fruity")

☐ fatigue

☐ nausea or vomiting

☐ fever

☐ rapid breathing or heartbeat

☐ mental fuzziness or confusion

to release glucose. Urinary tract infections are a common cause of ketoacidosis in patients with type 1 diabetes.

- Stress. Emotions can trigger a similar hormonal onslaught. The same is true of anything that stresses your body, such as trauma, a serious illness, or surgery.

- The "Oops" Factor. As in, "Oops, I forgot to inject insulin before lunch." (Physicians favor the term "noncompliance.") Some experts say the problem is particularly common among teenagers, though anyone with type 1 diabetes is capable of a potentially dangerous brain cramp. When ketoacidosis occurs in a patient over and over again, forgetfulness or some other cause of poor compliance is usually to blame.

- Other insulin problems. Patients who use insulin pumps may not notice if the device becomes clogged or for some other reason fails to deliver a scheduled dose, and ketoacidosis could result. Injecting outdated insulin could have the same effect.

- The "I've Got *What*?" Factor. Did those early symptoms of ketoacidosis—the unslakeable thirst, the well-worn path to the restroom—sound familiar? They should, since they are the early signs of type 1 diabetes. In

IT TAKES ALL TYPES

Many doctors believe that diabetic ketoacidosis is rare in patients with type 2 diabetes. There is also a common perception that when the condition does strike a type 2 patient, it's almost always triggered by a stressful event. However, in a 1999 study published in the *Archives of Internal Medicine,* researchers looked up 141 people who had sought treatment for symptoms of hyperglycemia two and a half years after they had been admitted to a hospital in Houston. It turns out that 39 percent of the patients actually had type 2 diabetes. What's more, there was no evidence in half of the cases that stress was the trigger. The moral: If you have any kind of diabetes and develop symptoms of hyperglycemia (such as extreme thirst, a frequent need to urinate, nausea, or vomiting), call your doctor.

HONK IF YOU HAVE HYPERGLYCEMIA!

Doctors sometimes call this condition *hyperosmolar nonketotic coma,* even though patients lapse into a coma in fewer than 10 percent of cases. However, this alternative name does allow physicians to refer to the condition by the amusing acronym HONK.

fact, some patients learn for the first time that they have the disease when they develop ketoacidosis and see a doctor for treatment.

Once again, be glad you weren't born a century ago. Before the discovery of insulin in 1922, ketoacidosis spelled certain doom. Today, ketoacidosis is fatal in fewer than five percent of cases. Treatment focuses not only on restocking your insulin but also on lowering glucose levels, whisking ketones out of the blood, and restoring all the water the condition drains from the body.

However, preventing ketoacidosis is as simple as taking a quick trip to the bathroom or doing an additional fingerstick. A urine or blood ketone test (described in Chapter 2) can pick up signs of ketoacidosis before the symptoms get out of control. As a rule, it's a good idea to give yourself a ketone test if

- your blood sugar is higher than 240 mg/dl (some doctors say 300 mg/dl is a better benchmark; ask your physician)
- you become nauseated or start vomiting
- you develop the flu, pneumonia, or any other serious illness
- you are pregnant (see Chapter 17 for a closer look at diabetes and pregnancy)

Talk to your doctor or diabetes educator about using urine ketone tests to detect ketoacidosis. Specifically, ask how often and when you should check for ketones and what you should do if a test turns up high levels.

HYPEROSMOLAR HYPERGLYCEMIC SYNDROME

Despite the name, this condition has nothing do with your molars. Instead, hyperosmolar hyperglycemic syndrome (HHS for short) occurs for lack of one of the most common elements—the clear, wet stuff that comes out of the tap in your kitchen or in overpriced bottles at the grocery store. Water is a critical player when glucose builds up in the blood. Normally, when blood sugar rises, the kidneys swing into action and lower levels by excreting excess glucose in the urine. But when the body's water supply runs low, the kidneys slow down urine production. Glucose builds up even more, further increasing demand for water.

Some of the symptoms of HHS resemble those of diabetic ketoacidosis, such as increased thirst, fatigue, and weakness. (However, HHS does not produce paint-thinner breath, since it doesn't cause ketones to flood the blood.) As HHS progresses, patients may develop rapid heartbeat and sunken eyeballs. They may also become confused and move awkwardly. At advanced stages, HHS can lead to convulsions and coma.

In some cases, a glass of H_2O is all it would take to prevent HHS. The condition often strikes elderly patients with type 2 diabetes (HHS is rare in type 1 patients), who become dehydrated because they can't tend to their own thirst or because whoever should be helping them to wet their whistles (nursing home attendants, for example) aren't getting the job done. Some other causes of HHS include

- poorly treated or undiagnosed type 2 diabetes
- weak kidneys or kidney dialysis
- infections, heart attacks, and strokes—or any other stress on the body, such as surgery.
- medications. Certain drugs used to treat hypertension, asthma, and allergies can cause dehydration, block insulin, or raise glucose.
- vomiting. Losing your lunch causes dehydration.

HHS is definitely a medical emergency. Doctors treat the condition with intravenous fluids to rehydrate the body and insulin to bring down soaring glucose levels. However, patients have often lapsed into a coma by the time they arrive in an emergency room. HHS is fatal in up to 40 percent of cases. As with diabetic acidosis, the key to preventing HHS is vigilant monitoring—in this case with a glucose meter. If levels rise and don't come down, for any reason, contact your physician. (See Chapter 2 for a refresher course on checking your blood sugar.)

ROUTINE MAINTENANCE

The goal for any diabetes patient is tight control of blood sugar. Follow these steps to help prevent glucose levels from dipping or soaring to extremes:

- Know the symptoms of hyperglycemia.
- Monitor your blood sugar regularly. As little as one check per day could spot a case of hyperglycemia before it causes symptoms.
- Ask your doctor or diabetes educator how often and when you should use urine ketone tests.
- If you feel thirsty, drink up—preferably water.

The Circulatory System and Diabetes

A century ago, the most serious threats to health in Western civilization were infectious diseases such as pneumonia and tuberculosis. Thanks to the invention of antibiotics (to say nothing of campaigns to promote hand washing and to discourage people from spitting in public), the number of deaths from most infectious diseases has plummeted.

Unfortunately, disorders of the blood vessels that make up the body's circulatory system have more than filled the void. Vascular diseases can cause heart attacks and strokes—the first and third leading causes of death in the United States—as well as serious damage to the limbs. Unfortunately, elevated blood sugar further increases the risk for diseases of the blood vessels. This chapter gives an overview of the problems that can plague the circulatory system, along with lifestyle changes and medications that can keep your heart ticking and your blood flowing.

Making the Blood Go 'Round: Your Circulatory System

It's a sad fact about diabetes: The disease has the uncanny ability to wreak havoc on just about any part of your body. However, the damage diabetes can cause to your circulatory system wreaks the greatest havoc. After all, every cell in your body relies on the heart and blood vessels for life-sustaining energy and nourishment. Many of the diabetes complications you will read about in other chapters, from blindness to kidney disease, begin with problems in the blood vessels.

Unfortunately, vascular problems that affect blood flow to some pretty important organs—the brain and the heart itself—are among the most common of all diabetes-related complications. Statistics tell the story: About two-thirds of people with diabetes die of vascular diseases, especially heart attacks and strokes.

There is good news, however. Death rates from cardiovascular disease dropped 18 percent in the United States from 1992 to 2002, according to the American Heart Association (AHA). Perhaps more people are responding to public health messages about the proper care and feeding of the cardiovascular system. However, cardiologists credit much of the reduction to therapies introduced during the last generation that help prevent and treat cardiovascular disease.

This chapter will detail how you can protect your cardiovascular system, but let's first take a peek inside your arteries to see how blood flows.

THE HEART AND BLOOD VESSELS

You have to use your imagination a little to see what's heart-shape about the familiar stylized heart that appears on Valentine's Day cards. On a real heart, which is about the size of a fist, the right and left upper chambers do indeed form rounded peaks with a cleft between them. But instead of being symmetrical, a real heart sags to one side and looks more like a big, misshapen potato. Although the heart weighs no more than a can of soda pop, it pumps about five liters of blood per minute.

You often hear or read that the heart's role is to circulate blood throughout the body. True enough, but the big beater in your chest has another job. Before it serves blood to awaiting cells in every tissue from your top to toes, the heart first sends the fluid to the lungs, where it picks up inhaled oxygen molecules. Newly oxygen-rich blood heads back to

STRINGING ALONG

If you were to string your blood vessels together end to end, they would stretch to about 54,000 miles. (But please don't try this at home.)

the heart, which then pipes the blood into the aorta, the body's main artery. The aorta divides into smaller arteries, then into even smaller arterioles, and lastly to capillaries. These tiny tubes supply blood to cells in organs, muscles, fat, and every other piece of flesh you can think of.

Cells use oxygen to stoke the flames of metabolism, the process of burning food as fuel for energy. Just as ashes are left behind after a fire, leftover unwanted stuff—namely carbon dioxide—is produced by metabolism. The blood carts off carbon dioxide and other waste products, traveling through the veins back to the heart. Before this blood can be reused, it has to be cleaned up and restocked, so the heart shuttles the thick fluid to the lungs. There, it gives up carbon dioxide (which is exhaled) and picks up a new load of oxygen, starting the process all over.

TROUBLESHOOTING CHECKLIST: SYMPTOMS OF A HEART ATTACK

Don't try to tough it out. Don't dismiss the symptoms as heartburn. Don't be silly. If you suspect you may be having a heart attack, get to a hospital, fast. (Calling 911 and letting emergency responders do the driving is the smartest move.) Emergency room doctors have at their disposal various clot-busting drugs that can break up the blockage that is depriving the heart muscle of nourishing blood. But the drugs are only effective if administered within three hours of the onset of a heart attack, so knowing the warning signs is crucial. They include:

- ☐ Chest pain or discomfort in the upper body
- ☐ Shortness of breath
- ☐ Nausea or vomiting
- ☐ Cold sweat
- ☐ Light-headedness
- ☐ Back or jaw pain

Males and females alike may experience chest pain as a warning sign that a heart attack is underway. But women are more likely to experience certain symptoms, including shortness of breath, nausea/vomiting, and back or jaw pain.

WHAT CAUSES HEART ATTACKS?

To reiterate: The heart pumps blood to every tissue in the body. That means *every* tissue, including the heart itself, which keeps beating on and on thanks to the contractions of fibers known as cardiac muscle. Like any other muscle, from your biceps to your gluteus maximus, the cardiac muscle needs a steady supply of fresh, oxygen-packed blood to contract.

Any interruption of blood flow to the cardiac muscle spells trouble, in varying degrees. Reduced flow can cause pounding chest pain known as *angina pectoris*. (Want to sound smart in front of your doc? Pronounce it "AN jih nuh," like he or she does, instead of "an JIE nuh," like the rest of the world says it.) Angina occurs when deposits of cholesterol and other gunk accumulate in the coronary arteries, which are the ones that bring oxygenated blood back to feed the heart. This narrowing of the arteries is known as *atherosclerosis*. Angina is most likely to strike during exercise or some other form of physical exertion, because the extra workload on your heart demands more oxygen. The pain usually fades after a few minutes of rest. But you can't dismiss angina as a mere inconvenience, since it represents a waving red flag that worse problems lie ahead.

That's because those clumps of cholesterol and other sludgy stuff in your arteries may be ticking time bombs, waiting to explode. Scientists are still trying to understand what causes these clumps (known as *plaques*) to form. It's pretty clear, however, that LDL cholesterol—the so-called "bad" kind—plays a role in the development of atherosclerosis. Some scientists believe that although large plaques reduce blood flow and cause angina, any plaque is capable of erupting, creating a clot that cuts off the flow of oxygen-rich blood to the cardiac muscle, resulting in the death of heart cells. Doctors call this phenomenon a *myocardial infarction*. But you can just call it a heart attack.

Diabetes and Your Heart

Okay, so heart attacks are scary and awful and everyone should fear them. But why should a diabetes patient be more concerned about having "The Big One" than any other Tom, Dick, or Harriet on the street?

Because, compared to the general population, people with type 2 diabetes are two to six times more likely to have a heart attack. Furthermore, heart attacks tend to be fatal more often in diabetes patients. Scientists aren't sure why diabetes seems to increase the risk of cardiovascular disease, but some intriguing theories are taking shape.

For starters, virtually all patients with type 2 diabetes have developed resistance to their own insulin, so their pancreases keep churning out this critical hormone in an effort to herd glucose into cells. There is some scientific evidence that high levels of insulin in the blood cause damaging changes to the lining of blood vessels that lead to atherosclerosis.

Another theory suggests that blood sugar itself is the culprit. In all humans,

93

a chemical reaction between glucose and proteins in the body produces compounds called advanced glycosylation endproducts, or AGEs. As the acronym suggests, your body produces greater numbers of AGEs as you get older. Since diabetes increases the amount of glucose in your blood that's available to be glycosylated, people with the disease tend to have high concentrations of AGEs. Unfortunately, these demon compounds may damage arteries, making them more likely to clog, in addition to increasing the risk for a long list of other common diabetes complications.

The role of AGEs and elevated blood sugar in heart disease remains up for debate. But there is no question that people with diabetes are more likely to have the following problems that increase the risk of heart attacks:

HYPERTENSION

More commonly known as high blood pressure, this condition is one of the leading contributors to heart attacks. Pressure in the blood vessels naturally rises when you're stressed out or exercising hard. But if you have hypertension, your blood pressure is always high. Although people frequently claim they can feel their blood pressure soaring when they are angry or frustrated, hypertension actually has no symptoms. That's why high blood pressure is called a "silent" disease. Chronically elevated blood pressure forces your heart to work too hard, which may cause it to weaken over time. High blood pressure also increases wear and tear on the arteries.

At least half of patients with diabetes have hypertension, though it's not clear why. According to one study, up to half of people with diabetes have poor control over their blood pressure. Hypertension also increases the risk for many of the other diabetes complications that you will read about later in this book.

HDL CHOLESTEROL

HDL (for "high-density lipoprotein") cholesterol is often described as the "good" kind, but what's so great about it? The liver makes cholesterol, which the body uses in a variety of roles, such as repairing cell walls. LDL (for "low-density lipoprotein") carries cholesterol around the body, but the process can get sloppy, with the fatty substance getting spilled here and there, slowly accumulating on artery walls.

NOT A RED ALERT

Sometimes when people feel upset or anxious, they insist that their blood pressure is soaring. In fact, emotional stress can cause blood vessels just beneath the skin to dilate, which may turn your face red. But don't worry, that doesn't mean your vessels are about to burst. This phenomenon does not cause blood pressure to rise.

That's why the liver also makes HDL, which acts like a DustBuster for the blood. HDL molecules travel around, sucking up leftover cholesterol, which it drags back to the liver to be eliminated. People who have high levels of HDL cholesterol have fewer heart attacks than people who have low levels.

HEAVY-DUTY LDL CHOLESTEROL

Although elevated LDL cholesterol levels increase the risk for heart disease, people with diabetes don't necessarily have too much of the fatty stuff. However, diabetes patients often have an especially sinister version of the so-called "bad" cholesterol. LDL cholesterol comes in several varieties. Some particles are puffy and buoyant, while others are small and dense. While puffy particles tend to float around in the blood, research suggests that small, dense particles are more likely to lodge in the arteries and form potentially deadly plaques. Unfortunately, people who have type 2 diabetes often have unusually high concentrations of these small, dense LDL particles in their blood.

"STICKY" BLOOD

People with insulin resistance—this means you, type 2 patients—also tend to have blood containing high levels of a protein called fibrinogen. You need some fibrinogen, since its job is to clot blood; without it, you could bleed to death from a paper cut. However, having too much fibrinogen can make blood thick or "sticky," causing it to form clots too easily. And you definitely do not want random blood clots turning up in your coronary arteries. People with diabetes also tend to have high levels of several other blood proteins that promote the clotting process known as *coagulation*.

HIGH TRIGLYCERIDES

When you eat more food than your body needs for energy, the leftovers are stored as triglycerides, a form of fat. You burn triglycerides as backup energy

IGNORING THE HEART OF THE MATTER

Despite the clear link between diabetes and cardiovascular disease, many patients don't seem to realize that their hearts require extra-special attention. In some cases, their doctors appear to be pretty clueless, too. A survey by the American Diabetes Association and the American College of Cardiology found that

- 60 percent of people with diabetes don't realize they are at risk for cholesterol problems.
- Only 8 percent of people with diabetes correctly identified lowering cholesterol as a critical step for reducing the threats of heart attacks and strokes.
- Nearly half the patients surveyed said their doctors had never talked about lowering cholesterol. Yet, according to one estimate, 70 to 90 percent of people with diabetes have a problem with blood cholesterol and other blood fats.

HINDERING YOUR HORMONES

Women who have not reached menopause have a far lower risk for heart disease than men do, possibly due to the beneficial effects of estrogen. However, having diabetes erases the hormone's protective effects: Women with diabetes have the same risk for heart disease as men, regardless of their age.

between meals, but high levels of this blood fat have been linked to heart disease.

OBESITY

Since triglycerides are the building blocks of a billowing belly and baggy buttocks, it's not surprising that people who have high levels of these fats wage a constant battle of the bulge. Many patients with type 2 diabetes are overweight or obese.

SMOKING

Smoking tobacco seems to increase the risk for just about every major medical condition, so why should diabetes be any different? To be sure, smokers are three times more likely to develop the disease than nonsmokers, according to a 2005 study by researchers at Wake Forest University. In one respect, the link could be explained away as guilt by association, since smokers are more likely than nonsmokers to be overweight, too, and extra pounds predispose the body to blood sugar problems. However, smoking a single cigarette also seems to raise glucose levels and blood pressure, as well as exacerbate insulin resistance. Cigarettes also contain toxins that have been associated with diabetes.

Alone, any one of these problems increases the risk for heart disease. As a group, they form a formidable cluster of conditions sometimes called insulin resistance syndrome or metabolic syndrome, which dramatically raises the threat of heart attacks and other cardiovascular chaos. If you have type 2 diabetes, chances are you have at least a few, if not all, of these risk factors. Fortunately, there are steps you can take to rein in these threats, so read on.

Preventing Heart Attacks and Other Vascular Diseases

Because you have diabetes, your doctor has already given you the obligatory stern lecture about diet and exercise. But in addition to improving your blood sugar, physical activity and better eating habits will lower your risk for cardiovascular disease and other circulatory problems. Some of the benefits are familiar, but others may surprise you.

- Eating less saturated fat and cholesterol reduces the load of cholesterol in your arteries.
- Reducing the sodium in your diet can help control blood pressure.
- Eating fruits, vegetables, and nonfat or low-fat dairy can lower blood pressure.

- Exercise boosts HDL cholesterol, the "good" kind, 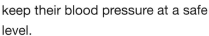 and produces a small drop in LDL cholesterol, the "bad" kind. Also, following a workout the volume of blood your heart pumps is reduced and your blood vessels relax, leading to lower blood pressure.
- A healthy diet and exercise help control obesity, which increases the risk of heart disease.

You will read all about how exercise and diet can help reduce your risk for cardiovascular and circulatory complications from diabetes in Chapter 13. But medications have become a mainstay in preventing heart attacks and strokes, especially in diabetes patients. This section offers a look at drugs your doctor may prescribe.

Drugs for Preventing and Treating Cardiovascular Disease

It's tempting to think of cardiovascular disease as a simple problem—sludge builds up in the arteries, blood flow stops, the heart starves, you keel over. In fact, atherosclerosis is a complex phenomenon that arises due to glitches throughout the circulatory system. Fortunately, your doctor can prescribe a wide variety of medications to help control the various conditions that increase the risk for heart attacks and strokes.

HYPERTENSION

If you have mild hypertension, you may be able to push your blood pressure back into the healthy range with lifestyle changes, namely exercise and a better diet. Chances are, however, that you'll need to take a drug—or more than one at some point—to get your blood pressure under control. A large study of patients with diabetes in the United Kingdom found that about one-third required three or more medications to keep their blood pressure at a safe level.

That may sound like a lot of pill popping, but consider the benefits: The same study found that patients who maintained tight control over their blood pressure reduced their risk of stroke (by 44 percent) and heart failure (by 56 percent). All diabetes-related deaths were reduced by 32 percent. The patients were also less likely to lose their eyesight, a common complication of hypertension and diabetes.

Furthermore, a 2004 Canadian study offers strong evidence that one class of drugs used to lower blood pressure—angiotensin converting enzyme (ACE) inhibitors—may offer diabetes patients a bonus. Researchers compared a large group of diabetes patients who took ACE inhibitors with a similar group of patients who did not use the drugs. None of the study participants had heart disease at the outset. After five years, researchers found that patients who took ACE inhibitors were 23 percent less likely to have died of heart disease. However, they were half as likely to have died of any cause, so ACE inhibitors appear to confer other healthful benefits in addition to protecting the heart and blood vessels.

Routine Maintenance

- [ ] Eat a healthy diet and exercise. (Read more about both in Chapter 13.)
- [ ] Take all prescribed heart medications. If side effects are intolerable, talk to your doctor (instead of skipping doses). There may be an effective alternative with fewer adverse effects.
- [ ] Have your blood levels of cholesterol and other fats checked on a regular basis. Your physician will decide how often.
- [ ] Know the symptoms of heart attack and stroke.

The major drugs used to treat hypertension include:

Diuretics

The usual description of diuretics, sometimes nicknamed "water pills," goes something like this: "These drugs act on the kidneys to draw fluid and salts from the body." That's a polite way of saying that diuretics make you urinate. A lot. To produce urine, the kidneys pull water out of the blood, which lowers the blood's volume and eases pressure in vessels. In small amounts, though, diuretics do not cause a perceptible increase in urination. But they *do* cause a perceptible decrease in blood pressure. So don't avoid taking a diuretic. They're an invaluable treatment for high blood pressure.

There are several varieties of diuretic drugs. One type, called thiazide, may increase blood sugar when taken in larger doses, so users who have diabetes must monitor their glucose. Other major side effects can include loss of potassium, which can be offset by taking supplements containing the mineral.

Beta-blockers

These drugs interfere with nerve signals that cause the heart to beat fast and hard. (In fact, performers with stage fright sometimes take beta-blockers to help them deal with anxiety.) Beta-blockers also cause blood vessels to dilate, or widen, which further lowers pressure.

Beta-blockers (sometimes called beta-adrenergic blockers) cover up some symptoms of hypoglycemia, such as a racing heartbeat, which would allow a period of low blood sugar to go unnoticed. Other possible side effects include insomnia, fatigue, cold extremities, and erectile dysfunction. Infants born to women who used beta-blockers during pregnancy frequently have medical problems, including low blood sugar.

ACE Inhibitors

This class of medications has a neat trick up its sleeve. ACE inhibitors prevent a harmless protein called angiotensin I from turning into its evil twin, a hormone called angiotensin II, which causes blood vessels to constrict. ACE inhibitors lower hypertension by keeping vessels relaxed, allowing blood to flow easily. ACE inhibitors may offer a twofer for diabetes patients, since they appear to reduce insulin resistance. Some studies show that these drugs (along with angiotensin antagonists) prevent the onset of diabetes.

One common side effect of ACE inhibitors is a dry cough. Users may also develop a skin rash, loss of taste, and, in rare instances, kidney damage.

Angiotensin Receptor Blockers (ARB)

These are similar to ACE inhibitors, with a different modus operandi. Instead of preventing angiotensin II from forming, these drugs (also known as angiotensin antagonists) simply get in the hormone's way as it tries to constrict blood vessels. (If you want to get technical about things, they block angiotensin receptor sites in the blood vessels.)

Unlike ACE inhibitors, ARBs are less likely to cause coughing, so doctors often prescribe the pills to patients who can't hack the hacking. However, ARBs are more expensive than ACE inhibitors and may cause dizziness.

Calcium Channel Blockers

You already know that contractions of the cardiac muscles make your heart beat so that it can pump blood into vessels. But your blood vessels aren't just stiff tubes. The inner walls of blood vessels contain tiny muscles that allow the tube to contract and expand. Muscles need calcium to contract, so drugs that block the mineral from entering muscle cells help blood vessels to dilate. Calcium channel blockers are also prescribed for angina.

Some possible side effects from calcium channel blockers include palpitations, swollen ankles, and constipation.

Alpha-blockers

Like beta blockers, these drugs interfere with nerve signals. But instead of acting on the heart, alpha-blockers prevent nerve impulses from triggering muscle contractions in blood vessels, allowing blood to flow easily. Doctors even prescribe the drugs to treat urinary problems caused by an enlarged prostate.

Some doctors avoid using alpha-blockers unless patients have failed on other drugs, since a large study found that they can cause heart failure and other cardiovascular problems. They may also cause dizziness or a sudden loss of blood pressure when you stand up.

Alpha-beta-blockers

Just what they sound like: A combination of alpha- and beta-blocking action, which slows the heartbeat and relaxes blood vessels, resulting in a drop in blood pressure.

Sympathetic Nerve Inhibitors

Talk about nipping a problem in the bud. Nerve inhibitors, sometimes called central agonists, act directly on the brain, snuffing out nerve signals that cause the heart to beat fast and blood vessels to constrict. These drugs, such as clonidine, alpha-methyldopa, and guanabenz, can cause dry mouth and fatigue; the latter probably explains why they are being studied as potential sleep aids.

Other Vasodilators

Several older medications, including hydralazine and minoxidil, also dilate blood vessels. But because they appear to worsen heart conditions in some cases, they

CARDIOVASCULAR DISEASE AND DIABETES, BY THE NUMBERS

Now that you know just how important it is to control blood pressure and cholesterol, let's answer the Limbo Question: How low (or high) should you go? Here are the standard goals for blood pressure and lipids that doctors have established for patients with diabetes.

Cardiovascular Risk Factor	Goal for People with Diabetes
Blood pressure	130/80 mmHg or lower
LDL cholesterol	100 mg/dl or lower
HDL cholesterol	40 mg/dl* or higher
Triglycerides	150 mg/dl or lower

*Some doctors feel that 50 mg/dl is a better goal for women.

aren't prescribed often these days. However, here's a bit of hair-raising trivia: Doctors noticed that some of their bald male patients who took minoxidil grew back a bit of hair. Today the drug is sold in liquid form under the name Rogaine as a hair-growth tonic.

CHOLESTEROL AND TRIGLYCERIDES

When the pipes in the bathroom sink are clogged, you pour in some liquid drain cleaner. Too bad you can't do the same thing for your arteries, but medications can do the next best thing: Keep cholesterol and other gunk from accumulating in the first place. If your doctor hasn't prescribed a pill for improving your blood fats yet, there's a good chance he or she will sooner or later. According to the Centers for Disease Control and Prevention (CDC), 70 to 97 percent of people with diabetes have unhealthy levels of cholesterol or triglycerides.

The following medications may help keep your pipes clear:

Statins

Once upon a time, you could watch television for an evening or read an entire magazine without seeing a commercial or ad for a statin drug. But the ubiquity of these heavily promoted cholesterol-lowering medications has had a major payoff: Doctors say the widespread use of statins has contributed heavily to an overall drop in total cholesterol and LDL cholesterol among adults in the United States since the drugs were introduced in the 1990s. Studies show that statins slash the risk of heart attack by about 30 percent.

Officially known as HMG CoA reductase inhibitors, statins knock out an enzyme the liver needs to make cholesterol. They also encourage the liver to reabsorb more LDL cholesterol, which we all know is the "bad" kind. Studies show that these drugs can decrease LDL cholesterol up to 36 percent in diabetes patients. Sharp-eyed readers may be thinking: Why should I care, since people with diabetes don't necessarily have super-high LDL in the first place?

Maybe not, but people with diabetes do have high concentrations of small, dense LDL cholesterol particles, which are more likely to plug up arteries. Statins wipe out all LDL particles, including the dangerous kind.

And that's not all. Statins also lower triglycerides, though not as effectively as they decrease LDL cholesterol. The drugs also cause a slight uptick in HDL cholesterol, and that's good news, too. In fact, scientists from other disciplines are studying whether statins fight other diseases, including various forms of cancer.

Doctors who treat heart disease are so grateful for the lives saved by statins that they sometimes suggest adding the drugs to our nation's drinking water. And they're only half kidding. Unfortunately, while these cholesterol crushers are considered quite safe, they carry a few risks. Some are mild and short term, such as gastrointestinal problems, headaches, and a rash. However, statins may also irritate the liver, so your doctor will keep tabs on it with occasional blood tests.

More controversially, statins have been linked to several conditions, particularly myositis (swelling of the muscles) and rhabdomyolysis (a breakdown of muscle fibers, which are then released into the circulation). Although they are rarely fatal, these conditions can cause muscle pain, cramps, and weakness. However, studies suggest that these problems are not very common. A 2003 survey in the *Journal of the American Medical Association* estimated that one to five percent of patients who take statins develop some form of muscle pain or weakness. What's more, the problem may be triggered by taking some other medication (such as fibrates

and niacin; see below) with a statin drug. Regardless, the symptoms fade once you stop taking a statin.

Fibrates

Unlike statins, these drugs (sometimes called fibric acid derivatives) aren't known for their LDL-lowering prowess. However, fibrates stimulate an enzyme that breaks down fats, so they lower triglycerides very effectively—by as much as 50 percent in some trials. Fibrates also produce a respectable increase in HDL cholesterol, more on the order of 10 or 15 percent.

Although they are considered safe, fibrates can cause gastrointestinal distress and may increase the risk of developing gallstones. If you're taking a statin, adding a fibrate may increase the risk of muscle pain or weakness.

Resins

Your multitalented liver not only makes cholesterol, but it can convert the waxy fat into bile acid, which you need to digest food. Resins (sometimes called bile acid sequestrants) lower cholesterol by forcing the liver into borrowing resources to get its work done. These drugs enter the gut and kidnap bile acids by binding to them, then carrying them through your GI tract to be excreted. The liver figures out that the intestines are low on bile, so to produce a fresh batch it pulls cholesterol out of the blood to use as raw material. Resins lower cholesterol levels by 10 to 20 percent.

Resins have a relatively clean safety record, too, though any time you start messing with business in your intestines you risk tummy trouble. As that goes, resins may cause nausea, gas, constipation, and other gastrointestinal unpleasantness. Convenience is a small matter, too, since resins come in the form of powders that must be mixed with water or juice and taken with a meal.

Niacin

Here's a drug that may make you red in the face in more ways than one. Niacin is a form of vitamin B that you will no doubt find in your multivitamin. However, it is also packed into pills at ultra-high doses (sometimes called nicotinic acid) for treating cholesterol problems. The good news is that niacin works wonders on all your blood fats, lowering LDL cholesterol and triglycerides while raising HDL cholesterol.

But there's a potential catch or two, especially if you have diabetes. High doses of niacin have a common, and infamous, side effect: flushed skin and hot flashes. Some users say their skin tingles. The pills can cause gastrointestinal problems, too.

Taking niacin with meals and starting with slow doses may alleviate the tomato-face issue. However, when taken at drug-level doses, niacin has another side effect that would frustrate any diabetes patient: It may raise blood sugar. Since you hold in your hands a book devoted to doing just the opposite, you may wonder why niacin is even worth mentioning. While many doctors won't prescribe niacin to diabetes patients, recent studies show that, when taken in small doses (no more than one or two grams), it doesn't seem to increase glucose levels.

Best bet: Ask your doctor whether small doses of niacin could improve your cholesterol and triglycerides. Worst idea: Self-treating with niacin supplements that are available over the counter. Too much niacin can cause liver problems, which your doctor may not notice or test for if unaware that you're taking high doses of the vitamin. What's more, if you're already taking a statin drug, adding niacin to the mix increases the risk for muscle problems.

VASCULAR DISEASE BY THE NUMBERS

- 1.2 million Americans have heart attacks each year.
- 700,000 Americans have strokes each year.
- About two-thirds of people with diabetes will die of heart disease, stroke, or other vascular diseases.

103

Ezetimibe

Hands up if you always thought the cholesterol in meats and milk is the same stuff that clogs arteries. While that's partly true, the reality is more complicated. Your liver can make its own cholesterol, thank you. In fact, that hardworking organ produces about 75 percent of the cholesterol in your body. However, that means the liver relies on cholesterol in the diet to produce the other 25 percent. Ezetimibe is a relatively new drug that prevents the liver from taking up cholesterol in the intestines. While reasonably effective on its own, ezetimibe has been paired in a single pill with a statin drug (simvastatin) to create a double-threat medication called Vytorin. Studies show that the duo can lower LDL cholesterol more than 50 percent. Side effects linked to ezetimibe include stomach pain and fatigue.

Aspirin

The little white tablets in your medicine chest don't lower cholesterol or triglycerides, but they are a potent weapon against heart disease. By some estimates, taking an aspirin a day lowers the risk of heart attack by about one-third. Aspirin makes blood less "sticky," meaning cells that cause coagulation (called platelets) are less likely to clump together. Furthermore, aspirin fights inflammation, which some scientists believe triggers plaques to erupt, causing heart attacks. Talk to your doctor before adding an aspirin to your daily regimen. Physicians who recommend preventive aspirin very often suggest taking a half tablet or child-size aspirin (75 milligrams, typically) to minimize possible side effects, which can include upset stomach. However, since your cardiovascular risk is heightened by diabetes, your doc may want you to pop a whole pill (162 milligrams).

Other Diseases of the Blood Vessels That You Should Know About

Blood-flow problems can crop up anywhere in the circulatory system. The symptoms can come on slowly, such as a little pain or shortness of breath. However, the first signs of trouble may come on suddenly. In either case, knowing what to look for could save your life.

STROKES

Doctors sometimes refer to strokes as brain attacks. The name calls to mind heart attacks, which is fitting since the two have much in common. Like heart attacks, strokes occur due to a sudden loss of blood circulation, in this case, to the brain. Both strokes and heart attacks are extreme—and often deadly or debilitating—medical emergencies. And, as with heart attacks, diabetes increases the risk of strokes. Compared to the general population, people with diabetes are two to three times more likely to suffer a stroke.

To be more precise, diabetes patients have a greatly increased risk for the most common variety of stroke. Ischemic strokes, which account for 80 to 85 percent of attacks, occur when a blood vessel to the brain becomes clogged. (*Ischemia* means "loss of blood flow.") They can occur due to the gradual build-up of fatty gunk on the vessel walls, the same way plaques accumulate in the arteries that feed blood to the heart. Or, a blood clot that formed somewhere else in the body may tear loose and float all the way to the brain's vessels before plugging up circulation.

The other major form of cerebrovascular disease is called a hemorrhagic stroke, which occurs when a weak spot in one of the brain's blood vessels bursts or leaks. The resulting blood flood puts damaging pressure on the brain. Hemorrhagic strokes make up about 15 to 20 percent of all strokes, and they don't seem to be linked to diabetes.

The results can be devastating with either kind of stroke. Although your brain makes up only about 2 percent of your body weight, the thinking machine

TROUBLESHOOTING CHECKLIST: SYMPTOMS OF A STROKE

The same clot-busting drugs that can stop a heart attack in its tracks can also be used to treat the majority of strokes, greatly reducing the threat of long-term disability from a stroke. However, these drugs must be administered within three hours of the onset of a "brain attack," so recognizing the symptoms—and responding by getting to an emergency room—is essential. The warning signs of a stroke include the sudden onset of

- ☐ weakness or numbness in the face, arms, or legs, especially if it occurs on one side
- ☐ confusion or difficulty understanding others
- ☐ trouble speaking
- ☐ blurry vision in one or both eyes
- ☐ difficulty walking, dizziness, or loss of coordination
- ☐ severe, unexplained headache

sucks up 20 percent of the body's oxygen and around 15 percent of the blood your heart pumps out. When supply routes for oxygen-rich blood are jammed, brain cells start to die. Whatever function those dying neurons govern in the body—such as talking, walking, and swallowing—will suffer and may be lost. Here's the clincher: Studies show that a person with diabetes is more likely to die or suffer irreversible neurological damage resulting in a permanent disability from a stroke.

The good news: If you're taking steps to cut your risk of heart disease, you're doing double duty, because the same measures also limit the risk of stroke.

HEART FAILURE

Many people think "heart failure" is a synonym for "heart attack," as in, *I nearly had heart failure when Carl gave me the new Engelbert Humperdinck CD for my birthday!* But while a heart attack can be a cause of heart failure, they are two different conditions. Heart attacks occur because a blocked artery prevents blood from reaching your ticker. When a person has heart failure, however, his or her heart can't pump an adequate volume of blood back into circulation. You could say that the heart still works, but it fails to meet the body's demands.

Furthermore, while heart attacks happen suddenly, heart failure is a chronic condition that gradually worsens over time. The first signs of trouble are usually fatigue and shortness of breath. Lying down can make the latter problem even worse. Eventually, the heart may become so weak that it can no longer efficiently push blood through the circulatory system. Stagnating blood begins to pool in the veins and cause swelling, usually in the legs and ankles, though any part of the body can be affected, especially the lungs. Because this condition causes blood in the circulatory system to become congested, it's often called congestive heart failure.

About five million Americans have heart failure. The condition has many causes, including heart attacks. Even before the Big One strikes, however, accumulating cholesterol and other crud in the arteries will narrow blood flow, making the heart work harder than normal, which may cause it to weaken. Hypertension, infections, and other diseases can cause heart failure, too. While atherosclerosis and high blood pressure often accompany diabetes, some doctors theorize that elevated blood sugar independently increases the risk for a weakened heart, a condition they have named cardiac myopathy. The theory remains controversial. However, there's no doubt that heart failure is a serious concern if you have diabetes. Men with diabetes have double the risk for heart failure, while women with diabetes are *five times* more likely to develop the condition than the general population.

Doctors usually order patients with heart failure to lose a few pounds and moderate their intake of sodium and fluids, especially alcohol, which could worsen fluid retention. Heart failure is often treated with many of the same medications prescribed for hypertension, including ACE inhibitors, beta-blockers, and diuretics, as well as digitalis, a class of drugs that makes the heart muscle contract more forcefully.

PERIPHERAL ARTERY DISEASE

Atherosclerosis, or the narrowing of blood vessels, is an equal opportunity disorder. While atherosclerosis in the coronary arteries leads to the number one cause of death in Western civilization, blood vessels throughout the rest of the body can get clogged, too. The problem, known as peripheral artery disease, or PAD, afflicts up to 12 million Americans, though only about half develop symptoms.

PAD can occur in the arms and other parts of the body but most often strikes below the belt. As blood flow to leg muscles slows down, pain and cramping can result in the calves, thighs, or hips while walking. The discomfort fades if you stop to rest. Because the pain comes and goes, it's known as *intermittent claudication.*

Many people who develop PAD symptoms never mention them to doctors, figuring a little pain now and then is part of aging. But over time, lack of adequate blood flow to the lower limbs can lead to some serious consequences. Poor circulation to the lower extremities can lead to nasty sores, gangrene, and even an amputated foot or two.

Here's why you should really care: People with diabetes are two to three times more likely than people who don't have the disease to develop PAD. In fact, as a diabetes patient, once you reach age 50, your odds are about one in three. Furthermore, when compared to other patients with PAD, people with diabetes are 10 to 30 times more likely to have a foot amputated.

And believe it or not, that isn't the scariest part. Doctors have come to think of PAD as a red flag—a warning that a patient is a heart attack or stroke waiting to happen. One study found that 70 percent of people who have PAD also have severe blockages in their coronary arteries. Another determined that intermittent claudication shortens lifespan by about 10 years.

There is much more to the PAD story, but because it is exacerbated by nerve damage—and because foot problems are a major part of managing diabetes—we'll cover this topic in greater detail in Chapter 10.

The Nervous System and Diabetes

Scientists and poets celebrate the brain as the body's supercomputer and seat of wisdom. But let's face facts: Take away the elaborate network of nerves that connects the brain to the muscles, organs, glands, and skin, and you're left with a three-pound lump of fat and protein. When we talk about the source of the human body's remarkable powers of perception and expression, we really mean the brain and the nerves, which make up the information highway in your body known as the nervous system.

Unfortunately, diabetes can create potholes in your neural highway. This chapter addresses one of the most common complications of diabetes: neuropathy, or nerve damage. On the following pages, you'll learn how to keep signals traveling on your nerves clear and static free.

Don't Lose Your Nerve(s): Diabetes and Neuropathy

Diabetes is the most common cause of nerve damage called neuropathy. You don't have to have diabetes to develop neuropathy; but if you do have the disorder, there is a good chance you will one day feel the effects of injured nerves. By most estimates, about half of all people with diabetes have some form of neuropathy. The figure may be even higher; in fact, some experts think that if you have diabetes, you have some degree of nerve damage, though the condition doesn't always produce symptoms. The longer you live with diabetes, the greater your chances of developing some degree of neuropathy; the first signs of nerve damage typically arise 10 to 20 years after a patient is first diagnosed with diabetes.

Diabetic neuropathy can instigate trouble all over your body, but the toes and the rest of the feet are especially vulnerable. In fact, for many people, diabetic neuropathy is synonymous with foot ulcers and other diabetes-related disorders of the foot. That's why Chapter 10 is devoted entirely to the topic of foot care. In this chapter, we'll look at the many other ways neuropathy can make life difficult, as well as how to minimize the threat of nerve damage.

The Nervous System

Although it resembles nothing more than a very large walnut, the brain assumes some mind-boggling responsibilities. The wonders of thought, speech, emotion, and the five senses all begin within the folds of the craggy organ inside your skull. The brain has three main regions: the cerebellum, the forebrain, and the brain stem. The latter is actually the upper end of the spinal cord, a tube of nerve tissue protected by the spine. The spinal cord connects the brain to the nerves, which are bundles of fibers (also known as axons) that connect the billions of cells in the nervous system, called neurons, to one another. Axons can be as tiny as a fraction of an inch or stretch to several feet. Many nerves are insulated with a protective layer of protein and fat known as a myelin sheath. If the myelin sheath is damaged, signaling between neurons may be delayed or shut down altogether.

From a structural standpoint, the nervous system has two main divisions,

A LIKELY STORY

You are more likely to develop diabetic neuropathy if you

- have a hard time maintaining glucose control
- have high blood triglyceride levels
- have high blood pressure
- smoke
- are overweight
- have had diabetes for a long time (highest rates are among people who have had the disease for 25 years or more)
- are tall, since long nerves become damaged first

the central nervous system and the peripheral nervous system. The central nervous system consists of the brain and spinal cord. The central nervous system, or CNS, acts as the body's corporate headquarters, processing information and making decisions. Meanwhile, the peripheral nervous system consists of the nerves that branch off the spinal cord and extend throughout the body. Think of the peripheral nervous system, or PNS, as the brain's field representatives, gathering information about the body's needs and carrying out executive decisions.

The nervous system is capable of operating in two modes, conscious and involuntary. On the conscious level, we take in information about the environment through our five senses, and we transmit that information to the brain via nerve signals. The brain crunches this data and decides how the body should act. For instance, say you're standing in line at Starbucks and you spot a coworker, Louise, sitting on one of the cozy sofas, sipping espresso. The optic nerves in your eyes deliver this information to the brain, which evaluates the situation and arrives at a conclusion: *Louise is such a bore—take immediate action to avoid eye contact.* With blazing speed, your brain sends instructions along the nerves back to the eye and neck muscles: *Avert gaze. Stare at display rack. Feign interest in the overpriced coffee mugs.*

At the same time, though, the involuntary side of the nervous system—often called the autonomic nervous system—runs day-to-day functions that we're too busy to think about. For example, we usually don't give much thought to maintaining a steady heartbeat, breathing, or blinking, but if the primal regions of the brain didn't oversee these basic needs, we would die. (We'd probably use a heck of a lot of Visine, too.)

Indeed, the nervous system controls everything humans do, whether it's catch a touchdown pass or drop a hot potato, write a love sonnet or a racy limerick, sing a Puccini aria or burp-speak the alphabet. Unfortunately, diabetes can gum up the works, in both direct and indirect ways.

ROUTINE MAINTENANCE

Diabetic neuropathy is a maddening condition. You can be a model diabetes patient, follow your doctor's orders to the letter, keep your glucose under control, and *still* end up with nerve damage. But there are steps you can take to keep neuropathy under control.

- Check your blood sugar often.
- Maintain tight glucose control by taking all the medications you have been prescribed, on schedule.
- Don't smoke.
- Don't drink alcohol to excess.
- Keep your weight down.
- Maintain healthy blood pressure and cholesterol levels.
- After your initial screening for diabetic neuropathy, get rescreened once a year.

WHAT CAUSES DIABETIC NEUROPATHY?

As you will learn in this chapter, diabetic neuropathy isn't one disease but an injury that can result in a long list of medical problems. So it's only appropriate that scientists have come up with a number of theories about how diabetes damages nerves. In fact, most experts agree that diabetic neuropathy is likely the result of several different biological changes that occur simultaneously.

That said, there is little doubt that chronically elevated glucose levels are bad for your nerves. Unlike your muscles, organs, and fat, the nerves don't need insulin to absorb glucose. So if blood sugar rises, nerves become saturated with the sweet stuff. Enzymes process the excess sugar, converting it to the compounds sorbitol and fructose, resulting in diminished levels of other important chemicals. As the protective myelin sheath erodes and the nerve's structure breaks down, signals traveling along the axons can go haywire. Some will be delayed, as if your brain suddenly reverted from broadband Internet access to dial-up. Other nerve signals may be blocked altogether.

Other culprits that may play a role in diabetic nerve damage include:

- Clogged arteries. Nerves need a fresh supply of blood to survive, and diabetes increases the risk of atherosclerosis, or narrowing of blood vessels.
- Advanced glycosylation end products, or AGEs, are nasty compounds the body produces when blood sugar is high. AGEs damage axons and promote the creation of free radicals, molecules that harm healthy cells.
- Low levels of nerve growth factor and insulin. Nerve growth factor (NGF) is necessary for healthy nerves; animals with very low levels of NGF tend to have severe diabetic neuropathy. Insulin, the vital hormone that people with type 1 diabetes lack, appears to promote healthy nerves, too.
- Inflammation. According to one theory, diabetic neuropathy may occur because the body's immune system launches a misguided attack on the nerves.

Diabetic neuropathy can produce symptoms and functional problems in just about any part of the body. Often, the early signs are merely annoying. The first clues that doctors look for are tingling or numbness in the feet, legs, arms, or hands. As nerve damage worsens, though, neuropathy can foul up the brain's signaling to muscles and organs in ways that cause debilitating pain, which may eventually deteriorate to loss of sensation in that part of the body. Neuropathy not only creates new medical problems, it also worsens existing conditions. It can even spoil your sex life.

Now do we have your attention? Read on to learn more about how diabetic neuropathy can produce a long list of complications, how you can protect your nerves, and what you can do to cope with the symptoms of neuropathy.

THE TYPES OF DIABETIC NEUROPATHY

The different types of diabetic neuropathy produce a variety of symptoms and cause a host of medical problems. But it can be difficult to diagnose the exact type of neuropathy that's at the root of your problems because the nervous system is so complex. Here are the basics to help guide you.

Peripheral Neuropathy

When your leg "falls asleep," it feels numb or tingly. You can poke or prod the skin and barely feel a thing. That's because your leg nerves have been squished for some reason—perhaps you sat in an awkward position for too long. Squished nerve fibers don't transmit clear signals, so for a moment or two your brain doesn't receive messages from the leg. As you stand and

stretch, the nerve becomes unsquished and your leg comes back to life. This familiar phenomenon offers a glimpse of what it's like to have peripheral neuropathy, the most common form of diabetes-related nerve damage.

In most cases of peripheral neuropathy, the nerve damage starts in the toes and feet, then slowly works its way north, spreading to the calves and thighs. Later, the hands and arms may be affected. Symptoms often occur symmetrically; that is, they arise in both feet or both legs, and they may be worse at night.

Symptoms of Peripheral Neuropathy.
- Numbness
- Tingling or prickly feeling
- Pain
- Burning sensation
- Inability to feel intense heat or cold
- Cramps
- Extreme sensitivity to touch
- Loss of coordination
- Weakness and loss of reflexes

Peripheral neuropathy produces this range of symptoms because different types of nerves perform distinct roles in the body. As a general rule, large sensory nerve fibers pick up sensations such as touching and vibration, so damage to these nerves can result in numbness and problems with balance.

Smaller nerves transmit pain and sensitivity to temperatures. Damage to these nerves can mask the pain and discomfort of a cut or wound, allowing it to become infected. Oddly enough, the opposite can happen, too: Nerves in the skin that detect pain or pressure can become oversensitized, making the softest touch hurt like a slap. Patients often say that a limb becomes so ultra-touchy that they can't even bear the weight of a bed sheet.

Damage to nerves in the feet can lead to one of the most common complications of diabetes, foot sores and other foot problems (which you can read about in Chapter 10).

Autonomic Neuropathy

Earlier in this chapter you read about the autonomic nervous system, the complex of brain cells and nerves that controls all the functions in your body that operate in the background, without any conscious thought or effort. While peripheral neuropathy often afflicts the feet, legs, and other extremities, autonomic neuropathy can affect any organ in the body.

One of the really scary things about autonomic neuropathy is the way it can cut off warning signs to the brain that the body sends out when trouble is

brewing. As a result, people with autonomic neuropathy may be well on their way to getting very sick but have no idea anything is wrong. Here are the major complications autonomic neuropathy can cause:

Unawareness of Hypoglycemia. While you don't have to have diabetes to develop autonomic neuropathy, one complication is of particular concern to people who have the disease. When a person who doesn't have autonomic neuropathy becomes hypoglycemic, the body releases compounds called catecholamines that cause trembling and a cold sweat. Anyone with diabetes should recognize these symptoms as evidence of low blood sugar, a problem that can be remedied by downing a glucose pill or a sweet snack or beverage.

However, autonomic neuropathy interferes with catecholamines, so diabetes patients who have this form of nerve damage don't develop the familiar trembling and sweating when their glucose plummets. Autonomic neuropathy can disrupt the body's ability to maintain glucose levels between meals. Normally, the pancreas releases the hormone glucagon, which triggers the liver to release glucose into the bloodstream when levels drop. This so-called *glucagon response* naturally weakens over time in patients with type 1 diabetes. But it's absent altogether if you have autonomic neuropathy.

Painless Ischemia and Other Forms of Cardiovascular Neuropathy. Ischemia is simply the medical term for a loss of blood flow to an organ. When that organ happens to be your heart, the result is very bad news indeed—a heart attack. Fortunately, heart attacks usually hurt like the dickens, causing chest pain and other symptoms (see Chapter 6 for a complete list). Recognize these distinctive signs early enough, and you can call 911 for help.

But if you have autonomic neuropathy and damaged nerves have blocked pain signals to the brain, you could be sitting around the house doing a crossword puzzle and have no idea that a clot had formed in your coronary artery and your heart is starving for oxygen. This condition is called painless, or silent, ischemia, and it occurs in about five percent of diabetes patients who don't have autonomic neuropathy. But if you have diabetes *and* autonomic neuropathy, your risk rises to 38 percent.

Painless ischemia is just one potential danger of cardiovascular neuropathy, which occurs in 17 percent of patients with type 1 diabetes and 22 percent of type 2 patients. For example, your body naturally makes adjustments to maintain normal blood pressure and heart rate to suit different circumstances. Autonomic neuropathy blocks the nerve signals that make these adjustments. Orthostatic hypotension is one common result of this signal interference. If you have this condition, simply standing up can cause blood pressure to plunge. You may only feel a bit dizzy or light-headed, though in some cases people faint. If damage occurs to the nerves that control heart rate, your cardiovascular system may stay on overdrive all day instead of revving up and relaxing to suit your body's various needs. These disturbances in blood pressure and heart rate increase the risk for cardiac catastrophe.

The following medical problems caused by diabetic neuropathy will be discussed in greater detail in chapters to follow.

DAMAGE CONTROL

Autonomic neuropathy is difficult to treat, but controlling your blood sugar levels can prevent or delay the onset of these troublesome symptoms. In the Diabetes Complications and Control Trial (DCCT), patients who maintained tight glucose control reduced their risk for autonomic nerve damage by 53 percent.

Digestive Distress. Autonomic neuropathy can cause just about any gastrointestinal disorder you can think of (as well as several others you would probably rather not think about at all). The longer you have had diabetes and the more trouble you have maintaining tight glucose control, the more likely you are to have digestive problems. Most GI woes are mild and treatable, but some can become serious.

Constipation is the most common complication caused by glucose-induced nerve damage; about 60 percent of diabetes patients have occasional or frequent bouts with this digestive discomfort. About one in four diabetes patients develops gastroparesis, another problem related to damaged digestive nerves. This condition causes food to empty out of the stomach slowly. Gastroparesis doesn't always cause symptoms, but in serious cases it can result in episodes of lost appetite, bloating, nausea, vomiting, and abdominal pain that can go on for months. Equally concerning, serious dips in blood sugar can occur if you inject insulin to blunt a post-meal surge of glucose, because gastroparesis delays food from reaching your intestines and

being absorbed into the blood. There is no extra sugar to process, and the insulin lowers glucose too much, leading to hypoglycemia.

Diarrhea is another digestive woe that plagues about one in five diabetes patients, and it seems to be more common in those with autonomic neuropathy. Normally, the autonomic nervous system ensures that the food you eat has a smooth and gradual trip through the stomach and intestines. But damaged nerves can disrupt the process, leading to loose bowels and the dreaded fecal incontinence (loss of bowel control). Finally, damage to nerves in the esophagus can cause difficulty swallowing in some patients.

Of course, lots of other things can cause gastrointestinal problems, so if you develop any of these symptoms, your doctor will want to rule out other potential causes. Constipation, for instance, can be caused by diseases such as hypothyroidism or colon cancer, and it can be a side effect of certain medications (such as calcium channel blockers used to treat hypertension).

Under- and Overactive Sweat Glands. Without sweat glands, we would probably have to pant like

115

dogs (which lack sweat glands) to cool down our bodies on hot days and during exercise. The nervous system controls sweat glands, so when damage strikes nerves in the extremities—one of the most common complications of diabetes—the result can be feet that don't sweat.

Eureka! Sounds like a cure for foot odor, right? If only it were that simple. Loss of sweating (known as anhidrosis) in the feet leads to severely dry skin, which is just one of the foot-related complications of diabetes you will read about in Chapter 10. What's more, your body makes up for not being able to sweat through the feet by gushing out extra perspiration in other parts of the body, often the face and trunk, a phenomenon known as compensatory sweating (or, if you want to sound brainy, compensatory hyperhidrosis, the medical term for excessive sweating).

Diabetes-induced nerve damage can cause a similar problem, known as gustatory hyperhidrosis. Anyone who has ever eaten in a Mexican restaurant knows that chomping on a habanero or some other type of hot pepper not only scorches your tongue but can make your brow perspire. Neuropathy can make you break out in a sweat when you eat or drink anything, no matter how bland. No one is sure why, but it may be that previously blunted sweat glands are reawakened by certain food ingredients, though no single dish is known to have the effect consistently in people who have this peculiar condition. For some reason, the glands overcompensate, glistening the skin on the face, neck, and scalp with sweat.

One study of 196 diabetes patients found that roughly one-third who had neuropathy suffered from gustatory hyperhidrosis (the condition is also linked to kidney damage). While any kind of excess sweating can be a social nightmare, gustatory hyperhidrosis worries doctors, since it may disrupt a normal, healthy eating plan, which in turn could cause fluctuations in blood sugar and produce bouts of hypoglycemia.

Urinary and Sexual Problems. Diabetes often strikes below the belt, in a manner of speaking. Normally, when the bladder fills up, nerve signals to the brain instruct you to visit the restroom, and the sooner the better. If those nerves become damaged, however, your bladder can fill up and bulge to three times its normal size, but you may never realize it. Eventually, you may become incontinent—that is, urine will spill out of the bladder, whether you

116

want it to or not. Studies show that people with diabetes are significantly more likely than the general population to develop incontinence.

Nerve damage can also weaken the bladder, making it difficult to empty completely during a visit to the powder room. Over time, bacteria may breed in urine left behind in the bladder, leading to a urinary tract infection (UTI). UTIs are no darn fun; they can cause pain while urinating and make you feel like you need to "go" all day and especially at night, among other symptoms. Having diabetes seems to raise the risk for this pesky problem. For example, a 2002 study found that postmenopausal women with diabetes were more than twice as likely to develop a urinary tract infection as postmenopausal women without diabetes. What's more, women with diabetes tended to develop more serious and painful infections.

Now, let's make our way from the bathroom to the bedroom, because it's time to broach an even more sensitive issue: Your love life and how nerve damage from diabetes can put a damper on it.

Erectile dysfunction is perhaps the most common male sexual disorder caused by diabetes-related nerve damage. In fact, men with diabetes are three times more likely to develop the problem than men who don't have the disease. Estimates vary, but between 20 and 85 percent of male diabetes patients will experience erectile dysfunction, often called simply ED. (Which is better than the older, somewhat offensive term "impotence," though guys named Ed may disagree.) For an erection to occur, the brain has to communicate with the penis via a network of nerves; damage to those nerves can spoil the fun.

Another problem, called retrograde ejaculation, occurs more often than normal in men with diabetes. When a male ejaculates, the bladder usually closes. If nerve damage disables the muscles that seal the bladder, semen backs into the organ. As a result, the man ejaculates little or no semen. Although retrograde ejaculation is physically harmless

OTHER CAUSES OF PERIPHERAL NEUROPATHY

Diabetes is a leading cause of peripheral neuropathy, but doctors need to rule out other potential culprits. They include

- inherited disorders, such as Charcot-Marie-Tooth disease
- physical injury to a nerve
- tumors
- infections
- exposure to toxic substances
- other autoimmune disorders
- nutritional deficiencies
- alcoholism
- kidney and liver disorders
- vascular disorders that constrict blood vessels
- hormonal disorders
- connective tissue disorders
- repetitive stress disorders (such as carpal tunnel syndrome)

for the man, it can cause infertility. It also turns urine cloudy.

Diabetes is an equal opportunity nuisance when it comes to sexual disorders, however. In fact, at least one study involving patients with type 1 diabetes found that sexual problems were more common in women (27 percent) than men (22 percent). In one survey, the most common sex-related complaint among women with diabetes was vaginal dryness, which results from damage to cells lining the vagina that provide lubrication. Lack of lubrication can make intercourse painful. Add side effects from medications you might be taking, plus anxiety or depression about your health, and it's no surprise that women with diabetes often lose interest in sex or have trouble having orgasms, too.

Night Blindness and Related Visual Problems. Loss of vision is one of the most ominous threats people with diabetes face. That's why Chapter 11 of this book is devoted entirely to the subject. However, damage to the autonomic nervous system causes a specific vision problem in people with diabetes. The problem is your pupils, the openings in the irises that allow light into the eye. In the dark, pupils dilate to allow more light in. If you have autonomic neuropathy, your pupils may respond more slowly to changes in light and have a smaller diameter. In some cases, the pupils of a diabetes patient are so small and slow that they develop night blindness, making driving after dark risky.

Proximal Neuropathy. If you have read this far and think diabetic neuropathy can be a big pain in the butt, you're right—literally. Proximal neuropathy causes discomfort in the buttocks, hips, and thighs. Pain may subside after a few months, but it's often followed by weakness in the legs that can make it difficult to stand from a sitting or squatting position or to climb stairs. Pain and disability usually occur on one side of the body.

Proximal neuropathy goes by several other names, including lumbosacral plexus neuropathy, femoral neuropathy, and diabetic amyotrophy. It's most common in type 2 diabetes patients and usually occurs after age 50.

Focal Neuropathy. When you focus on something, your attention zeroes in on a specific item. Focal neuropathy is damage that occurs to a nerve controlling a specific muscle, often resulting in severe pain. Some of the symptoms of focal neuropathy include

- double vision or difficulty focusing your eyes
- an ache behind one eye
- paralysis or drooping of one cheek (Bell's palsy)
- severe pain in the lower back or pelvis
- pain in the front of a thigh or in the chest, stomach, or side
- pain on the outer shin or inner foot
- sudden weakness of the ankle, known as "foot drop"
- chest or abdominal pain that mimics a heart attack or attack of appendicitis

Focal neuropathy usually afflicts older patients. It flares up suddenly but seems to fade on its own after a few weeks or months. A related problem, called entrapment syndrome, occurs when nerves become compressed. The wrists are a common location for entrapment, which is well-known to anyone who has developed carpal tunnel syndrome from using a keyboard or computer mouse for an extended period. (Bones in the wrist called carpals form a tunnellike structure; repetitive

TROUBLESHOOTING CHECKLIST

Many of the symptoms of diabetic neuropathy can be caused by other problems; a bout with constipation, for instance, may simply mean you haven't been eating your bran buds every morning. However, because you have diabetes, these signs should be taken seriously, since they may be evidence of nerve damage. Talk to your doctor if any of these symptoms persist:

- ☐ Numbness, tingling, pain, burning, or loss of sensitivity to temperature in a limb
- ☐ Unexplained changes to your limbs, especially your feet
- ☐ Extreme sensitivity to touch
- ☐ Loss of coordination or weakness
- ☐ Low blood sugar that's not accompanied by symptoms of hypoglycemia
- ☐ Dizziness or feeling faint upon standing
- ☐ Gastrointestinal problems, such as constipation, nausea, or diarrhea
- ☐ Dry skin
- ☐ Excessive sweating (which may occur after eating)
- ☐ Urinary problems
- ☐ Erectile dysfunction, vaginal dryness, or other sexual problems
- ☐ Difficulty seeing in dim light, double vision, or difficulty focusing
- ☐ Pain or feeling of weakness in the buttocks, hips, or thighs
- ☐ An ache behind one eye
- ☐ Paralysis or drooping of one cheek
- ☐ Severe pain in the lower back, pelvis, thigh (especially in the front), chest, stomach, side, outside of the shin, or inside of the foot
- ☐ Sudden weakness of the ankle

motions cause tendons in the wrist to swell, compressing nerves.)

DIAGNOSING DIABETIC NEUROPATHY

A doctor may suspect neuropathy based on a patient's particular complaint, a physical exam, and medical history. To confirm the diagnosis, a physician may use some of the following tests, depending on the suspected source of nerve injury. The American Diabetes Association recommends that patients be screened for diabetic neuropathy when they are initially diagnosed with type 2 diabetes. (In fact, symptoms of nerve damage are the first signs of diabetes in some patients.) Patients with type 1 diabetes should be screened for neuropathy five years after their initial diagnosis. Both groups should be screened annually thereafter. These are tests that help diagnose diabetic neuropathy:

A complete foot exam. Kick off your shoes and relax—your doctor wants to spend some time checking out your feet. Read why this isn't as weird as it sounds in Chapter 10.

Nerve conduction studies. Doctors use special devices to measure how well signals travel along nerves in the arms and legs, much like electricians use voltage testers to find out whether

there's any current running through the wiring in your house. Using an electrode attached to the skin near the nerves in question, the doctor delivers a tiny zap. Other electrodes measure the strength of electrical signals given off by nerves and muscles in reaction to the shock. Slow or weak nerve signals may indicate damage.

Electromyography (EMG). This test looks for nerve damage with fine needles, which the doctor inserts directly into muscle. You may be asked to flex the muscle. The needles transmit information about the muscle's response to a computer. Again, slow or weak signals may be a sign of nerve damage. Electromyography is often performed at the same time as a nerve conduction study.

Quantitative sensory testing (QST). If you have been feeling tingling, burning, or numbness in any part of your body, a doctor may use quantitative sensory testing to determine if nerve damage is to blame. Nerve fibers play different roles, depending on their size. Big ones detect vibrations, medium nerves sense cold, and small fibers are the ones that tell you to drop a hot casserole dish if your oven mitts are too flimsy. (That is, they detect heat.) Instead of needles and electrodes, quantitative sensory testing uses various tools to produce vibrations, as well as hot and cold temperatures. The examiner will test affected and unaffected parts of your body, asking you what you feel and recording your responses.

Ultrasound. Doctors use sound waves to take a peek at your internal organs. If you have diabetic neuropathy and have been experiencing urinary problems, your physician may use ultrasound to take an image of your bladder to determine whether it is emptying completely.

Cardiovascular testing. If you have been feeling dizzy or faint, your doctor may measure how your blood pressure and heart rate change in response to standing. (This can be accomplished using the "tilt table test," in which the patient lies on a flat surface that is gradually tilted upright while machines measure blood pressure and electrical activity in the heart.) An electrocardiogram may also be conducted to measure the heart's response while the patient tries to force air from his or her lungs while blocking the airway, which increases blood pressure in the head. (This is known as the Valsalva maneuver, which is the same thing you do naturally when lifting a heavy object or sneezing.)

Sweat testing. There are several ways to test for abnormal perspiration patterns

produced by damage to autonomic nerves. The most exotic method is called thermoregulatory sweat testing. The patient is coated with a special powder, then steps into a warm chamber designed to induce sweating. Perspiration makes the powder change color, which can help diagnose sweating disorders that may be related to diabetes.

COPING WITH THE SYMPTOMS OF DIABETIC NEUROPATHY

Doctors don't pester diabetes patients about keeping blood sugar low just to exercise their jaws. Maintaining tight control over glucose levels prevents complications, including nerve damage. In the Diabetes Control and Complications Trial (DCCT), patients who received aggressive insulin therapy and maintained reasonably low blood sugar reduced their risk for neuropathy by 60 percent. (Patients in the DCCT who kept their blood sugar low for an average of 6.5 years also cut their risk for blindness and kidney disease, as you will read in later chapters.)

That means preventing and minimizing nerve damage is as simple as eating right, exercising, and taking the medications you have been prescribed. Other can't-hurt-might-help measures include getting your blood pressure, cholesterol, and other blood lipids under control; quitting smoking; and drinking less alcohol.

However, since half of all people with diabetes eventually experience some degree of nerve damage, you may one day develop symptoms that can range from annoying to debilitating. We'll discuss treatments for several common categories of symptoms caused by nerve damage here; treatments for limb, digestive, visual, urinary, and sexual problems caused by diabetic neuropathy will be covered in later chapters.

Hypoglycemia unawareness
- Check your blood glucose frequently, especially before going to bed or driving a car.
- Treat low blood sugar whether or not you have symptoms.
- Your doctor may adjust your insulin dose to minimize the risk of hypoglycemia.
- Explain to friends and family that you may become hypoglycemic without realizing it. Be sure they know what symptoms to look for and what to do.
- If your blood sugar dips below 50 mg/dl without any symptoms, tell your doctor.

Pain
While foot pain (covered in Chapter 10) may be the most notorious form of

diabetes-related discomfort, neuropathy can produce aches and sores all over the body. Severe pain may require a combination of complementary medications, such as an antidepressant and an anticonvulsant.
- Aspirin, acetaminophen, or non-steroidal anti-inflammatory drugs (NSAIDs) such as ibuprofen. These pills are all available over the counter, but ask your doctor which pain reliever is best for you. For instance, people with kidney problems should avoid NSAIDs, which could worsen their condition. Don't expect miracles, however. While OTC pain relievers are cheap and convenient, they may not be potent enough to fight most forms of neuropathy-related pain.
- Antidepressants. Many patients get at least moderate relief from an older class of antidepressant drugs known as tricyclics (such as amitriptyline, imipramine, and desipramine), which seem to block pain signals from reaching the brain. However, many patients find these drugs hard to tolerate because they produce a wide range of side effects, from dry mouth and headaches to seizures and hallucinations. Some newer mood medications may provide relief from neuropathic pain, with a lower risk of side effects. In 2004 the Food

and Drug Administration approved duloxetine (Cymbalta) for the treatment of neuropathy caused by diabetes. In one trial, 51 percent of patients who took duloxetine achieved at least a 30 percent sustained reduction in pain. At higher doses, duloxetine may cause nausea, fatigue, dizziness, and other side effects.

- Capsaicin, a skin cream that contains the substance that puts the fire in cayenne peppers. As you might expect, a balm made from hot peppers stings at first, but after repeated uses capsaicin appears to desensitize pain receptors.
- Anticonvulsant drugs, including carbamazepine, gabapentin, and topiramate. A 1998 study published in the *Journal of the American Medical Association* found that diabetes patients with neuropathy who took gabapentin suffered significantly less pain compared with patients who took placebos. However, about one in four patients taking gabapentin complained of dizziness and sleepiness.
- Codeine. Your doctor may prescribe a short course of this narcotic if you go through a period of severe pain. However, codeine can be habit-forming, so it's not a good choice for long-term pain control.

PAIN PILLS WITH POTENTIAL?

Scientists are studying whether the following three treatments can ease the pain, burning, and other symptoms of diabetic neuropathy. One or more of these treatments may eventually prove valuable in managing the pain of neuropathy. However, at present, the scientific jury is out until larger, more authoritative research studies are done. Although you can purchase alpha-lipoic acid and evening primrose oil supplements without a prescription, do not be tempted to take either of these products—or any other form of therapy for diabetes—without first talking with your physician.

Aldose reductase inhibitors. According to one theory, diabetic neuropathy is caused by the buildup of a compound called sorbitol. These drugs block aldose reductase, an enzyme the body needs to produce sorbitol. Studies of these experimental drugs have so far failed to show any benefit in humans, but research continues.

Alpha-lipoic acid. This powerful antioxidant appears to protect nerves from damage by free radicals, which may contribute to diabetic neuropathy. Several studies have found that intensive treatments with alpha-lipoic acid reduce neuropathy symptoms.

Evening primrose oil. Herbalists have long recommended evening primrose oil to relieve the pain of inflammation, particularly in rheumatoid arthritis. Studies have had mixed results, but some evidence suggests the oil may benefit patients with peripheral neuropathy, too. One small study found that patients who took evening primrose supplements for six months had improved nerve function and fewer symptoms. High doses of evening primrose oil can interfere with the blood's natural clotting ability.

- Mexiletine. This drug is normally used to regulate heart rhythm, but at least three studies have found that it can help ease neuropathic pain. Side effects can include upset stomach.
- Electrical stimulation. Want to zap away your pain? TENS might help. TENS stands for "transcutaneous electrical nerve stimulation." Electrodes are applied to the skin above the area of pain and deliver a small jolt of electrical current. (It's painless, though it causes a tingling sensation.) A related therapy, percutaneous electrical nerve stimulation, or PENS, uses acupuncturelike needles. Doctors believe that electrical stimulation closes the "gate" that pain signals must pass through to reach the brain. The electrical charge may also stimulate the brain to produce endorphins, the body's natural painkilling hormones. TENS units are small enough to wear or carry. In one study, 75 percent of patients using TENS devices reported significant pain reduction; in another, 90 percent of patients treated with PENS felt better. However, pain seems to return eventually if you stop receiving treatment.
- Anodyne therapy. *Anodyne* is an old-fashioned word for medicine or anything that soothes stress or discomfort. However, anodyne therapy is a high-tech treatment that relieves pain with near-infrared photo energy. (That's a term describing a special type of light that the human eye can't detect.) Devices used to deliver anodyne therapy have flexible pads equipped with light-emitting diodes that wrap around the skin. In theory, the light increases levels of nitric oxide in blood vessels, which improves circulation. Anodyne therapy is not a miracle cure for neuropathy (though you may see it touted as such). However, it may be a resonable treatment alternative for some people with this common complication. In a 2004 study, patients with mild neuropathy had less pain and greater sensation after just six treatments with anodyne therapy. At the beginning of the study, 90 percent of those with neuropathy had balance problems, but that number dropped to 17 percent after the treatments. However, those who had severe neuropathy didn't experience any improvement in pain or sensation. Some clinics offer anodyne therapy, but you can also purchase devices for self-treatment at home.
- Acupuncture. If you inject insulin and check your glucose regularly, the tiny needles acupuncturists use to treat pain and other conditions won't faze you a bit. In one study, nearly 90 percent of patients with peripheral diabetic neuropathy experienced pain

relief; needle therapy appeared to improve mood, sleep, and mobility, too. In another study, patients receiving acupuncture were able to cut back on pain medications. Traditional healers say that acupuncture works by altering the flow of *qi,* a mystical inner force in the body. Skeptical western-trained doctors say *qi* is more mythical than anything else and that needle therapy probably treats pain by producing painkilling endorphins.

- Magnet therapy. One study found that magnetic insoles improved burning, numbness, and tingling caused by diabetic neuropathy; see Chapter 10.
- Polyurethane film. One novel approach that seems to help protect tender spots is to wrap them up like last night's leftovers using polyurethane film dressings. Studies show that creating a physical barrier around sores caused by damaged nerves can help reduce pain and improve the patient's overall quality of life by increasing mobility and improving sleep and mood.

Sweating disorders

- Identify and avoid foods that trigger outbreaks of perspiration.
- The drug glycopyrrolate (Robinul) is usually used to treat ulcers, but some patients with gustatory sweating may benefit from it.

Dizziness upon standing and other symptoms of orthostatic hypotension

- Rise slowly when getting up from a chair or out of bed.
- Raise the head of your bed.
- Wear compression stockings, which will improve circulation in the legs (but take them off when you go to bed).
- Avoid hot baths.
- Take insulin injections lying down, if possible.
- Your doctor may recommend a surprising therapy: Eat more salt. Sodium helps regulate blood pressure, so if your diet includes too little salt, upping your intake of the white crystals may help. You may also get a prescription for salt tablets or a drug called fludrocortisone (Florinef), which causes the body to excrete less sodium. While effective, fludrocortisone therapy can have serious side effects, ranging from swollen ankles to heart failure.

Other drugs sometimes prescribed for orthostatic hypotension include

- clonidine (Catapres), a drug for hypertension
- midodrine, a drug that increases blood pressure
- octreotide, a drug that has a variety of actions, including treating low blood pressure

The Kidneys, the Urinary System, and Diabetes

The kidneys are a bit like trash haulers: No one thinks about them until they quit working. As key players in the body's waste-management system, the kidneys keep the blood free of impurities while retaining protein and other healthy substances. Diabetes creates conditions that can cause the kidneys to go on strike as well as problems with the other parts of your urinary system. If you have been diagnosed with hypertension, this chapter is a must read. Your blood pressure is intimately linked to your kidney function. Learn how to keep these critical organs on the job.

Don't Fail Me Now: Diabetes and the Kidneys

Each year, about 100,000 Americans develop kidney failure. Diabetes is the culprit in more than 40 percent of all new cases, making it the most common cause of the condition that is also known as renal failure. Likewise, kidney failure is one of the most common complications of diabetes, affecting up to 21 percent of patients. Kidney failure caused by diabetes goes by a variety of names, including diabetic nephropathy (*nephro* means "relating to the kidneys"), diabetic glomerulosclerosis, diabetic kidney disease, and Kimmelstiel-Wilson disease (for the two doctors, Paul Kimmelstiel and Clifford Wilson, who first described the condition).

As with heart failure, the phrase "kidney failure" doesn't necessarily mean that the organ has stopped working altogether. More commonly, the phrase is used to describe a kidney whose main functions are grinding to a halt, either quickly (acute renal failure) or gradually (chronic renal failure). Trauma, infections, and urinary tract obstructions can cause acute renal failure. Although the condition requires urgent medical care, acute renal failure is often reversible.

Diabetes, meanwhile, can cause chronic kidney failure, which has a much more gradual onset. In fact, obvious symptoms rarely occur until the condition is in an advanced stage. Patients whose kidneys have stopped functioning altogether are said to have end-stage renal disease, which means the kidneys must be replaced with a transplanted organ or their function must be performed by a dialysis machine.

Of the two major forms of diabetes, type 1 is more likely than type 2 to cause kidney failure. In fact, 20 to 40 percent of patients with type 1 diabetes receive a diagnosis of kidney failure by the time they turn 50. It's not uncommon for type 1 patients to develop symptoms of nephropathy before age 30.

Catching kidney failure early on is critical, and fortunately, simple tests can uncover the first silent signs. While the damage caused by diabetic nephropathy can be controlled with proper treatment, it is much more difficult to reverse. If you haven't discussed kidney disease with your doctor yet, do so soon. But read this chapter first to understand the threat kidney failure poses and how you can face it down.

LEADING CAUSES OF KIDNEY FAILURE

Diabetes: 42.3 percent

High Blood Pressure: 23 percent

Glomerulonephritis: 12.3 percent

Polycystic Kidney Disease: 2.9 percent

Other causes: 18.6 percent

The Kidneys

The kidneys are shaped like, well, kidney beans. Or kidney-shape pools. You have two of them—kidneys, not pools—one on each side, just above the waist in the back of the abdomen. (In most people, the right kidney sits slightly lower than the left in order to make room for the liver above.) Each kidney is about five inches long and weighs just four to six ounces. Yet these relatively small organs receive roughly 25 percent of the blood pumped from your heart. However, the kidneys quickly put all but a small fraction of that fluid back into circulation. In fact, while these hard-working organs process 200 quarts of blood per day, they only retain about 2 quarts, though they don't keep it for long.

The process goes like this: Kidneys receive blood from large vessels called renal arteries that branch from the aorta, the body's main artery, which delivers blood pumped from the heart. Once inside the kidney, the *renal arteries* divide into smaller blood vessels, which divide into even smaller blood vessels, and so on until they're just tiny capillaries that end in structures called *nephrons*.

There are about one million nephrons in each kidney. (Each nephron consists of two parts: clusters of capillaries called *glomeruli*, which are connected to tube-shape channels aptly known as *tubules*.) Since you have so many of them, nephrons must be pretty important, right? You bet—nephrons filter excess, unnecessary, and downright dangerous stuff from the blood. Yes, it's true: Blood is full of junk. For example, when proteins in the body outlive their usefulness, they break down into waste products. When cells use food as a source of energy and to rebuild tissue, they toss out the leftovers. And it all ends up in the blood, like toxic sludge dumped into a river.

The nephrons act like mini water treatment plants, filtering out all this gunk. Nephrons also remove excess water from the blood. As this crude urine passes through the tubules, much of it returns to circulation. That's because it contains substances your body needs,

BUSY BLOOD

More than 2,500 pints of blood pass through the kidneys every day, which would fill about 28 beer kegs. Every drop of blood in your body passes through the kidneys once an hour. However, nephrons only filter about one-fifth of that volume.

including protein and electrolytes such as sodium, phosphorus, and potassium. (Electrolytes are molecules that control various processes in the body.) The kidneys determine whether current levels of these chemicals in the blood need adjustment and reabsorb whatever is necessary through the renal veins to achieve a healthy balance. The waste-filled fluid left behind is plain old urine, which the kidneys ship south to be eliminated.

The kidneys do more than just control water quality and levels in the body, however. As a side job, these hard-working organs also release an array of hormones, enzymes, and other critical substances, including the following:

- Calcitriol, the hormone made from vitamin D that's necessary for healthy bones, among other things.
- Erythropoietin, a hormone that regulates the manufacture and distribution of red blood cells from bone marrow.
- Renin, an enzyme that the kidneys produce when blood pressure dips too low; it causes the blood to make angiotensin, which constricts blood vessels, causing blood pressure to stabilize. Angiotensin, meanwhile, also causes the adrenal gland to release a hormone called aldosterone, which acts on the tubules to regulate electrolytes.

Diabetes and Your Kidneys

Spaghetti, anyone? The handy kitchen device known as a colander works by letting water pass through its tiny holes, leaving behind pasta or whatever food you're straining. But what if the holes in a colander suddenly expanded to the size of, say, the pockets on a pool table? Obviously, the noodles would slip through easily, dropping into the sink and possibly down the drain. Result: You go hungry.

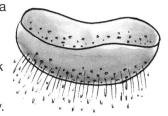

The nephrons are kind of like colanders, allowing very small waste particles to pass through but holding back proteins and other larger molecules, ushering them back into circulation. However, elevated blood sugar fouls up this process. As you have read earlier, glucose reacts with proteins in the body to produce demon compounds called advanced glycosylation end products, or AGEs. Over time, if blood sugar is not well controlled, AGEs accumulate on the walls of the blood vessels in the kidneys, which makes the nephrons' filters too porous or leaky. As a result, protein molecules begin to slip through the kidneys' filters and into the urine. This phenomenon is called proteinuria, though when it's detected at an early stage doctors call it microalbuminuria (albumin is a simple form of protein).

At first, losing a little protein in the urine is no big deal. In fact, you won't even notice the problem, though as proteinuria progresses, you may observe that your urine looks a bit frothier. (If you're in the habit of observing such things.) Even though some of your nephrons are struggling, each kidney packs a million of the filtering units, so the organs are able to keep up with the body's demands for the first few years. (The body is capable of running just fine if you donate a kidney or one of yours quits working.)

Over time, however, exposure to high glucose levels—as well as the effects of hypertension, smoking, and certain other conditions—begins to destroy huge numbers of glomeruli, dramatically reducing the kidney's filtering capacity. Not only does the body lose protein, but more waste products remain in the blood, especially substances called creatinine and urea. About 80 percent of type 1 diabetes patients who develop persistent microalbuminuria but don't receive adequate medical care will progress to full-blown kidney failure within 10 to 15 years.

Symptoms of advanced kidney failure may include

- high blood pressure (though hypertension causes kidney problems, too; more on that later)

- swelling, especially around the eyes or ankles. Excess amounts of protein and salt in the urine cause water to pool in tissues. This may be accompanied by weight gain.
- loss of appetite
- nausea, vomiting
- headache
- itchiness
- fatigue and poor sleep
- frequent need to urinate at night
- difficulty concentrating
- an all-around blah feeling
- and, of all things, frequent bouts of the hiccups, which for some reason often accompany kidney failure

In addition to these symptoms, you may also begin to feel anemic, since all that toxic sludge in your blood can poison the kidneys, interfering with production of erythropoietin. As you recall, kidneys make this hormone, which triggers bone marrow to produce red blood cells. One of the main roles of red blood cells is to carry oxygen to cells throughout the body. A drop in red blood cells means cells lack the needed spark—oxygen—to make energy.

Furthermore, kidney disorders tend to go hand-in-hand with hypertension. See "Kidney Failure and Hypertension" on the opposite page for more on this dangerous duo.

Testing for Kidney Problems

If you have diabetes, your doctor should be on the lookout for all of the major complications the disease can cause, including kidney failure. He or she may suspect the condition based on symptoms, but certain medical tests can confirm a diagnosis or, even better, spot kidney failure in its earliest stages.

URINE TESTS

When kidneys work properly, they ignore protein; only minute traces of these building-block molecules are removed from the blood and passed in the urine. In the early stages of kidney failure, however, the kidneys' filters spring leaks. That allows some protein to be filtered out of the blood and

KIDNEY FAILURE AND HYPERTENSION

It's a medical chicken-or-egg question: Does hypertension cause kidney failure? Or does kidney failure cause hypertension? In fact, there's no mystery here, because the two conditions go hand-in-hand. To explain how that can be, first a quick refresher course on hypertension.

Hypertension, or high blood pressure, is a problem of too much fluid in too-narrow a space. Specifically, the condition occurs when there is too much fluid in blood that is trying to force its way through a blood vessel. Or when a blood vessel becomes constricted or narrowed, putting the squeeze on a normal volume of blood. Left untreated, hypertension not only strains the heart, it also damages blood vessels.

Government statistics show that high blood pressure is the second leading cause of kidney failure, after diabetes. Yet, doctors tell us that hypertension is a common result when kidneys poop out. The problem begins with blood vessels in the kidneys. Hypertension does not discriminate, meaning it damages blood vessels everywhere in the body, including your two filtration organs. When blood vessels in the kidneys sustain injuries, the filtering process suffers. So, instead of being turned into urine and excreted, metabolic garbage and excess fluid keep circulating in the blood. The added volume increases blood pressure—which, in turn, damages blood vessels in the kidneys even more. If this destructive cycle continues long enough, kidney failure is inevitable.

escape the body via the urinary tract. We're still talking tiny amounts of protein, though, measured in millionths of grams. Simple tests that measure protein in urine, such as so-called "dipstick" tests (in which a strip of treated paper is dipped into a urine sample), can be performed in a doctor's office. Unfortunately, they aren't sensitive enough to detect ultrasmall concentrations of protein. That's why your doctor should screen for microalbuminuria.

Albumin, as mentioned earlier, is a simple protein found in all human tissue that can be measured in urine, even in minuscule traces. There are several ways to test for microalbuminuria. In one method, your doctor will send you home with a kit designed to collect one day's worth of urine. When you're done, you drop off the sample at a lab, which measures its albumin content. If the urine you produce over a 24-hour period contains 30 micrograms of albumin or more, your doctor will suspect kidney failure. However, other conditions can cause albumin levels in the urine to rise, including high blood glucose, stress, fever, urinary tract infections, heart failure, and even a vigorous workout. With that in mind, your doctor will ask you to repeat the test in a week or two. If the lab results from round two come back positive, it's

official: Your kidneys are struggling, and you need to take prompt action to prevent end-stage renal disease. (We'll discuss the recommended steps in the next section.)

There are several other versions of the microalbuminuria test. One uses a random sample of urine, while another analyzes a sample of urine collected overnight. Each measures albumin in a slightly different way.

At the same time your doctor screens for microalbuminuria, he or she may also test your blood for waste products, namely blood urea nitrogen (BUN) and creatinine. High levels indicate that your kidneys aren't doing their job, which is to filter toxic substances from the blood. Results of these tests are usually expressed as total BUN and BUN-to-creatinine ratio. The range for a normal BUN is 8 to 20 milligrams per deciliter. A healthy BUN-to-creatinine ratio is 10:1 to 20:1 (or up to 30:1 for infants less than 12 months old).

Patients with type 2 diabetes should have their urine tested for protein when they are diagnosed. Type 1 patients should start urine testing five years after diagnosis. Once initiated, urine testing of protein levels should be repeated annually for both groups.

OTHER TESTS

In rare cases, a doctor may order an ultrasound to observe the size of a kidney. In the early stages of kidney failure, the organ may be slightly enlarged; advanced chronic kidney failure, on the other hand, can shrink a kidney. An ultrasound exam can also rule out urinary obstruction as the cause of kidney failure. Biopsies are rarely necessary but may be ordered if some other cause of kidney failure is suspected.

Treating Kidney Failure

While there is no cure for chronic kidney failure, it is possible to slow the condition's progress considerably with the following three-point plan:

TIGHT GLUCOSE CONTROL

Chalk up another good reason why your doctor nags you to keep your blood sugar down: Scientific studies show that maintaining glucose control could save your kidneys. For example, in the landmark Diabetes Control and Complications Trial (DCCT), sponsored by the National Institutes of Health, researchers followed more than 1,400 patients with type 1 diabetes for a decade. In that study, patients who received the most aggressive glucose-lowering therapy slashed their risk for developing kidney disease by 50 per-

cent. Several other large studies have similarly shown that diabetes patients who keep their blood sugar in check have healthier kidneys.

BLOOD PRESSURE MEDICINE

Within minutes of diagnosing a patient with kidney failure, doctors often find themselves scribbling prescriptions for antihypertensive drugs. It's not hard to

ROUTINE MAINTENANCE

Kidney failure is one of the most common complications of diabetes. Following the steps below can minimize your risk and help you spot the condition early.

- Have your blood pressure checked at least twice a year. If it's high, your doctor will prescribe diet, exercise, and medication to bring it back down below 130/80. Stick with the plan.
- Even if your blood pressure isn't high, ask your doctor whether you would benefit from an ACE inhibitor or ARB.
- After your initial screening, have your urine checked annually for microalbuminuria. If the test is positive, have your blood checked for creatinine, blood urea nitrogen, and other waste products.
- Discuss your diet with your physician and decide whether you should reduce your protein intake.
- You can't hear it enough: Keep your blood sugar under control. Get your A1c level checked twice a year. Follow all of your doctor's instructions regarding lifestyle and medications.

see why. Earlier, you read about the link between kidney health and blood pressure. Not only does hypertension damage kidney function, but as the organs lose their ability to filter waste from the circulatory system, blood volume increases, pushing blood pressure even higher. Many studies have shown that blood pressure drugs can help slow the progress of kidney failure, even in patients who do not have hypertension. In particular, research shows that aggressive treatment with antihypertensive drugs can

- improve the kidneys' ability to filter waste from the blood
- reduce the likelihood of requiring dialysis or a kidney transplant
- increase life expectancy

There are many types of medications for lowering blood pressure. Doctors prescribe the following two categories of antihypertensive drugs most frequently to patients with diabetic kidney failure:

Angiotensin-converting enzyme (ACE) inhibitors. These drugs block production of an enzyme that causes blood vessels to narrow, which raises blood pressure. There is also some evidence that ACE inhibitors may protect glomeruli, the kidneys' filtering units, from damage. Even patients with failing kidneys but normal blood pressure appear to benefit from taking ACE inhibitors. Doctors prescribe these medications with great care to patients with serious kidney failure, since they may increase blood potassium to dangerous levels, a condition called hyperkalemia that can lead to muscle weakness and electrical disturbances in the heart. A dry cough is one of the more common side effects that ACE inhibitors may cause.

Angiotensin receptor blockers (ARBs). Like ACE inhibitors, ARBs prevent blood vessels from narrowing, though they work in a slightly different way. ARBs offer an advantage over ACE inhibitors, since they're less likely to cause coughing. However, like ACE inhibitors, they also increase the risk of hyperkalemia. ARBs are more expensive, too.

Your physician may also prescribe other hypertension medications, including beta-blockers, calcium channel blockers, or diuretics. In fact, you may need more than one antihypertensive drug to get below the recommended blood pressure threshold for patients with diabetes, 130/80 (which is lower than the rest of the population, for whom lower than 140/90 is considered safe).

MODERATE-PROTEIN DIET

If you have developed microalbumin-uria, you might think it's time to beef up your diet—literally. After all, wouldn't a nice, juicy porterhouse steak replace some of the protein you're losing? Unfortunately, extra protein only increases the kidney's 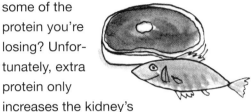 workload, placing further strain on its ability to filter waste. In fact, as protein breaks down it produces nitrogen, which can poison the kidneys. For that reason, many doctors order patients with kidney failure to reduce the amount of protein in their diets.

Some controversy exists over the benefit of reduced-protein diets for patients with chronic kidney failure. Skeptical doctors say the diets are too hard to follow and could result in some patients developing nutritional deficiencies. However, several studies have shown that eating less protein can help slow the deterioration of the kidneys' filtering capacity, known as the glomerular filtration rate.

Besides, it's not like you have to give up beef and other protein-rich foods altogether. The general recommendation for most patients with kidney failure is simply to adopt the National Academy of Sciences recommended daily allowance for protein—that is, the amount you should be eating anyway. The fact is, most Americans consume far more protein than the body needs for the ongoing job of rebuilding muscle and other tissue. If your physician recommends a cutback on protein, he or she will probably refer you to a registered dietitian, who will design a healthy meal plan for you.

End-Stage Kidney Disease

When a patient's kidney function drops below 10 percent of normal capacity or quits working altogether, he or she is said to have end-stage kidney disease or end-stage renal disease. That means the kidneys can no longer eliminate waste through urine or regulate electrolytes. Tight glucose control, drugs, and diet are no longer enough. Since these life-sustaining organs no longer work, something must replace them, permanently. Patients with end-stage kidney disease have two options: kidney dialysis or a kidney transplant.

KIDNEY DIALYSIS

The term dialysis comes from a Greek word meaning "separate." That's just what these machines do, separating nourishing blood and proteins from

toxic metabolic waste products. The first dialysis machine was invented in the 1940s, though the technology wasn't widely used until the 1960s. There are two main types of dialysis. One removes the patient's blood from the body to sift out impurities, while the other approach performs the cleanup inside the patient's body.

Hemodialysis

Simply put, a hemodialysis machine acts as an artificial kidney. The patient first undergoes minor surgery to create an opening in the skin, usually in the forearm (though the leg or neck may be used), to allow access to the bloodstream. Blood is pumped out of the body through a tube and into a dialyzer. Inside, the blood passes through a membrane that filters out tiny particles of waste and other toxic junk, which is discarded. The newly "clean" blood continues through the dialyzer and then is pumped back into the patient's body.

To keep their blood healthy, patients undergo hemodialysis about two or three times a week. Sessions can last three to five hours, though speedier new machines can shorten the process to two hours. Patients usually report to a hospital or special dialysis center for hemodialysis, though with the proper training and equipment, the process can be conducted at home.

Peritoneal Dialysis

This method transfers the work of the kidneys to another part of the body. The peritoneum is a membrane filled with blood vessels that lines the abdomen. In peritoneal dialysis, blood remains in the body, with the peritoneum acting as a filter. First, a doctor surgically installs a catheter (a type of flexible tube) into the patient's abdomen. The catheter remains in the patient permanently. During peritoneal dialysis, a special solution called dialysate is pumped into the abdomen, where it remains for up to five hours. The dialysate draws excess fluid and waste from blood vessels, leaving behind blood and other healthy stuff. When the session is over, the waste-filled dialysate is drained and discarded.

There are two types of peritoneal dialysis. They are:

SOME FACTS ABOUT END-STAGE KIDNEY DISEASE

- 400,000 patients in the United States are currently receiving long-term kidney dialysis
- 16,500 Americans received kidney transplants in 2005
- 67,000 Americans are waiting for a kidney transplant
- 2 to 4 years is the average wait for a kidney transplant in the United States

Continuous Ambulatory Peritoneal Dialysis (CAPD). Call it do-it-yourself dialysis. CAPD uses no machines; instead, gravity does the work. A bag of dialysate is attached to the catheter and suspended shoulder high until it empties into the abdomen, where it remains for several hours. After draining the dialysate, the procedure is repeated. CAPD offers one big advantage, in that you can continue daily activities during the process.

Continuous Cycling Peritoneal Dialysis (CCPD). This method is popular with people who want to sleep through dialysis. Instead of a suspended bag, a machine called a cycler pumps dialysate into the abdomen, then automatically drains it during 60- to 90-minute cycles. CCPD is typically performed at home, usually overnight.

Your doctor will help you choose the form of dialysis that's right for you. Hemodialysis is associated with more potential side effects and complications. What's more, unless you can afford to have a dialyzer installed in your home, hemodialysis requires frequent lengthy visits to a hospital or clinic. However, some patients may have physical limitations that would make performing at-home peritoneal dialysis difficult or impossible.

KIDNEY TRANSPLANTS

The choice between having a kidney transplant or undergoing dialysis for the rest of your life appears an easy one. Who wouldn't rather get a new kidney instead of being tethered to a machine several days a week? However, choosing to have a replacement kidney installed is no simple matter. The most obvious issue is availability. You may be fortunate enough to have a friend or relative (or very kind stranger) donate one of their kidneys. However, there are more people seeking new kidneys than there are available organs. (See "Some Facts About End-Stage Kidney Disease" on page 136.) Not just any kidney will do, of course, because the organ must be compatible with your blood and tissue type.

But finding a suitable kidney is only the beginning. A kidney transplant candidate must undergo a lengthy medical evaluation to determine whether he or she is physically, mentally, and emotionally prepared for the procedure. There will be X-rays and other imaging studies to make sure everything else is running smoothly inside, along with blood and urine tests. The candidate answers many, many questions about his or her medical history, lifestyle, and other issues. For instance, doctors will want to know that a candidate is capable of following the strict medication regimen all new transplant patients must adhere to.

Although kidney transplants are a major deal, the procedure isn't particularly

tricky. The surgeon makes an incision in the side of the abdomen, inserts the new kidney, and attaches arteries, veins, and ureters. (Your natural kidneys are usually left in place because it is a huge surgery to remove them.) The patient goes home from the hospital after about a week with orders to take it easy for a month or so.

While most kidney transplant patients go on to lead reasonably normal lives, maintaining the new organ requires daily vigilence and care. The most important responsibility is preventing your immune system from "rejecting" the new organ. You see, your body knows this new kidney isn't part of your original equipment. Your immune system will try to attack the transplanted kidney, as it does any other foreign object that gets inside.

To prevent this phenomenon, transplant patients must take antirejection, or immunosuppressive, drugs for the rest of their lives. There are several categories of these medications, but most interfere with a step in the cascade of events that triggers the body's immune response. Unfortunately, these drugs often have some pretty lousy side effects, such as elevated blood pressure, weight gain, and others.

More concerning, blocking the body's ability to mount a defense against

TROUBLESHOOTING CHECKLIST FOR KIDNEY FAILURE

The first signs of kidney failure are silent. In fact, you can have the condition for years and not realize it, when all the while your kidneys are slowly losing their ability to remove waste from the blood. In addition to having your kidney function tested on schedule, be on the lookout for these symptoms:

- ☐ Swelling, especially around the eyes or ankles
- ☐ Unexplained weight gain
- ☐ Loss of appetite
- ☐ Nausea, vomiting
- ☐ Headache
- ☐ Itchiness
- ☐ Fatigue, lack of energy
- ☐ Poor sleep
- ☐ Frequent need to urinate, especially at night
- ☐ Difficulty concentrating
- ☐ Persistent hiccups

suspected invaders could have unwanted consequences, such as increasing the risk of infections and certain cancers. However, these risks are balanced by impressively high success rates. Survival rates for kidney transplant patients are about 90 percent at one year and 80 percent after three years. About one-half of all transplanted kidneys are still functioning and filtering a decade after surgery.

Diabetes and the Rest of the Urinary Tract

Your busy, overworked kidneys don't have time or space to hold urine until your coffee break or you reach the next rest area, so the organs pass the fluid through long tubes called *ureters* (each kidney has a pair) to the *bladder*. This hollow organ, which sits behind the pubic bone, stores urine.

An adult's bladder normally holds up to a pint of urine. As the organ fills with fluid, it begins to stretch. When the urine level reaches anywhere from five to nine ounces, it triggers nerve signals to the brain that deliver the message: Time to start looking for a bathroom. While you search, the urethral sphincter muscles remain tightened, keeping the bladder's trap door closed. When the time is right, the brain returns signals to the urinary tract,

instructing the urethral sphincter to relax and bladder muscles to contract, forcing urine downward through the bladder neck and into another tube called the urethra, through which the waste-filled fluid exits the body.

You may laugh or blush when someone mentions urinating, but this essential process is necessary to maintain a healthy water balance in the body. The average person produces about a quart or two of urine every 24 hours. But how much you void on any given day depends on your diet—especially how much fluid you have been drinking—and how much water you have lost through other avenues, such as perspiration or simply breathing. If you wash down a hot tamale and spicy burrito with a few ice-cold beers, chances are you will soon require a trip to the *hombres* or *mujeres* room for bladder relief. That's because the water concentration of your body rose higher than necessary to keep tissue hydrated. Sensing the imbalance, the kidneys pulled the excess water out of the blood and turned it into urine. Likewise, if your car breaks down and you have to walk through the desert without a canteen, you can thank your kidneys for preserving body water by producing less urine (and kick yourself for not charging your cell phone battery).

139

As you read earlier in this chapter, hypertension is the primary cause of diabetes-related kidney disease. However, when a person with diabetes develops difficulty or discomfort with urinating, damage to the nerves is usually to blame. By now, you should guess that the cause of nerve damage is the usual suspect: elevated blood sugar levels. As Chapter 7 explains in greater detail, uncontrolled glucose causes nerves to become saturated with sugar, which produces other compounds that destroy nerves or disrupt their signals.

Problems with urinating may not be life threatening, but they can produce annoying, and even painful, symptoms, while creating inconvenient, awkward, and embarrassing moments in daily living. As a diabetes patient, you have a heightened risk for two urinary problems, in particular: loss of bladder control and urinary tract infections.

LOSS OF BLADDER CONTROL

When everything is operating smoothly along the urinary tract, muscles in the bladder and other organs contract and relax at all the right times, making for uneventful trips to the restroom. However, neuropathy can cause your plumbing to spring leaks or clog up. Doctors sometimes refer to urinary difficulties caused by nerve damage as neurogenic bladder, which may cause the organ to become overactive (it releases urine when you don't want it to) or underactive (the bladder doesn't respond when you need it to). If you have neurogenic bladder, you may have one or more of the following symptoms:

Urinary frequency. Are you wearing out a path to the bathroom? The National Institute of Diabetes and Digestive and Kidney Diseases defines frequent urination as eight or more times during the day and more than twice at night.

Urinary incontinence. Also called leakage. Damaged nerves may behave erratically, sending signals out of the blue to the bladder muscles, telling them to contract and force urine into the urethra when you're sitting in a board meeting or having dinner. (Damage to the nerves of the urethral sphincter may also cause incontinence or the inability to start a urine stream— see next item.) Urinary incontinence is often preceded by urinary urgency: the sudden, desperate need to void.

Urine retention. The nerves connecting the bladder to the spinal cord may lose sensation, reducing or eliminating the brain's ability to tell when the organ is filling up with urine. Your friends may stare in awe as you guzzle a sixth tall glass of ice tea without budging from your chair, unaware that your bladder is ready to burst. Although it won't burst, the bladder may leak if it remains full too long; this is known as overflow incontinence. Again, due to nerve damage, you may not feel urine escaping. What's more, weakened signals from the brain to the detrusor muscle in the bladder may cause urinary hesitancy—you feel like you have to "go" but produce little or no urine. As a result, you may not be able to empty your bladder completely.

Urinary Tract Infections (UTIs)

If you can't empty your bladder efficiently, the urine left behind can become a breeding ground for bacteria. The irony here is that, even though urine is full of waste products, under normal circumstances it's a sterile fluid. Furthermore, a usual pattern of urination flushes germs out of the body. But if bacteria sneaks into the bladder and finds a stagnant pool of urine, it has time to reproduce and flourish. Bacteria may even keep swimming upstream and find its way into the kidneys, causing an infection known as pyelonephritis. If not treated in time, these

BEAT BACTERIA FOR FEWER INFECTIONS

UTIs have a nasty habit of recurring, so working with your physician to eliminate urinary difficulties that allow bacteria to breed is essential. Meanwhile, you can further reduce your risk for UTIs by following these simple steps:

- Take showers instead of baths.
- If you do take a bath, don't use bubble bath products.
- Avoid feminine hygiene sprays and scented douches.
- Clean the genital area before sexual intercourse; as unromantic as it may sound, always urinate afterward.
- For women and girls: After urinating, wipe from front to back to avoid introducing bacteria from the anus into the urethra.

infections can result in kidney scarring and permanent organ damage.

To make matters worse, diabetes compromises the body's ability to fight off infections. For these and other reasons, urinary tract infections (UTIs) are unusually common in people with diabetes.

Symptoms of a urinary tract infection include

- pain or burning sensation while urinating
- pressure in the lower pelvis (in women)
- a feeling of fullness in the rectum (in men)
- a persistent feeling that your bladder needs emptying, often urgently

141

- frequent trips to the bathroom, especially at night, among other symptoms. Having diabetes seems to increase the risk for this pesky problem.
- cloudy urine, or traces of blood in the urine
- urine that smells really bad
- nausea, vomiting
- fever or chills
- fatigue
- the "jitters"
- mental fuzziness

Diagnosing a Neurogenic Bladder

If your doctor suspects nerve damage in the urinary system after taking a medical history and conducting a physical exam, he or she may ask you to take the following steps and tests to confirm the diagnosis of neuropathy.

Keep a Urinary Diary

Dear Urinary Diary, I ate at a fancy restaurant today that had the most marvelous restroom. It had marble walls and cloth hand towels.... Not quite. A urinary diary (also called a "voiding diary") is a log of how much fluid you drink, whether you consumed any beverages containing alcohol or caffeine, and how many times you urinate on a given day. It should also list any problems experienced, such as incontinence or hesitancy. Knowing the details of your urinary difficulties can help a doctor figure out the cause.

Urodynamic Testing

This is a blanket term for any of several tests used to measure how well your bladder works. Specifically, these tests will determine the following:

- How much urine your bladder can hold. To measure your bladder's capacity to hold urine, your doctor may perform a cystometrogram. A catheter (a long slender tube) is inserted—don't flinch—into the urethra and snaked into the bladder. Then the doctor pumps a sterile solution into the bladder to determine how much it will hold. He or she will ask how you feel during the exam to determine how much fluid it takes for your bladder to feel full. A cystometrogram can also determine what volume of urine your bladder can hold before it leaks. Some doctors use special video urodynamics equipment to create live-action pictures of the bladder.
- The speed of your urine stream, known as the flow rate. Your doctor may ask you to urinate into a toilet that's equipped with a special device that measures not only how much urine you produce but also how fast it comes out. If your flow rate is

abnormal (meaning it's slow or hesitant or produces dribbles), your doctor will suspect problems with bladder muscles (though an obstruction can't be ruled out).

- How much urine remains in your bladder after you have voided. Your doctor may use the catheter again to siphon any remaining urine from the bladder, known as the postvoid residual urine volume. An ounce or two is normal, but nerve damage is likely if you have six or more ounces of fluid in your bladder after urinating.

Imaging

Visualizing your insides aids diagnosis.

Electromyography. Nerve signals can be measured in much the same way electrical current can be detected in household wiring. Your doctor may use a device called an electromyograph to test the strength of nerve signals between the brain and bladder by measuring muscle activity with sensors placed on the skin near the urethra.

Electroencephalography. Images of the brain can help with the diagnosis, too, so your physician may also perform an electroencephalograph. Using sensors taped to the forehead, doctors can check to see if an abnormality in the brain is creating urinary difficulties.

Other imaging technology. To look for other potential problems along the urinary tract and nervous system, a doctor may use other medical imaging equipment, including X-rays, computed tomography (CT) scans, and magnetic resonance imaging (MRI).

Diagnosis of Urinary Tract Infections

If you have a UTI, chances are your urine holds the telltale signs. A urinalysis conducted by a lab will look for bacteria, white blood cells, or pus—the yellow-green slimy stuff infections often produce. If the symptoms of a UTI don't respond to standard drug treatments or the symptoms are accompanied by a fever, doctors may order imaging tests to look for changes or damage in the urinary tract. They may include

- Intravenous pyelogram (IVP), a type of X-ray that creates images of the kidneys, ureters, and bladder. This test requires the injection of contrast material (iodine), which creates more distinct X-ray images.

- Ultrasound, which uses sound waves to create images of internal organs.
- Cytoscopy, which uses a narrow scope to examine the inside of the urethra.

Treatments for Neurogenic Bladder

Although scientists are developing artificial nerves, doctors are not yet able to replace faulty wiring in your body. However, there is help for bladder problems.

TROUBLESHOOTING CHECKLIST

Urinary problems are common among men and women with diabetes. One study found that 60 percent of postmenopausal women with diabetes had at least one instance of urinary incontinence per month. Another, by researchers at Harvard, showed that women with type 2 diabetes were twice as likely as women without the disease to develop severe urinary incontinence (considered leakage heavy enough to dampen outer clothing). Urinary tract infections are more common in people with diabetes, too. If you develop any of the following signs or symptoms, talk to your doctor.

☐ Frequent urination (eight or more times per day and more than twice at night)

☐ Urinary incontinence (the inability to stop urine from leaking)

☐ Frequent urgent need to urinate

☐ Loss of impulse to urinate; you know your bladder is full, but you feel no need to urinate

☐ Inability to empty your bladder completely (that is, you often feel as though you still need to "go," but nothing comes out)

☐ Pain or burning sensation while urinating

☐ Pressure in the lower pelvis (women) or a feeling of fullness in the rectum (men)

☐ Cloudy urine or traces of blood in the urine

☐ Foul-smelling urine

☐ Nausea, vomiting

☐ Fever, chills, or nervousness

☐ Fatigue or mental problems

TIMED VOIDING

Here's where a urinary diary comes in handy. The log will likely show patterns indicating the approximate times of day when you need to urinate urgently or experience leakage. Using this information, you can design a urination schedule. Instead of leaving things to chance, you can plan on attempting to empty your bladder at timed intervals. (If nothing happens when you try to urinate at the appointed hour, your doctor can teach you a form of bladder massage that can help get a urine stream started.) Setting up a urination schedule can also ensure that you are near a bathroom, should you need one, during times of day when leakage tends to be a problem. With practice, you can extend the length of the intervals between planned trips to the restroom.

KEGEL EXERCISES

These exercises are named for their creator, Arnold Kegel, M.D., of the University of Southern California, who introduced them a half century ago. Designed to reduce urinary incontinence, Kegel exercises strengthen the muscles that hold urine in the bladder by contracting and relaxing them over and over. Although you can teach yourself how to do Kegel exercises, it may be wise to work with a trainer to make sure you're contracting the right muscles. Some studies suggest that biofeedback devices can improve the effectiveness of this form of bladder re-training. Like any muscle workout, Kegel exercises lose their effectiveness if you stop doing them. Some patients also are able to empty their bladders by learning to execute the Valsalva maneuver (the same tightening of internal muscles you perform while passing stool).

DRUG THERAPY

Depending on your symptoms, a doctor may prescribe one or more medications for the following problems:

Urinary urgency. The sudden urge to urinate occurs due to unwanted bladder-muscle contractions, resulting in leakage. Medications that relax bladder muscles and reduce these contractions include dicyclomine (Bentyl), flavoxate (Urispas), hyoscyamine sulfate (Anaspaz), imipramine (Tofranil), oxybutynin (Ditropan), tolterodine (Detrol), and propantheline (Pro-Banthine).

Muscle spasms. Neuropathy can cause nerve signals to go haywire, producing twitches and glitches that foul up the movements of muscles needed to urinate. These timing problems can cause leakage and difficulty urinating. The usual solution is to relax the sphinc-

145

ROUTINE MAINTENANCE

Although urinary difficulties often accompany diabetes, you can control symptoms and prevent problems from worsening by following these healthy habits:

- Tell your doctor about any changes in your urinary habits soon, especially symptoms of urinary tract infections (which can spread to the kidneys).
- Keep a urinary diary, which will provide your doctor with valuable information about your condition.
- Stick with Kegel exercises if you try them to control incontinence. Results may take some time, but any improvements will disappear if you quit exercising.
- Avoid baths and keep your genital area clean if you have recurrent urinary tract infections. Take all prescribed antibiotics if you have a urinary tract infection, even if symptoms clear up.

ter muscle. Some drugs that may help include baclofen (Lioresal), diazepam (Valium), alfuzosin (UroXatral), tamsulosin (Flomax), terazosin (Hytrin), and doxazosin (Cardura).

Incontinence. If your doctor suspects your problem is muscle weakness, you may get a prescription for a drug that bolsters the urethral sphincter, such as ephedrine, phenylpropanolamine (Dexatrim), or pseudoephedrine (Sudafed). If overflow incontinence is the problem, bethanechol (Urecholine, Duvoid) may help; it triggers bladder contractions. Meanwhile, clonidine (Catapres) is a drug that can relieve pressure on the urethra.

These drugs can produce a wide range of side effects, from common and annoying (such as headaches) to rare and scary (hallucinations). However, if one medication is intolerable, your doctor has plenty of other options that may be more suitable.

CATHETERS AND STENTS

Doctors can use catheters to drain urine from an uncooperative bladder. However, a process developed in the 1970s called clean intermittent self-catheterization (CISC) allows patients who are willing and able to self-catheterize to empty their bladders at home at intervals throughout the day. It's awkward at first, but with practice most people can learn how to self-catheterize. Obviously, CISC must be performed in a very clean environment to avoid infection. For patients who can't or won't self-catheterize, indwelling catheters are another option. With this method, a health professional inserts a catheter into the bladder, and it's left in place for extended periods. Patients with indwelling catheters are at risk for infection and have a higher incidence of bladder stones and tumors.

You may have heard of stents used to open clogged arteries. Similar devices are also used in patients who retain urine in the bladder. Inserted into the urethra in a minor surgical procedure, a stent expands the sphincter muscle, allowing urine to flow more easily.

ELECTRICAL STIMULATION

If the muscles that control urination aren't receiving signals from the brain, then it may be possible to create an artificial signal. A device recently approved by the Food and Drug Administration called InterStim delivers a mild electrical pulse to nerves in the lower back that control the bladder and sphincter muscles. Surgery is required to implant the stimulation device under the skin. In a 2001 study, 83 percent of patients receiving an InterStim showed some improvement in symptoms. However, these devices are reserved for patients who have not had any luck with more conventional, conservative approaches.

OTHER FORMS OF SURGERY

If all else fails, doctors may recommend surgical procedures that can improve urine output. If a sphincter that's clenching too tight is causing urine retention, it can be weakened by trimming away part of the muscle in a procedure known as a sphincter resection. Or the whole thing may be removed in a sphincterotomy. (This procedure causes loss of bladder control, so the patient must wear a condomlike device that collects urine; since condomlike devices won't fit on the female anatomy, sphincter surgery is only performed on men.)

A bladder that fills too quickly can be enlarged (a procedure called augmentation cytoplasty) with tissue taken from the intestines. In another approach, urine may be diverted from the bladder to a pouch outside the body through an artificial opening called a stoma. All of these surgical procedures carry the risk of infection and other side effects.

Treatments for Urinary Tract Infections

Bacteria are the problem, so antibacterial drugs are the obvious solution. However, antibacterial drugs—you know them better as antibiotics—come in all shapes, sizes, and flavors. Fortunately, when labs analyze urine samples, they harvest some of the bacteria and grow it in a petri dish. Next, they test various antibiotics on the bacteria to determine which one does the best job of wiping it out. The most common choices include

- trimethoprim (Trimpex)
- trimethoprim-sulfamethoxazole (Bactrim, Cotrim, Septra)
- amoxicillin (Amoxil, Trimox, Wymox)
- nitrofurantoin (Macrodantin, Furadantin)
- ampicillin (D-Amp, Omnipen, Polycillin)
- fluoroquinolones (Levaquin, Cipro, Noroxin)

147

A New Wrinkle in the Treatment of Overactive Bladder

Botox injections, which smooth wrinkled skin, may help relieve symptoms caused by an overactive bladder. Botox is a drug made from a protein produced by a bacterium called *Clostridium botulinum*. In its natural form, the protein contains a toxin that can cause food poisoning. When purified, however, the protein is harmless, although it prevents muscles from contracting. In a 2005 study published in the *British Journal of Urology International,* researchers in Scotland injected Botox into the bladder muscles of 15 women with urinary incontinence. All but one of the women experienced improvement in urinary urgency and frequency. A single Botox injection appeared to remain effective for up to six months.

In many cases, taking the right antibiotic for a few days clears up most UTIs, though your doctor will likely instruct you to take the pills for a week or two in order to make sure the bacteria have been eliminated. Better safe than sorry, since allowing a few straggler germs to survive in your urinary tract could lead to a kidney infection. Two forms of bacteria put up a particularly tenacious fight, however, so they always require a longer course of treatment: *Chlamydia trachomatis* and *mycoplasma hominis.* In addition to trimethoprim-sulfamethoxazole, doctors prescribe tetracycline (Achromycin) and doxycycline (Periostat) for these harder-to-treat infections.

If you have ever had to take antibiotics, you know the drill: Keep popping those pills until the bottle is empty, even if your symptoms improve. As Charles Darwin taught us, the weak die first, while the strong survive longest. If you quit a course of antibiotics too soon, you may allow the most stubborn germs to live and reproduce. In a worst-case scenario, you could end up being the patient whose laziness created a new breed of superbacteria that antibiotics can't destroy. And that's a lousy way to become famous.

While antibiotics are waging war on the bacteria in your urinary tract, your doctor will probably recommend over-the-counter pain relievers such as ibuprofen (Advil) or acetaminophen (Tylenol) to ease any pain you may be experiencing.

The Gastrointestinal System and Diabetes

Does any part of the body take more ribbing than the gastrointestinal system? Although it carries out critical roles—absorbing life-sustaining nutrients and expelling life-threatening toxins—the digestive tract gets no respect. There is even an entire category of comedy, known as "potty humor," that celebrates the quirks and foibles of the body's food-processing facility.

However, there's nothing funny about the various problems that can plague the gastrointestinal system. The symptoms can be transient and mild or chronic and debilitating—either way, having diabetes increases the likelihood that you will have to cope with one or more of the problems described in this chapter.

It Takes Guts

In case you were bonked on the head and developed amnesia since you read Chapter 7, here's a quick reminder of a key fact: High blood sugar can injure nerves. That includes the wiring in your digestive tract. In fact, some studies suggest that damage known as gastrointestinal autonomic neuropathy produces at least one symptom of digestive distress in roughly 75 percent of patients with diabetes. Some gastrointestinal problems resulting from nerve damage are only mildly bothersome, while others can pose serious threats to your health. They can even interfere with careful and conscientious efforts to control blood sugar.

THE DIGESTIVE SYSTEM

While we may hesitate to associate our mouths with certain other parts of the gastrointestinal tract, make no mistake: Your piehole is where food processing begins. As the jaws move up and down, teeth chop and mince your meals into smaller pieces, while your tongue shapes bits of food into little balls that will fit down your windpipe. Digestion actually begins the instant you chomp on a hot dog or bagel, as enzymes in saliva are already at work, turning big, bulky molecules into smaller ones. In particular, the enzyme amylase starts to break down starchy carbohydrates.

As little chunks of food move to the back of the mouth, they enter a chamber called the pharynx, continuing south into the esophagus. Once they enter this narrow tube, food and drink move through the digestive tract thanks to the contractions of tiny smooth muscles, the process known as peristalsis. After a quick trip through the esophagus, your most recent meal drops into the stomach. Digestion continues in this big pouch, which—when you're really pigging out—can hold up to three pints of food and drink. The stomach produces acids that start breaking down proteins. What's more, muscles in the stomach contract and relax, churning food and converting it into a semi-liquidlike substance. (Extra credit: This goo is known as chyme, which is pronounced "kime" and rhymes with "slime.")

After about four hours, your lunch empties from the stomach into the intestines. Now the serious digestion begins. In the uppermost section of the small intestine, known as the duodenum, fat is dissolved by bile, which is made by the liver. Meanwhile, digestive juices (produced in the lining of the intestines and by our old friend the pancreas) break down carbohydrates, fats, and protein. After these nutrients are converted to smaller molecules, they are absorbed into the bloodstream through the walls of the small intestine, along with vitamins, minerals, and water.

After all that usable material has been extracted from the food making its way through the digestive tract, the leftovers are pushed into the colon, where they form feces. This waste product (also known as stool, along with countless other unprintable synonyms) is made up of water, used-up bile and digestive juices, old cells sloughed from the walls of the intestines, and anything you eat that your body can't digest, namely dietary fiber. (What's more, rest assured that if your child swallows a crayon you will likely see it again before long.)

After a day or so, the feces continue through the remainder of the large intestine, into the rectum, and out of your body through the anus. That assumes, of course, that all of the parts of this complex system are in working order. Unfortunately, diabetes can lob a wrench into the works, causing gastrointestinal discomfort and distress.

DIGESTION AND DIABETES

Since it takes a meal 24 hours or so to travel from one end of the gastrointestinal tract to the other, it wouldn't be practical if you had to spend all day thinking about digesting the waffles you had for breakfast. Instead, the autonomic nervous system, which you read about in Chapter 7, oversees food processing. The autonomic nervous system is a complex of brain cells and nerves that controls breathing, body temperature regulation, and all the critical functions that occur inside you without your conscious thought. Elevated blood sugar damages nerves throughout the body, and your gut is no exception. However, many of the problems discussed next can also be caused or worsened by aging, poor diet, obesity, and lack of exercise.

Heartburn

Heartburn is one of the most common medical complaints, and not just among people with diabetes. More than 60 million Americans feel flames in their chest at least once a month, according to the American College of Gastroenterology. Heartburn can occur as a symptom of other conditions triggered by diabetic neuropathy, though it may also be a diabetes patient's sole digestive complaint.

NOT-SO-SMALL INTESTINES

Ever notice how the intestines have an accordionlike appearance, kind of like a vacuum cleaner tube stretched out? That's because they're made up of folds of tissue. If you unfolded a small intestine, it would have the surface area of a sheet of cloth 3 feet wide and nearly 1,000 feet long.

Heartburn is a misnomer, of course (though the heart muscle can become inflamed, that unrelated condition is called carditis). When you feel an inferno in the chest minutes after scarfing down a bowl of three-alarm chili, the pain and burning occur in the esophagus, or windpipe. The trouble starts at the southern end of the esophagus. To get into your stomach, food passes from the pharynx to the esophagus to the lower esophageal sphincter (LES). The LES is like a trapdoor, relaxing to allow food into the stomach but snapping shut quickly to prevent caustic gastric acid from splashing upward and burning the lining of the esophagus.

Heartburn happens when the LES relaxes any old time, opening the door for stinging acidic juices to slosh into the gullet, producing the familiar fiery feeling. (Reflux is the term for the backward movement of fluid through any channel in the body, such as the digestive tract.) Everyone has had heartburn at one time or another, but if you're reaching for the Rolaids twice a week or more, doctors say you may have a condition called gastrointestinal esophageal reflux disease, or GERD.

G.I. Woes

Poor blood sugar often results in gastrointestinal problems. Here is the prevalence of three of the most common digestive conditions among people with diabetes:

- Constipation: 60 percent
- Gastroparesis (delayed stomach emptying): 25 percent
- Diarrhea: 20 percent

There's a good chance that you've got GERD if any of these symptoms accompany frequent heartburn:

- Burning in the chest that worsens when you lie down
- Regurgitating bits of undigested food or sour-tasting fluid
- Coughing or wheezing
- Recent onset of asthma
- Hoarseness or sore throat

Difficulty Swallowing

It's one thing to have a hard time swallowing a known prevaricator's tall tale. It's another to develop a hard time swallowing, period—a condition called dysphagia. Although gulping down a banana or chocolate bar might seem like a simple act, swallowing is actually a complex event that involves a number of muscles and nerves. As for the latter, damage to one in particular, the vagus nerve (pronounced like the hedonistic paradise in Nevada) can result in dysphagia, though this problem is considerably less common than other diabetes-related gastrointestinal conditions. Other causes of swallowing difficulty include untreated GERD, which can burn the lining of the esophagus, producing scar tissue that can clog the windpipe.

The symptoms of dysphagia may include

- chest pain
- food getting stuck in the throat, especially solid food
- a sensation of heaviness or pressure in the neck or upper chest
- coughing while eating or drinking

Gastroparesis

This term is just a fancy way of saying that food stays in your stomach too long; it's also known as delayed gastric emptying. As we explained earlier, after food enters the stomach, it usually remains there for about four hours before emptying into the intestines, giving stomach acid time to perform its digestive duties. Normally, the food doesn't just sit there; churning motions by the stomach muscles puree your most recent meal, then push it along into the duodenum, the first section of the small intestine.

Unfortunately, nerve damage can slow down and even halt food from emptying out of the stomach. Specifically, injuries to the vagus nerve block signals from the brain to the smooth muscles in the stomach. If these miniature muscles don't get the message to contract, peristalsis—the natural movement of food through the digestive tract—slows or stops altogether. Roughly one in four diabetes patients develop gastroparesis, which means "stomach paralysis."

Symptoms of delayed gastric emptying include

- early satiety, or the feeling of being full after just a few bites of food
- bloating
- constipation
- nausea and vomiting (may occur in cycles, lasting for days or weeks at a time)
- regurgitating undigested food
- heartburn
- abdominal pain
- poor appetite
- weight loss
- blood glucose levels that rise and plunge erratically

The last symptom is particularly worrisome for people with diabetes, of course. When food empties from the stomach on schedule, glucose levels rise and fall in a predictable manner. But if you have gastroparesis, you're never really sure when your postmeal glucose rise will occur. And most people who inject insulin or take insulin-regulating medications will agree that getting the timing right is hard enough as it is. Taking insulin to lower glucose levels that won't be rising any time soon can cause hypoglycemia.

Delayed gastric emptying can lead to other problems. For instance, food lingering in your belly may begin to

153

TROUBLESHOOTING CHECKLIST

Everyone has a touch of stomach trouble now and then. But frequent or chronic gastrointestinal problems can interfere with daily life and generally leave you feeling lousy. Worse, they may be signs of more serious illnesses, so talk to your doctor if you have any of the following symptoms for an extended period.

- ☐ Abdominal discomfort, including pain, nausea, or a persistent sense of fullness
- ☐ Vomiting
- ☐ Burning sensation in the sternum, regurgitating food or acidic fluid
- ☐ Feeling full after only a few bites of food
- ☐ Loose, watery bowels
- ☐ Hard, dry bowels
- ☐ Infrequent bowel movements (three days or more without passing a stool)
- ☐ Too frequent bowel movements (more than three in a day)
- ☐ Excessive straining to produce a bowel movement
- ☐ Difficulty swallowing
- ☐ Any sudden change in bowel habits
- ☐ Poor appetite
- ☐ Weight loss
- ☐ Blood sugar levels that dip and soar erratically

ferment, which could produce bacteria and cause infections. Stagnant stomach contents can even begin to stick together and form hairball-like masses (see "The Bizarre World of Bezoars," page 157).

Constipation

There are many worse medical conditions than constipation. But try telling that to someone whose bowel activity has come to a standstill. Surprisingly, although constipation is the most common gastrointestinal complaint in the United States (and the most common digestive problem for diabetes patients), there is a great deal of misunderstanding about what it is. Some people believe that if they go a day without a bowel movement it's time to break out the laxatives. However, perfectly healthy people can go two or three days without passing a stool.

Although there is no standard medical definition of constipation, most doctors look for the following signs:

- Three or more days without a bowel movement
- Hard, dry stools
- Pain when passing a stool
- Inability to pass a stool after trying for more than 10 minutes

Like gastroparesis, constipation occurs when motion through the digestive tract becomes sluggish, which may be a result of damaged nerves. Ideally, as stool chugs through the intestines, it loses some water, which is drawn into the bloodstream. But if transit time slows down, the stool loses too much water. Instead of a soft, bulky mass that's easy to pass, the stool turns hard and is painful to pass.

Diarrhea

Although diabetes can cause constipation, the disease is also capable of inducing its evil opposite: diarrhea. Chronic diarrhea tends to be a particularly serious problem for patients who have had type 1 diabetes for many years, even more so if glucose levels aren't well controlled. Damage to certain nerves in the intestines can prevent water in stools from being absorbed into the blood. That means feces retain too much fluid, making them slip through the intestines too rapidly. Bacterial infections resulting from gastroparesis can also cause diarrhea.

Symptoms of diarrhea typically include
- three or more bowel movements per day (some patients have reported up to 30)
- loose, watery stools
- urgent or sudden need to pass a stool
- straining to pass a stool

Patients may battle diarrhea for periods of weeks or months that alternate with stretches of normal bowel activity or constipation.

Bowel Incontinence

For obvious reasons, the inability to control the passage of feces or intestinal gas can be a nightmare, creating the potential for embarrassing moments in public and private. Normally, a pair of sphincter muscles manages the timely and appropriate movement of stool through the rectum and out of the body. Damage to nerves regulating these sphincter muscles or diminished muscle tone that may come with old age can lead to a loss of sensation and control, resulting in soiled undergarments and quick exits from social settings.

DIAGNOSING GASTROINTESTINAL AUTONOMIC NEUROPATHY

In many cases, a doctor can identify the source of a patient's digestive disturbance based on reported symptoms and a physical exam. However, special tests may be necessary to confirm a diagnosis or rule out other medical conditions. For instance, the symptoms of gastroparesis may mimic a peptic ulcer or even a cancerous tumor in the gastrointestinal system. Getting the diagnosis right means getting proper therapy as soon as possible.

155

Some tests your doctor may order include:

Upper endoscopy. Open wide! A doctor inserts a slender, flexible tube with a video camera on the tube's business end into the mouth and guides it down the esophagus. If you can't even brush your molars without gagging, don't worry. Before the procedure, which takes only 10 or 15 minutes, your doctor will either spray your throat with a local anesthetic or give you a sedative. The camera sends images to a video monitor, allowing the doctor to scan the esophagus, stomach, and duodenum for anything that might be causing gastrointestinal problems, including tumors, ulcers, or inflammation. Endoscopes can also take a biopsy if any tissue looks suspicious. A doctor may also use this test if he or she suspects you may have a bezoar.

Colonoscopy and sigmoidoscopy. Kind of like an endoscopy, with one key difference: the scope enters the body at the other end of the digestive tract. If a patient has severe or worsening constipation, persistent diarrhea, unexplained pain in the abdomen, or any other gut abnormalities, a doctor may order one of these tests. A colonoscopy examines the inside of the entire colon; a sigmoidoscopy only offers a view of the lower

third of the intestines. To ensure that these scopes take clear pictures, your intestines must be empty and squeaky clean. That means no solid food for a day or two before the exam, though you are allowed to sip broth and drink all the juice you like right up until the night before the test. On the day before the exam you'll take laxatives and give yourself enemas to flush the contents of your intestines. (Plan on spending the day within a very short walk of a bathroom.) Right before the exam, you will be given a sedative and pain reliever. During the procedure, the doctor may take biopsies with tiny forceps or remove polyps (little nubbins in the colon that can turn cancerous).

Esophageal motility testing. If you're having difficulty swallowing, your doctor may use this exam to determine whether the muscles in your esophagus have suffered nerve damage. The procedure involves slipping a slender tube called a catheter into one nostril, then guiding it into the esophagus. The tip of the catheter is equipped with sensors that record pressure inside the esophagus, then send the information to a recorder. The test can also measure how well the LES is working.

Gastric emptying study. Your doctor may order this test if you have symptoms of gastroparesis. Although you may not have much of an appetite, you will be asked to eat a small meal (such as a scrambled egg) that has been laced with radioactive material. The doctor then places a special scanner over your stomach that traces the movement of the radioactive material, measuring how long it takes to empty into the intestines. The gastric emptying study is considered the gold standard for confirming the diagnosis of gastroparesis.

Gastroduodenal manometry. Although this test isn't commonly performed or universally available, your doctor may order it. The physician inserts a small plastic tube through the nose, down the esophagus, and into your stomach and small intestine. The tube measures muscle contractions in the gut and sends the information to a computer. Doctors use this test to learn whether muscle contractions in the stomach are strong enough to mash food and move it down the pipe, and whether muscles in the stomach and intestines are working in a coordinated manner. A related test may be used in cases of bowel incontinence to measure the strength of anal muscles.

Electrogastrogram. Didn't Buck Rogers use an electrogastrogram to fight the

THE BIZARRE WORLD OF BEZOARS

In extreme cases of gastroparesis, bits of vegetable fiber and other food elements that the body has a hard time digesting can clump together. Over time, these clumps grow into gnarly balls of crud called *bezoars*. These masses can further block food from emptying into the intestines and worsen feelings of fullness and nausea. And if that wasn't industrial-strength icky enough for you, did you know that humans can have hairballs? People with certain mental or emotional problems sometimes eat their own tresses, which can form into bezoars, too.

Martians? Although it sounds like a ray gun or some other science-fiction gadget, an electrogastrogram is actually a new medical imaging tool (similar to an electrocardiogram) that measures the strength and rhythm of electrical signals traveling between the brain and the stomach muscles. You'll be relieved to know that no tubes down the throat are needed; this device senses muscle activity with electrodes taped to the abdomen. Stomach contractions normally have a steady pace and speed up after a meal; an electrogastrogram study showing that your belly muscles move slowly, or not at all, offers strong evidence of gastroparesis.

Stool sample. Your doctor may want to obtain a sample of your stool to deter-

COULD IT BE MY MEDS?

If you develop persistent digestive problems, talk to your doctor about any medications you are taking. Many prescription and over-the-counter drugs cause gastrointestinal difficulties. That includes pills your doctor may have prescribed to treat diabetes. For instance, metformin, which helps regulate glucose levels, may cause nausea, diarrhea, and bloating. Likewise, sulfonylurea can cause heartburn, while alpha-glucosidase inhibitors may induce diarrhea. The annoying symptoms often fade over time, but if they don't, your physician may be able to prescribe an alternative drug.

The following gastrointestinal symptoms may be triggered by drugs:

- Constipation: drugs used to treat pain, depression, psychosis, and hypertension, as well as sedatives and drugs used to prevent seizures. Also antacids that contain aluminum and dietary supplements that contain large amounts of iron.
- Diarrhea: antacids that contain magnesium; antibiotics; chemotherapy drugs; laxatives; orlistat (Xenical), a weight-loss drug; some drugs used to treat arthritis and gout.
- Bowel incontinence: antacids, laxatives, sedatives, narcotics, and muscle relaxants.
- Gastroparesis: drugs used to treat pain, bipolar disorder, depression (specifically tricyclic drugs), and Parkinson's disease; progesterone.
- Heartburn: drugs used to treat asthma, angina pectoris (chest pain), hypertension, and irritable bowel syndrome.

mine the cause of a gastrointestinal problem, especially persistent diarrhea. For instance, traces of blood—although not a cause for panic—may be an early sign of colon cancer. Large amounts of bacteria, on the other hand, suggest that an infection has arisen in the digestive tract. Typically, you will be given a special kit for collecting stool samples at home. The samples will be sent to a lab for analysis.

Upper GI series. If you have ever had an upper GI series, you may recall the experience as "the time I had to guzzle the milkshake that tasted like chalk." Also known as a barium suspension, the thick drink coats your innards, which makes abnormalities or defects that may be causing trouble in the digestive tract show up better on an X-ray. After downing the barium beverage, you will sit or stand before a device called a fluoroscope. This device tracks the progress of barium as it travels through the esophagus, stomach, and small intestines.

Other imaging tests. To rule out obstructions and tumors (such as pancreatic cancer) a physician may order some other imaging tests, including magnetic resonance imaging (MRI) or computerized tomography (CT) scans.

Treating Symptoms of Gastrointestinal Problems Caused by Diabetes

The first order of business when taking on tummy trouble if you have diabetes is to be sure you're doing everything you can to keep your glucose levels low and stable. That's often easier said than done, since many medications—including certain diabetes drugs—can wreak havoc in the digestive tract. Fortunately, there are various treatments for most of these conditions, so quelling queasiness and other gastrointestinal symptoms may just be a matter of finding the right therapy.

HEARTBURN

Tackling heartburn is like forming a football team: You will be most likely to succeed if you have a strong offense and defense. Going on the offensive means attacking stomach acid, the source of the problem. But a sound defensive strategy will block searing gastric juice from burning your windpipe in the first place.

Sick of sports metaphors? In plain English, making simple lifestyle changes and judicious use of medications can help put heartburn on ice.

Lifestyle changes

These self-help methods are an important part of your offense in the battle against heartburn.

Watch what you eat. Most people who experience frequent bouts of heartburn know that certain foods may as well be hot coals, though some sufferers are more sensitive to certain dishes than others. Spicy or acidic foods, such as tomato and citrus products, are obvious culprits. But seemingly innocuous foods trigger heartburn in some people, too, probably by causing the LES to relax and open. For instance, chocolate, peppermint and spearmint, and high-fat foods are common suspects. Caffeinated and carbonated beverages, such as alcohol, may also cause heartburn.

Lose weight and quit smoking. If you need just one more reason to shed pounds and kick the habit, here it is. Excess heft can push stomach contents upward and into the esophagus. And—surprise!—inhaling smoke may cause a burning sensation in the chest, though that's probably because chemicals in tobacco cause the esophagus's trapdoor to swing open.

Chill out. Despite widespread belief, stress doesn't cause heartburn. But doctors who treat gastrointestinal problems say feeling anxious and bothered can make heartburn seem worse. Find-

159

ing a way to mellow out and cope with life's frustrations and fears may make heartburn more manageable, among other benefits for the mind and body. Meditate, try yoga, or stare at the fish tank for a spell—whatever it takes to relax and hush the panicky voice in your head.

Use gravity. Heartburn is often worse at night, especially when you're trying to sleep. Blame gravity. When you lie down, the contents of your stomach slosh against the LES, forcing their way into the windpipe. Avoiding eating before bed will reduce the amount of food in the stomach, lowering pressure on the esophagus. Moreover, many doctors send their patients with night-time heartburn to the lumber- or brick-yard, instead of to the pharmacy, to buy some wooden blocks or bricks. Slide your purchases under the legs at the head of your bed to raise it six inches or so. (Old books or any other flat, sturdy objects will do, too; just be sure they're secure.) As an alternative, you can get the same benefit from "bed wedges" that fit under the mattress, which are sold in specialty stores and by mail order. Elevating the upper half of your body should help prevent stomach acid from pushing upward; the stuff may be potent, but it's not immune to the laws of physics.

Medications

Heartburn drugs work by making the stomach contents less bitter and harsh or by reducing acid production in your belly.

Antacids. For occasional heartburn, antacids are cheap and effective therapy. These pills and potions are packed with minerals that neutralize stomach acid, so while you may still have reflux, it won't sting. Bonus: Many antacids are little more than calcium tablets, which can help bolster bones. But don't pop them like Pez candy; super-high doses of calcium, or any other mineral, can be toxic. And if you have to treat heartburn every day, you probably need stronger medicine, so talk to your doctor about the following medications:

- H2 blockers. If your doctor feels that your heartburn has turned into full-blown GERD, he or she will likely recommend an H2 blocker (or a proton pump inhibitor; see next item). These drugs reduce stomach acid levels by blocking a protein called histamine. Don't worry, reducing acid won't affect your food processing capability; your digestive tract has plenty of enzymes along the way to get the job done. A few commonly used H2 blockers include famotidine (Pepcid), ranitidine (Zantac), and cimetidine (Tagamet).

- Proton pump inhibitors. Proton pump inhibitors reduce acid levels even lower than H2 blockers by blocking an enzyme in the stomach wall. You can purchase one of these drugs, omeprazole (Prilosec), over the counter (and in larger doses by prescription). Other proton pump inhibitors are sold by prescription only. They include esomeprazole (Nexium), pantoprazole (Protonix), lansoprazole (Prevacid), and rabeprazole (Aciphex). Although more expensive than H2 blockers, proton pump inhibitors can help heal tissue in the esophagus damaged by long-term exposure to stomach acid.

Surgery

People with severe GERD that doesn't respond well to medical therapy sometimes opt for surgery. A procedure called fundoplication can improve the effectiveness of the LES, making it more difficult for stomach acid to singe the lining of the esophagus. Although this operation once left large scars and carried the risk of heavy blood loss, surgeons now use smaller instruments, making for a less-invasive procedure.

DIFFICULTY SWALLOWING

Several categories of drugs can relax muscles in the esophagus, including the LES, though doctors say this treatment doesn't always make it easier or less painful to swallow. Acid-blocking drugs will be prescribed if GERD has produced scar tissue. In some cases, doctors manually widen a narrowed esophagus with a dilator. Using an endoscope, the doctor inserts a balloonlike device into the esophagus. As the balloon is inflated, the windpipe widens. In severe cases, a type of surgery called myotomy may be necessary, in which certain muscles are cut, allowing food to pass through the esophagus. As with other nerve disorders, doctors are also reporting success in treating dysphagia with Botox injections (see more about this therapy in the gastroparesis entry, next).

GASTROPARESIS

If you are experiencing a slowdown in your stomach, your doctor will likely ask you to make some changes in diet in order to get things moving again. Be sure to follow all recommendations to the letter. While medications are available that promote motility, or the movement of food through the digestive tract, they may lose effectiveness quickly and can cause serious side effects.

Diet Changes

Your stomach is struggling to move food to the intestines, so why overbur-

ROUTINE MAINTENANCE

- Maintain a healthy weight and quit smoking.
- Exercise.
- Eat a healthy diet. If your doctor has advised you to increase your fiber intake, start slowly to reduce flatulence.
- Take all prescribed medications. With antibiotics, be sure to take all prescribed pills, even if symptoms subside.
- Tell your doctor about any changes in gastrointestinal symptoms.

den it with mega portions? You may find some relief by switching from the traditional three square meals to more frequent repasts featuring junior-size servings. Doctors suggest trying four to six small meals per day. While you're at it, cut back on fat, which slows down stomach emptying. Because gastroparesis increases the risk of bezoars, eating less fiber may be necessary; ask your doctor or a dietitian how much you should consume every day. During difficult periods, your doctor may recommend that you replace solid foods with soups.

Medications

Doctors prescribe various types of drugs to treat vomiting and nausea that may be caused by gastroparesis. Prokinetic drugs can help speed up the movement of food out of the stomach and into the intestines. They include:

Metoclopramide (Reglan). This drug has several benefits for patients with gastroparesis. Not only does it make stomach muscles contract, which helps push food on its way, but metoclopramide also blocks messages to the brain that cause vomiting, so it relieves nausea, too. What's more, it makes the LES work better, so doctors sometimes prescribe the drug to patients with GERD who don't respond to other medications. However, it carries a greater risk of side effects than the heartburn medications mentioned above, especially when used long term. Patients who take metoclopramide may experience jitteriness, drowsiness, muscle spasms, confusion, depression or anxiety, and facial twitching, among other side effects.

Cisapride (Propulsid). Like metoclopramide, this medication increases stomach muscle contractions and reduces severe GERD symptoms. However, cisapride has been linked to rare but serious cardiac problems, primarily in patients with certain pre-existing conditions and who take some types of medication. The Food and Drug Administration has cautioned doctors not to prescribe cisapride to patients with a history of heart disease, kidney disease, lung disease, and several other conditions. Nor should patients who use allergy medication, certain heart drugs, antidepressants, and several other drug categories take cisapride.

Erythromycin. An antibiotic, erythromycin has an added benefit: It locks into cell receptors in the stomach and small intestine, which triggers muscle contractions. However, as with any antibiotic, taking erythromycin for an extended period can render it useless, as the patient may eventually develop a tolerance to its effects.

Other drugs. Some doctors have had success treating patients who have gastroparesis with medications designed for other gastrointestinal conditions. Two such drugs are tegaserod (Zelnorm), usually prescribed for irritable bowel syndrome, and octreotide (Sandostatin), designed to treat severe diarrhea.

Surgery

During periods of particularly severe gastroparesis, a patient may become malnourished, because nutrients in food can't reach the intestines, where they would normally be absorbed into the blood. To bypass the clogged stomach, a patient may need to undergo a jejunostomy, a surgical procedure in which a doctor inserts a feeding tube into the small intestines. The patient receives nutrients pumped through the tube until stomach empty-ing improves. As an alternative, a patient with severe gastroparesis may receive parenteral nutrition; that is, liquid nutrients delivered through a tube inserted directly into a vein, usually in the chest.

Botox

In the previous chapter, we described how some doctors use injections of Botox (a purified version of the botulinum toxin) to treat urinary problems. Doctors are now using Botox to relieve gastroparesis, too. Using an endoscope, a surgeon injects the drug into the pyloric sphincter, a ring of muscle separating the stomach and small intestine. By numbing the activity of certain nerves, Botox causes the pyloric sphincter to relax, which may improve stomach emptying. In a 2005 study at Temple University in Philadelphia, 63 patients with gastroparesis received Botox injections. Nearly half (43 percent) of the patients experienced at least some improvement of symptoms for about five months, on average. (For some reason, men were more likely than women to respond well to Botox injections.)

Gastric Electrical Stimulation

A few hospitals in the United States use tools that jolt damaged stomach nerves back to life, increasing muscle contractions and improving transit speed through the digestive tract. Electrical stimulation can be performed with electrodes taped to the skin on the abdomen or with a small battery-operated "neurostimulator" implanted in the body. The device works like a pacemaker, delivering electrical impulses that trigger muscle contractions. In a 2005 study published in the *Archives of Surgery,* 29 patients with debilitating gastroparesis received implanted gastric neurostimulators. After 20 months, 19 of the patients (70 percent) had "good to excellent" results.

CONSTIPATION

Although constipation and gastroparesis both occur when movement in the digestive tract slows to a halt, their treatments differ.

Diet

The food cure for constipation consists of three words: Fiber, fiber, and fiber. Your doctor or dietitian will instruct you to add whole-grain bread, bran cereal, and plenty of fruits and vegetables to your diet. Dietary fiber keeps a stool soft and bulky, making it easier to pass. Your goal should be 25 grams a day; the typical American diet includes far less. If you have never had a prune, now would be a good time to develop a taste for the wrinkly fruit: ten prunes

contain about seven grams of fiber. Just remember that prunes are carbohydrates (there are about six grams of carbohydrate per prune), so be sure to check your glucose and also have your doctor adjust your medications if needed.

Always drink plenty of water or other liquids when consuming a high-fiber diet. Getting plenty of exercise helps keep you regular, too.

Medications

If you're having trouble getting adequate fiber from your diet or the recommended amount hasn't gotten things moving, your physician may recommend laxatives. First choice is usually a regimen of fiber supplements, which contain either psyllium (derived from the seeds of a type of plantain) or methylcellulose (a synthetic version of indigestible material in plants). Like the fiber in food, these supplements make stool bulkier.

If adding fiber doesn't work, other types of laxatives may. Osmotic agents contain indigestible substances, such as minerals (like magnesium—think milk of magnesia) or sugars (sorbitol). They work by holding water in the intestines. For even more intractable constipation, stimulant laxatives (including senna, cascara, and bisacodyl) cause contractions in the intestines, which can force stools to move along.

Caution: Laxatives are serious medicine, and that includes products sold over the counter as dietary supplements with cutesy names like "Nature's Broom." Laxative abuse can lead to dehydration, cardiac problems, kidney failure, and a long list of other conditions. If you have chronic or frequent constipation, talk to your doctor before using laxatives.

People with persistent constipation often develop impacted stools, which are hard, dried masses of fecal matter that lodge in the rectum. To loosen an impacted stool, your doctor may attempt to remove it with a gloved finger or send you home with instructions to pick up an enema kit at the pharmacy. Neither method of dealing with an impacted stool will be the highlight of your day, but one or the other should remedy the problem.

DIARRHEA

While nerve damage can cause loose, watery bowels, so can a number of other conditions that affect the intestines. With that in mind, your physician may try one of several treatment approaches.

Diet

Adding roughage to your diet, either with high-fiber foods such as whole grains, fruits, and vegetables or with fiber supplements, may help sop up some of the excess water in the intestines that can cause diarrhea. Drinking plenty of fluids can help prevent dehydration.

Medications

Some cases of diarrhea may clear up with a few swigs of the pink drink, Pepto-Bismol, or some other product containing bismuth subsalicylate. (Follow instructions on the product label.) Another over-the-counter medication, loperamide (found in Imodium and other products) may help, too. Like loperamide, the prescription drug diphenoxylate (Lomotil and others) slows the movement of stool through the intestines. Doctors need to closely monitor patients taking these drugs, since they can cause the intestines to expand, causing a life-threatening condition known as megacolon.

Clonidine, an antihypertensive drug, may improve nerve function in the gut, slowing down bowel activity. If a physician suspects that overgrowth of bacteria in the gut is causing diarrhea, he or she will prescribe a course of antibiotics. When all else fails, doctors try octreotide (Sandostatin), an injected drug sometimes used in patients receiving chemotherapy.

BOWEL INCONTINENCE

Treatments for this embarrassing problem range from simple lifestyle changes to surgery.

Diet and Medication

When bowel incontinence produces loose, watery stools, treating diarrhea is an essential first step. Patients are advised to consume more dietary fiber and take one or more of the medications described above in order to produce bulkier stools, which are more easily controlled.

Biofeedback

Biofeedback is any form of training that provides information about bodily functions with the goal of helping people gain conscious control over them. One common method for treating bowel incontinence is to insert a balloonlike device in the patient's rectum. Inflating the balloon helps the patient relearn how it feels to pass a stool. The patient then practices contracting rectal muscles in order to control the stool's passage. Some biofeedback proponents claim 70 percent of patients with bowel incontinence who undergo the training have improved symptoms, though in some studies actual success rates have been less impressive.

Surgery

In cases of severe bowel incontinence that doesn't respond to other therapies, surgery may be the next best hope. Surgeons have several options for restoring healthy bowel function. In patients suffering from nerve damage, muscles may be harvested from elsewhere in the body (such as the thigh) and transplanted to strengthen contractions in the rectum. Artificial bowel sphincters are another option; they ensure that the feces cannot pass until the patient manually deflates a special "cuff." Fecal diversion is a final alternative. Also called a colostomy, this approach empties stool from the colon through a portal surgically implanted in the abdomen and into a special collection bag.

Sacral Nerve Stimulation

This experimental treatment is similar to electrical devices implanted in the gut to improve stomach muscle contractions. Studies in Europe have found that patients who have these small devices implanted in the lower back have better bowel control. However, the treatment is not yet available in the United States.

Your Feet and Diabetes

Whether you have big, floppy flippers or prim, petite paws, your feet absorb a beating like no other part of the body. Every step you take exerts hundreds of pounds of pressure on the foot, and even a do-nothing lazybones takes 2,000 to 3,000 steps per day. (If you're moderately active, you pound the pavement 5,000 to 7,000 times.)

Is it any wonder, then, that foot injuries are among the most common medical complaints? Unfortunately, diabetes can add to these woes by causing diabolical problems for the feet, as well as the ankles and lower legs. In fact, foot disorders are among the most frequent and feared complications of diabetes. In the following pages, you'll learn how to stay on your toes (and hold on to them) for years to come.

Keep Your Footing: Your Feet and Diabetes

There's no sense in pussyfooting around: Diabetes poses a serious danger to your dogs. Having the condition doubles the risk for foot disease. In fact, about 30 percent of people with diabetes who are older than 40 develop medical problems with their feet. The damaged nerves and poor blood circulation that often accompany elevated blood sugar ensure that there is no such thing as a minor cut, scrape, bump, or bruise on the foot when you have diabetes. While blood-sugar problems can create a dizzying range of hard-to-treat complications, lower-limb diseases that are not properly treated can deteriorate so quickly and so badly that doctors have no other choice but to eliminate the problem altogether. That's another way of saying that people with diabetes account for 60 percent of all lower-limb amputations in the United States. In fact, a patient with diabetes is 10 to 30 times more likely to have a lower limb amputated than a person without the disease.

THE FEET

For two sturdy performers who take a daily pounding, the feet are surprisingly complex structures. Combined, your two feet have more than one-quarter of the bones in your body—26 each.

Although they form the foundation for the body, the feet aren't static blocks but agile and dynamic machines of movement, with more than 100 tendons, muscles, and ligaments apiece. Given their workload and all those moving parts, it's not surprising that about 75 percent of Americans experience one foot condition or another in their lifetime, according to the American Podiatric Medical Association. (Podiatrists are foot doctors; you'll read more about them later in this chapter.)

THE FEET AND DIABETES

As you know all too well by now, chronically elevated glucose levels can damage the nervous system, the wiring that transmits signals from the brain throughout the body. The nervous system works the other way, too: It detects information about the environment and how it affects the body through the five senses. Damaged nerves, or neuropathy, can lead to an array of physical problems and disabilities anywhere in the body. But nerve injuries and other diseases that affect the feet (and lower legs) may be the complications most frequently associated with diabetes. What's more, the various foot conditions linked to diabetes may be the complications patients dread most.

Annoying and painful symptoms can occur when the brain can't successfully send messages to the feet. But the even greater threat posed by diabetic neuropathy happens when the feet can't send information to the brain because they've become numb from overexposure to blood sugar. What do your feet have to report to mission control? Plenty. But cuts, bumps, and other injuries that once would have made you wince or howl in pain go unnoticed when your feet lose their feeling.

To make matters worse, dulled nerves probably aren't your only problem if you have diabetes. The disease can also cause poor blood circulation. Like the heart's arteries, blood vessels anywhere else in the body can become stiff and narrowed. In fact, 1 in 3 people with diabetes who are older than 50 has clogged arteries in the legs, a condition known as peripheral artery disease, also called peripheral vascular disease. Narrowed arteries diminish blood flow to the lower legs and feet, which, as you'll learn later in this chapter, can cause pain while walking long distances. More ominously, the loss of blood flow to the

feet can prevent wounds and sores from getting the oxygen and nutrients they need to heal, allowing them to grow and spread.

So while occasional bumps, blisters, or cuts are trivial medical concerns for most people, for diabetes patients these minor injuries can turn serious in a hurry. Left ignored and untreated,

ROUTINE MAINTENANCE

Avoiding foot ulcers and other diabetes complications that affect the lower limbs means following general, big-picture health advice (such as watching your weight and eschewing tobacco) and paying attention to minute details, such as keeping an eye out for tiny cuts and bumps that might turn into large, limb-threatening wounds. These rules can help:

- Keep your blood glucose under control.
- Have your physician check your feet often; undergo a comprehensive examination at least once a year.
- Give yourself a daily foot exam; learn what signs to look for and report anything suspicious to your doctor.
- Maintain a healthy weight and low cholesterol.
- Don't smoke.
- Exercise; develop a suitable regimen with your physician.
- Learn proper toenail cutting technique.
- Wear comfortable shoes (and socks or hose) that fit and protect your feet. Don't go barefoot.

minor sores on the skin of the foot can turn into severe problems with potentially devastating consequences—namely, foot ulcers.

FOOT ULCERS

Most people think of ulcers as burning sores that cause bellyaches. But while gastric and peptic ulcers that form in the stomach and intestines are usually easy to cure with drugs, ulcers on the skin of the feet and legs can pose a more serious threat. These craterlike wounds can arise from seemingly inconsequential injuries to the feet. In extreme cases, they can deteriorate and develop into crippling and positively medieval-sounding complications. (We'll save the details about extreme disorders of the extremities for later in this chapter.)

According to the Centers for Disease Control and Prevention, about 15 percent of people with diabetes develop foot ulcers. The problems begin with nerve damage. Specifically, ulcers arise due to a loss of sensation in the foot caused by peripheral neuropathy (see Chapter 7 for a detailed explanation), which afflicts about half of people with diabetes who are older than 60. If you lose feeling in the lower limbs, the risk of foot ulcers soars 700 percent.

When you lose sensation in the feet, small injuries can go unnoticed and degenerate into large, open sores. There are endless scenarios for how a foot ulcer may begin to form, including the following:

- If you have damaged nerves in the lower limbs, you may not be aware that a pair of ill-fitting shoes is causing blisters, corns, or other foot conditions that can lead to ulcers.
- If your skin can't tell hot from cold, you could scald your foot in steaming-hot bathwater; the burned skin may blister.
- You could step on a sharp rock and cut your heel while walking barefoot.

WHO GETS FOOT ULCERS?

Having diabetes increases the chances of developing serious sores on the feet. But some patients have a greater risk than others. To find out what qualities increase the risk, doctors at the University of Washington studied 749 veterans with diabetes. At the outset, none of the veterans had foot ulcers. After an average of 3.7 years, the doctors reexamined the veterans and their medical records. Patients with the following traits were among the most likely to have developed foot sores:

- Evidence of nerve damage (including both peripheral and autonomic neuropathy)
- Insulin use
- Deformities, such as Charcot's foot or hammertoe
- Poor vision
- Obesity

- If your foot is numb from nerve damage, you may get in the habit of banging it into hard objects because you don't feel any pain. Over time, damage to joints and other structures in the foot could cause a deformity that puts pressure on the skin.
- If you have arthritis in the ankle or toes, you may lose joint mobility and alter the way you walk so that too much pressure is placed on the ball of the foot. Or, your normal gait may simply apply excessive force on certain sections of your soles. Over time, wear and tear could cause the skin to erode, forming a sore.
- Simply cutting your toenails the wrong way can damage skin and produce sores.

In addition to nerve damage, people with diabetes tend to have several other problems that further increase the risk of foot ulcers. As we have already mentioned, peripheral artery disease may reduce or cut off blood flow to the lower limbs, which will slow or prevent healing of sores (as well as make walking around the block a painful experience). High blood sugar doesn't help matters any, since bacteria feasts on glucose, helping the germs to thrive, which causes infections. To make matters worse, diabetes interferes with the immune system's ability to kill germs,

and that allows infections to worsen. If blood sugar has damaged your optic nerves (which it may; see Chapter 11), blurry vision can make detecting cuts and sores more difficult. Finally, if you're overweight, as many type 2 diabetes patients are, simply bending over to examine or treat your feet may be difficult, if not impossible.

Feet First: Antiulcer Strategies

Foot ulcers and the complications they can cause are not an inevitable part of having diabetes. Along with maintaining healthy blood sugar, here are steps to keep the nasty sores at bay.

- Meet your feet. Get to know them intimately. Make a point of examining your feet at least once a day. Be on the lookout for any cuts, sores, bumps, or bruises. Be sure to check between your toes. If necessary, use a hand mirror with a long handle or place a mirror on the floor to check areas that are hard to see. Report any problems to your doctor. If you have poor vision, ask someone else to give your feet a once-over. (Which is all the more reason to heed the next piece of advice.)
- Clean up your act. Washing your feet daily will not only keep them from smelling like, well, feet; but more importantly, frequent cleaning can help prevent infections. Test water

temperature with your hand before stepping into a bath to avoid burns. (Better yet, use a thermometer; 90 to 95 degrees Fahrenheit is about right.) Use nonabrasive, unscented soap that contains lanolin, a moisturizer. Dry carefully with a clean towel, especially between the toes, to prevent athlete's foot. Most doctors discourage patients with foot ulcers from soaking their feet for too long, which, ironically, may dry the skin.

- Wear sensible shoes. *These shoes are killing me* is the familiar refrain from sore-footed sorts after a day wearing too-tight pumps or wingtips.

WHAT'S GOOD FOR THE FACE...

...may be good for the feet if you have ulcers. A 2005 study in the *Archives of Dermatology* found that the anti-acne treatment tretinoin (Retin-A) may help relieve these nasty sores. Researchers at the University of California, San Diego, asked one group of patients to apply tretinoin cream to their foot ulcers every day. A similar group received a placebo cream that contained no medication. After four months, nearly half (46 percent) of the ulcers treated with tretinoin had vanished, while just 18 percent of the placebo-treated ulcers had healed. The study was small, including just 22 subjects, and excluded any patient who had evidence of infection or poor circulation in their extremities. However, the study's authors believe that this potent pimple potion may be an option for people with hard-to-treat foot ulcers.

While uncomfortable shoes may not be deadly weapons, they can cause foot problems that may turn serious if left untreated. One study of 669 patients with foot ulcers found that about 20 percent of the sores were linked to ill-fitting footwear that caused rubbing on the skin.

A good pair of shoes should be snug but comfortable, without producing friction against the foot or cramming the toes together. Tip: Shop for new shoes in the afternoon, since your feet swell slightly during the day. You don't have to stomp around in work boots, but choose styles that protect your tender feet. Avoid sandals and shoes with a thonglike strap between the toes. If new shoes are stiff, break them in by wearing them no more than an hour or two per day. Better yet, stick with easygoing footwear. Shop for shoes that feel like you've owned them for years the first time you slip them on.

Therapeutic shoes and inserts may help prevent pressure sores from developing. Specially designed shoes do not eliminate the risk of ulcers, however, and some studies suggest that they may be most beneficial to patients with severe lower-limb problems, such as foot deformities, or to those who have already had a foot amputated.

- Get hosed. Wearing hosiery or socks will help prevent foot problems. Stockings made from natural fibers, such as cotton and wool, will keep your feet drier than polyester and other synthetic fabrics. Tight hose can reduce circulation. Change your socks every day.
- Don't go barefoot in the park. Or the backyard, beach, or anywhere, including indoors. Hot pavement or sand can burn your feet, sharp pebbles or shards of glass can cause gashes, and you can stub your toe or whack an ankle just about anywhere. When you visit an ocean or lake, wear beach shoes, which offer more protection than flip-flops. (Wear them in public locker rooms and pools, too, to protect against viruses and fungi.) Find a sturdy pair of slippers to wear around the house.

THE FOOT EXAM

Plan on having a thorough foot exam at least once a year, more often if you smoke or have other conditions that raise the risk of ulcers and complications, such as heart disease. If you have been diagnosed with neuropathy, ask your physician to have a look at your feet every chance you get. Pretend you're visiting your mother's house, and take off your shoes the instant you walk through the door as a way to remind your doc to examine your feet for signs of trouble. (Removing your socks would help, too.)

Before a doctor lays a hand on your hooves, he or she will want to collect some information, such as how long you have had diabetes, how well you control blood sugar, and whether you have had any foot ulcers before. Then the doctor will give your feet a good going over, checking the blood vessels for pulses and looking for corns, calluses, and any of the other potentially prickly problems described in Common Foot Problems and How to Fight Them, beginning on page 176.

Your physician may also use one or more of the following tests to detect or predict nerve damage in your feet.

Monofilament test. You might call it the "tickle test." The doctor performs this exam using a small device with a plastic handle and a slender nylon fiber. After the patient removes his or her shoes and socks, the doctor touches the tip of the nylon fiber to various points on the patient's soles to check for the presence of sensation. Some doctors diagnose neuropathy if a patient is unable to feel the monofilament at any spot on their sole, while others believe nerve damage isn't significant unless there are several locations that lack sensation.

Tuning fork test. In this simple, low-tech test, the doctor taps a two-pronged metal fork against a hard object, which causes the device to vibrate, then holds the fork to the patient's foot. In some studies, patients who could not feel the vibration had an increased risk for developing foot ulcers.

"Electrical tuning fork" test. Like plain old tuning forks, these high-tech tools test whether a patient can detect vibration. (One widely used model is called the Biothesiometer.) Unlike tuning forks, the sensitivity of these devices can be adjusted. Some studies suggest that they may more accurately identify patients at risk for foot ulcers.

Pressure mat. Your doctor may have you walk on a special pressure-sensing mat to measure how much force you place on the soles of your feet. High pressure may indicate an increased risk for foot ulcers.

Treating Foot Ulcers

After a doctor cleans dead tissue and dresses the wound, the following measures will speed the healing of a foot ulcer:

Kick back and relax. Better yet, just relax—your feet are in no shape to do any kicking. Rest is essential while an ulcer heals, so avoid walking as much as possible. Keep the affected foot elevated to take pressure off the wound. You may need crutches or even a wheelchair.

Go shoe shopping. But you're probably not going to want to splurge on those Manolo Blahniks you've always wanted.

Comfort is more important than style when you have foot ulcers, which often result from tight or poor-fitting footwear. Read more about buying shoes on page 172.

Go for a cast-ing call. You may need a cast to protect the ulcer and take pressure off the foot. One commonly used variety is known as a *total contact cast,* which is made of fiberglass and has a bar on the sole to absorb pressure while you stand or walk. The cast fits very closely and has a foam layer to protect the ulcer. Other types of casts may be used.

Kill the bacteria. If an ulcer is infected, your doctor will prescribe antibacterial drugs. Be sure to take all antibiotics prescribed.

Speed it up. Becaplermin (Regranex) is a prescription gel that speeds up ulcer healing by attracting molecules in the body that repair wounds.

Get some closure. Sounds like science fiction, but skin implants can be used to heal deep or stubborn ulcers that don't respond to other treatment. Two products, Apligraf and Dermagraft, are made from actual human cells called fibroblasts, which promote tissue growth. (Fun fact: Apligraf and Dermagraft are produced with cells extracted from the foreskins of infant boys.) These padlike devices are applied to an ulcer and are gradually absorbed, replacing lost skin (though they lack blood vessels, hair follicles, and other components of your real skin).

Treat blood-flow problems. Ulcers will not heal well and will become a recurring problem if blood vessels in the leg

WHAT IS A PODIATRIST?

In an episode of the TV show *Seinfeld,* Elaine boasts that she is dating a podiatrist. Jerry is unimpressed. "Anyone can get into podiatry school," he tells her. "*George* got into podiatry school."

Maybe he did, but that well-known goof-off probably wouldn't have lasted long in a rigorous podiatry program. Podiatrists (sometimes known as "chiropodists") are specialized doctors who treat disorders of the foot, ankle, and lower leg, including the various diseases and injuries that frequently afflict people with diabetes.

Instead of an M.D., for "medical doctor," they add a D.P.M. after their names, for "doctor of podiatric medicine." But first they must complete four years of extensive medical education and training, including courses in anatomy, chemistry, pathology, and pharmacology. Podiatry students also perform clinical rotations in private practices, hospitals, and clinics. Most states require podiatrists to complete a one- to three-year postdoctoral residency program, too. Finally, before a podiatrist can hang a shingle, he or she must pass an oral and written licensing exam.

are blocked (or ischemic). Steps must be taken to restore circulation to the lower limbs and feet. You will read about this problem and measures to relieve blood flow problems later in this chapter.

COMMON FOOT PROBLEMS AND HOW TO FIGHT THEM

Diabetes patients have an unusually high number of foot problems, including those described below. Many of these nuisances can deteriorate into sores that may cause serious foot ulcers. Fortunately, following the daily care suggestions detailed in Feet First, pages 171–173, especially wearing good-fitting shoes, can reduce the risk for these nagging foot woes.

AGONY OF THE FEET

Ulcers and other forms of foot disease linked to diabetes are a major public health problem. The numbers are telling:

- 300,000 people with diabetes are hospitalized annually for treatment of serious foot infections and ulcers.
- Each year, more than 82,000 nontraumatic lower-limb amputations are performed on diabetes patients.
- Amputation rates in people with diabetes can be reduced by 45 to 85 percent with comprehensive foot care programs.

Athlete's foot. A notorious menace in locker rooms, athlete's foot is a risk for anyone who does a lot of sweating. Moisture between the toes promotes the growth and spread of fungus. The skin between the digits can become dry, scaly, itchy, and sore. The skin may crack, exposing it to bacterial infection. Blisters may form, too.

Treatment: Over-the-counter antifungal creams are usually effective. But if you don't see improvement in five days or so, contact your doctor.

Blisters. Wear a new pair of high heels all day before they're broken in, or decide to skip the socks when you go for a long jog, and you may pay the price in the form of blisters. These sores form when skin rubs against a surface for an extended period. Over time, layers of skin beneath the area that's rubbing become damaged and blood vessels leak fluid called serum, which collects just under the top layer of skin. (Other influences, such as sunburn and certain diseases, can cause blisters to form, too.)

Treatment: Never pop a blister. Instead, cover it with a sterile gauze pad and bandage. Leave it alone, and the body will eventually reabsorb the fluid. The blistered skin will slide off on its own, probably while you're bathing. If a blister opens, wash it with soap and water, then cover it with gauze and a bandage.

Charcot's joint. If nerve damage in the foot is severe enough, you may be able to bang it against the wall or a table leg and not feel a thing. Unfortunately, being impervious to pain may mask mounting damage to joints in the foot caused by a series of minor injuries. Over time, a joint may become so damaged that it stiffens and becomes deformed. Named for a nineteenth-century French neurologist, this condition can affect any joint, though it occurs most frequently in the foot (which is called Charcot's foot). About 15 percent of people with diabetes develop Charcot's joint, which is also known as neuropathic joint and neuropathic arthropathy.

Treatment: A surgeon can remove abnormal bone growth and fragments of cartilage in a procedure known as an ostectomy. The surgeon may also insert screws and plates to realign and stabilize a weakened joint.

Corns. If you swear your feet are size 6s when they're really size 7s, you may develop corns as proof of your denial. When you cram your feet into tight shoes, the toes may end up jammed against the inside. As protection against all that pressure and friction, the skin thickens with dead skin cells, which may eventually form small, pea-shape bumps on the tops and sides of the toes. (So why not call them "peas"? Because the layer of skin that accumulates to form a corn is called the stratum *corn*eum.) People who have high arches are more at risk for corns, since the shape of their feet adds pressure on the toes. Some corns are painless, while others hurt like heck.

Treatment: Soft toe pads or cushions, available in pharmacies, may help relieve pressure that causes a corn to hurt. Moleskin works, too. But avoid corn remover treatments, which contain acid and may damage your skin. And don't even think about playing amateur surgeon. If a corn needs to be trimmed, let a doctor do the cutting.

Calluses. Like corns, calluses are areas of thickened skin created by friction. They can turn up anywhere on the body, but they usually form over joints and other bony parts. On the feet, calluses most often appear on the soles, often in joggers, walkers, and other people who pound a lot of pavement. Some calluses are painless, while others hurt and may mask the presence of a foot ulcer.

Treatment: Special pads and shoe inserts may help relieve pain, if any. Soaking your feet briefly in warm water may help, too, though patients with neuropathy must be careful not to scald their skin with too-hot water. Some doctors recommend smoothing the callus with a pumice stone, but others say the risk of injury is too great, especially if you have diabetes. As with corns, do not attempt to remove a callus with a knife or blade. That's why your doctor gets the big bucks.

Dry skin. Damage to nerves in the feet can block signals to the brain. That means the skin may lose moisture, since the body doesn't realize it needs to retain enough water to keep the tissue hydrated. When skin becomes very dry, it may crack, creating an open door for bacteria and other germs, raising the risk of infection.

Treatment: Apply a small amount of moisturizing cream or lotion to your feet once or twice a day, avoiding the spaces between the toes.

Ingrown toenails. Ingrown toenails may sound like no big deal, but if they aren't treated promptly and properly, they can be a nightmare. They can occur if the nail becomes deformed and its edge grows inward, pushing its way into the skin. In other cases, the skin on the big toe grows too much and overwhelms the nail. Wearing too-tight shoes is a common cause of ingrown toenails. Improper nail trimming is a problem, too. While a strange-shaped toenail alone is of little consequence and probably won't cause symptoms, an ingrown toenail can become painful and inflamed if the skin becomes infected.

Prevention and treatment: Wear comfortable shoes that don't strangle your feet. Learn proper nail-trimming tech-

CUTTING EDGE NAIL CARE

For the newly diagnosed diabetes patient, the news may come as a shock. *C'mon, doc. Are you really saying that I need to relearn how to cut my toenails? What next? A seminar on eyebrow plucking?* Yet, understanding the proper way to care for your nails can spare your feet a lot of grief. Cutting them improperly can promote ingrown toenails, which can lead to infections and ulcers. In fact, some doctors discourage patients with diabetes from using toenail scissors or trimmers at all. One slip and you could cut your skin, opening the door to infection. If you do trim your toenails, follow these rules:

- Cut across the top in a straight line, no shorter than the front edge of the toe.
- Use an emery board to file down sharp corners.
- Never trim the sides of a nail, which exposes sensitive skin to puncturing from the growing nail.

nique from your doctor or diabetes educator. (See "Cutting Edge Nail Care," above.) If a toenail is digging into your skin, don't attempt at-home surgery; ask your doctor to trim it. If the toe is infected, you'll be given a prescription for antibiotics.

Bunions. Once again, tight shoes, especially narrow high heels, are the most common culprit; not surprisingly, 90 percent of bunion sufferers are women. In fact, according to the American Academy of Orthopaedic Surgeons, about half the women in the United States have a bunion. (However, the problem seems to run in families, too.) Bunions occur when the metatarsophalangeal joint—the joint at the base

of your big toe—rubs against the side of your shoe, becomes swollen, and begins to jut outward. That forces the big toe to push inward on the second toe. A domino effect may happen, in which the second toe leans in on the third toe. The swollen joint is usually quite painful, especially when you walk, and can become infected. (A bunionette is a small swollen lump on the outside of your foot, below the little toe. Like its big brother, a bunionette can usually be traced to tight shoes.)

Treatment: The first step your doctor orders may be to clean out your shoe closet, or at least get rid of any footwear with pointy toes or heels over 2¼ inches. In severe cases, surgery can realign the bones, tendons, and other structures inside the foot that have shifted out of position.

Hammertoe. Although it sounds like what you get if you drop a heavy tool on your foot, hammertoe is yet another deformity that can result from ill-fitting or tight shoes, especially if they squish the toes. Muscle abnormalities in the toes can cause the problem, too. When the front of the foot has to fit into a narrow space, the second, third, and fourth toes may be forced to arch upward to make room. Over time, the muscles in the toe freeze, leaving the digit in a hook or clawlike position. The toe may also ache and develop a corn.

Treatment: Your doctor may instruct you to do exercises to strengthen the toe muscles, such as using your foot digits to pick up small objects. Corn pads may help relieve some discomfort. If switching to roomier shoes doesn't solve the problem, minor surgery may be necessary to repair hammertoe.

Plantar warts. All warts are caused by a virus, known as human papillomavirus, that can lurk on floors where people tend to walk around barefoot. But that's where the similarity ends between plantar warts and warts that turn up elsewhere on the body. *Plantar* refers to the sole of the foot, where these warts grow. While other warts are round growths that protrude from the skin, plantar warts are flat, since you spend all day standing on them. And while warts elsewhere on the body are harmless (if a bit unsightly), plantar warts may hurt, especially when you walk. They may also become infected or bleed.

Treatment: Plantar warts often go away on their own, but if you have one that's painful or persistent, do not attempt to remove it. Do not perform bathroom surgery, and do not use over-the-counter wart treatments because they can contain harsh chemicals. If your blood glucose control is poor, you can get into trouble rapidly. See a doctor for any foot problems. Your doctor may apply a mild acid solution that can shrink warts or remove the growth with a scalpel or by freezing it (a technique known as cryotherapy).

When You Can't Walk the Walk: Peripheral Artery Disease and Intermittent Claudication

It's a cruel irony: One of the most important things you can do to delay the progress of diabetes is to drop the remote, jump off the sofa, and get some exercise. Unfortunately, one of the disease's most common side effects is throbbing leg pain that makes the idea of a good, long walk on a sunny summer day sound like a masochistic march. What's more, the condition that causes sore legs when you walk briskly or uphill, known as peripheral artery disease (PAD), comes with even more ominous implications.

Peripheral artery disease is simply another way of saying clogged or narrowed arteries. Sound familiar? It should, since the most common cause of death in the Western world, cardiovascular disease, occurs when the major blood vessels that keep heart muscle alive become blocked with cholesterol, calcium, and other circulatory garbage. Partial blockages of the heart's arteries can produce chest pain called angina pectoris. Likewise, clogged pipes cause most strokes. Doctors use the phrase "peripheral artery disease" (or "peripheral vascular disease") to describe blockages in blood vessels that occur anywhere in the circulatory system other than the heart or brain.

Diabetes patients are two to three times more likely than others to develop peripheral artery disease, which occurs more often in men than in women. For some reason, the condition strikes most frequently in the legs. Many people with blocked leg arteries, perhaps as many as three-quarters of them, never develop any symptoms. In some cases, that may be due to the phenomenon known as "collateral circulation," in which smaller blood vessels sprout up to reroute blood flow around blocked arteries.

However, many diabetes patients who have peripheral artery disease experience a problem called intermittent claudication. The term claudication comes from the Latin word for "limp." Indeed, sufferers develop problems with perambulation, typically while walking quickly or a long distance. (Some people with intermittent claudication can't make it longer than a block 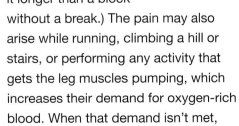 without a break.) The pain may also arise while running, climbing a hill or stairs, or performing any activity that gets the leg muscles pumping, which increases their demand for oxygen-rich blood. When that demand isn't met,

181

TROUBLESHOOTING CHECKLIST

Both nerve damage and poor circulation can herald the onset of serious foot and lower-limb disease, so the earliest symptoms may vary. Talk to your doctor promptly if you develop any of these signs:

☐ Persistent tingling, burning, or pain

☐ Numbness—you can't feel touch, heat, or cold

☐ Change in skin color

☐ Dry, chapped skin

☐ Change in shape

☐ Loss of hair

☐ Toenails turn thick and yellow

pain sets in. Just as reduced blood flow to the heart produces a crushing, viselike sensation in the chest, intermittent claudication produces tightness, cramps, fatigue, and aches. (Some doctors call intermittent claudication "angina of the legs.")

Most people feel the discomfort of intermittent claudication in the calves, but it may also affect the buttocks, thighs, or feet. The good news: If you stop and rest, the pain subsides quickly, usually within two or three minutes. The bad news: The anguish comes back just as quickly if you start working those leg muscles again. (That's where the "intermittent" part comes from.)

Some other signs that you have peripheral artery disease include
- lack of a detectable pulse in the feet
- cold or numb extremities, especially the feet

- skin color changes; the legs may turn pale if you elevate them, for instance, or ruddy if you sit on an exam table with legs hanging over the side
- loss of hair on top of the foot
- dry, scaly skin
- thickening of toenails
- weakness in the legs and loss of muscle, usually in the calves
- foot ulcers

Peripheral artery disease can be an early warning sign that a patient has clogged arteries in other critical parts of the body. Studies show that a person with PAD is four to six times more likely to suffer a heart attack or stroke than nonsufferers. What's more, about one person in ten who develops intermittent claudication goes on to develop serious loss of blood flow to the feet, though the risk is much higher among people with diabetes. In one study, 40 percent of patients with diabetes who had intermittent claudication developed foot sores or other serious complications. Diabetes patients tend to develop more severe symptoms of peripheral artery disease, at a younger age, than the general population.

DIAGNOSING PERIPHERAL ARTERY DISEASE

If you report symptoms that sound like peripheral artery disease, your doctor will take a complete medical history and conduct a physical exam. As part of the exam, your doctor will check the arteries in your feet to determine whether a pulse can be detected. If not, he or she will suspect that the blood vessels in your legs may have one or more blockages, also known as plaques. The following tests will help confirm the diagnosis.

Ankle-brachial index test. If a doctor suspects PAD, he or she may use this exam to determine how severe the problem has become. While you lie down on an exam table, the doctor will measure the blood pressure in your upper arm and at the ankle. (Your doctor may also ask you to repeat the test after you spend a few minutes walking on a treadmill.) Now the doctor crunches some numbers, dividing the highest systolic blood pressure obtained from the ankle by the highest pressure in either arm to establish an ankle-brachial index. Normally, the blood pressure in the ankle should be higher than the pressure in the upper arm, so an index of 1 or 1.1 is normal. A lower index offers solid evidence of PAD. Doctors use slightly different values to evaluate the severity of PAD, but the numbers in the box below may be associated with the accompanying symptoms.

While the ankle-brachial index test is generally a useful tool for diagnosing PAD, its value is limited. Some patients, including many with diabetes, have heavy calcium deposits in their blood vessels. The resulting stiffness can cause blood pressure readings to be artificially high, which means PAD

INTERPRETING THE ANKLE-BRACHIAL INDEX

If your ankle-brachial index is:	then you probably have:
0.9 or lower	One or more blood vessels in the legs with significant narrowing. You may have symptoms of intermittent claudication, or pain in the foot, leg, or buttocks during exercise.
0.5 or lower	Severe PAD; you may feel pain in the lower limbs all the time, even while resting.
0.25 or lower	A high risk for losing a limb to amputation.

183

may not be diagnosed. (As an alternative, your doctor may perform a photoplethysmography exam; see next item.) If your ankle-brachial index test is abnormal or you have other symptoms of PAD despite a normal ankle-brachial test, your doctor will likely order further studies to locate the blockage or blockages in your legs' blood vessels.

Photoplethysmography (PPG) exam. If the arteries in your ankle have become too stiff to yield accurate blood pressure readings, then your doctor may use this exam. The exam uses a small blood-pressure cuff that's slipped over a toe. The doctor also measures blood volume in the toe with an instrument that emits infrared light. A special sensor detects how the light is absorbed inside the toe. The intensity of the light recorded reflects the blood's density.

Angiogram. An angiogram is simply an X-ray of the blood vessels. Doctors use them to search for blockages and other vascular problems, such as aneurysms. To perform an angiogram, the physician first inserts a slender, flexible tube called a catheter into an artery through a small incision near the groin. Then the physician injects a dye, or contrast medium, into the artery and takes an X-ray of the legs. The contrast helps highlight blockages and narrowed areas

in the artery. Although angiograms require a small incision in the skin, they have an advantage over other imaging techniques, since the doctor can use the catheter to repair blockages during the procedure. (See page 189 for more information.) Angiograms are sometimes called arteriograms and can be combined with computed tomography to create three-dimensional images.

Duplex ultrasound imaging. This procedure uses two types of ultrasound (which is why it's called "duplex"), which allows doctors to get a picture of the insides of your blood vessels and measure the speed of the blood and which way it's flowing. (Conventional ultrasound bounces sound waves off structures, while Doppler ultrasound measures the movement of moving objects, namely, blood.) Unlike an angiogram, ultrasound is noninvasive; that is, no incision is required and you won't have any tubes poked inside your body. Instead, a special gel is painted onto the skin of the legs. Then the doctor slowly traces the skin with a wand, which transmits color images, including details about any blockages, back to a monitor.

Magnetic resonance angiography (MRA). Simply put, this is an MRI (magnetic resonance imaging) scan of the blood vessels. MRIs create two- and three-dimensional images using magnetic fields and radio waves. MRA is not only noninvasive, it also requires no exposure to X-rays. However, since the test does require lying still in a loud, narrow tube, MRA may not be appropriate for people who are claustrophobic, very obese, or easily agitated.

RISK MANAGEMENT: FOUR WAYS TO PREVENT PERIPHERAL ARTERY DISEASE

A blood vessel is a blood vessel, whether it's in your heart or big toe. That's why many of the same steps you may already be taking to prevent heart attacks and strokes could also help lower your risk for peripheral artery disease. Here are four ways to lower your risk for leg and foot pain as well as other complications of PAD.

Control glucose levels. Is there an echo in here? You hear this advice over and over for a reason: Chronically elevated blood sugar damages countless structures in the body, including blood vessels. Scientists aren't sure how, but evidence suggests high glucose levels produce armies of dangerous compounds called advanced glycosylation end products, or AGEs, which contribute to artery clogging. For example, the huge United Kingdom Prospective Diabetes Study found that every 1 percent increase in A1c (the standard measure of blood glucose) increases the risk for PAD by 28 percent. Additionally, other studies show that using intensive insulin therapy to keep glucose under control reduces the risk for claudication and other complications of PAD, including amputation.

Don't smoke. Although keeping blood sugar in check is vital, research shows that the most important step you can take to prevent PAD or slow its progression is to avoid tobacco. A 1999 study in the *Archives of Internal Medicine* found that smokers with PAD who gave up cigarettes reduced their risk for limb amputation and for foot pain while resting. The message is clear: If you smoke, quit. If you don't smoke, don't even think about acquiring the evil habit.

Control familiar (and not-so-familiar) cardiovascular risk factors. High blood pressure and elevated cholesterol often go hand-in-hand with PAD. If you have either of these conditions, taking steps to lower them will reduce your risk for heart attacks and strokes. What's more, studies show that lowering elevated

185

cholesterol minimizes symptoms of intermittent claudication and that lowering blood pressure may help, too. However, research also suggests that a less-familiar cardiovascular threat may play a role in PAD, too. Homocysteine is an amino acid found in the blood that some researchers believe plays a role in clogging arteries. Patients with PAD tend to have high homocysteine levels. B vitamins, including folate, help reduce homocysteine levels. While there are no studies showing that high doses of B vitamins reduce the risk or symptoms of PAD, taking a multi-vitamin (which should contain the recommended daily intake of B vitamins) can't hurt.

Lose weight. Taking off a few pounds will relieve pressure on your legs, lightening their burden, which will ease pain.

TREATING PERIPHERAL ARTERY DISEASE

If you have occasional or mild intermittent claudication and other symptoms of PAD, making lifestyle changes and getting some exercise may be all you need to do. If not, your doctor can offer a variety of medical treatments.

Exercise

Your doctor is not a sadist. But, chances are, he or she wants you to exercise your legs, even if it hurts. *Especially* if it hurts, in fact. Although walking long distances and running can cause the pain of intermittent claudication, exercise is an effective treatment for PAD. In fact, more than 20 well-designed studies show that regular exercise is the best therapy for PAD, according to the medical journal *American Family Physician*. A 2005 scientific review of ten studies found that frequent workouts can increase walking time by an average of 150 percent.

A typical regimen for a patient suffering from intermittent claudication might require walking for at least 30 minutes, three times a week, usually supervised by a doctor or a physical therapist. Over time, the patient should try to increase walking time gradually to reach 50 minutes per session. Other exercises may be substituted, but only if they induce claudication; bicycling, for instance, probably won't be much benefit, since it largely involves muscles in the upper legs. Walking or running, meanwhile, uses muscles in the lower legs; as those muscles demand more blood flow, the patient will feel discomfort. Patients are typically encouraged to push themselves right up to the point where the discomfort in their legs reaches about a 3 on a scale of 1 to 5. This is one instance in which you have a lot to gain from a little pain.

Medication

In addition to exercise, your doctor will probably prescribe one or more medications. Unfortunately, physicians steer clear of one effective drug for intermittent claudication, ticlopidine (Ticlid), since it causes a dangerous drop in white blood cells, which the body needs to fight infections. However, one or a combination of these medications may keep you on your feet longer:

Aspirin. Relief from intermittent claudication is cheap and might already be in your medicine chest. The little white pills prevent blood from getting "sticky"; that is, aspirin stops proteins called platelets from clumping together and forming clots. Of course, if you have cardiovascular disease, your doctor may have already instructed you to take

OTHER PILLS FOR PAD

If you surf the Internet or talk to a natural health buff, you may have heard about some of the following treatments for intermittent claudication and other symptoms of PAD. While several are available over the counter, others aren't yet approved for use in this country. One or more of these therapies may hold promise, but more scientific scrutiny is needed.

Naftidrofuryl. A 2005 review found that this medication may relieve pain and increase walking distance in patients with intermittent claudication. However, although it is used in Europe, it is not approved for use in the United States.

Buflomedil. Although it has been approved for use in Europe, this drug has not been adequately studied for treating intermittent claudication.

Ginkgo biloba. This herb, derived from the oldest living species of tree, may offer modest relief from intermittent claudication. (Some studies suggest it works about as well as pentoxifylline.) Keep in mind, however, that the Food and Drug Administration does not closely monitor the quality and efficacy of medicinal herbs and other dietary supplements.

Policosanol. Another dietary supplement, policosanol is made from honeybee wax. Small studies suggest it may ease leg pain caused by circulation problems, but more research is necessary.

Vitamin E. Few reliable studies are available to recommend vitamin E for treating intermittent claudication. It's worth noting, however, that researchers have failed to find much evidence that this vitamin lowers the risk for heart attacks, another problem caused by narrowed arteries.

On the horizon. Scientists are studying the use of amino acids, prostaglandins, and drugs that promote the growth of new blood vessels to treat PAD symptoms. Stay tuned.

an aspirin a day to keep heart attacks away. Aspirin is sometimes recommended in combination with other drugs, including clopidogrel and dipyridamole (see descriptions below). You don't need a prescription to buy aspirin, of course, but talk to your doctor before self-treating leg pain.

Cilostazol (Pletal). This drug widens arteries in the legs and prevents clots from forming. Patients who take cilostazol may feel improvement in as little as two weeks, though it could take up to three months before the medication has any effect. An analysis of eight studies found that diabetes patients with severe PAD who took cilostazol increased the distance they could walk by 34 percent. The most common side effect of cilostazol is headache. Patients with heart failure should not take the drug.

Clopidogrel (Plavix). Although it's chemically similar to ticlopidine, clopidogrel is safer to use. Like aspirin, it prevents blood platelets from sticking together. Studies suggest that clopidogrel reduces symptoms of intermittent claudication somewhat more effectively than aspirin, though it's much more expensive. Clopidogrel may cause fatigue, upset stomach, and other side effects.

Dipyridamole (Persantine). Like clopidogrel, dipyridamole is an antiplatelet drug. It's most commonly used to prevent blood clotting during some types of heart surgery. Some studies have shown that patients with intermittent claudication who combine the drug with aspirin can walk greater distances.

Pentoxifylline (Trental). Although it probably will not be your doctor's first choice, this drug is sometimes prescribed to relieve leg pain and cramps caused by circulation problems. Pentoxifylline changes the shape of red blood cells, which improves blood flow. However, studies consistently find that other drugs do a better job of increasing walking distance in patients with intermittent claudication.

Minimally Invasive Surgery
"Minimally invasive" describes surgery that doesn't require a long incision (which produces an equally long scar and carries the risk of blood loss). Instead of large scalpels, surgeons use small, delicate instruments that are inserted through tiny incisions. To open up a blocked artery in the leg, your doctor may recommend a minimally invasive procedure called balloon angioplasty.

You may have heard this term associated with cardiovascular disease, since the technique is used to clear blockages in the heart's arteries. The same procedure may help improve PAD symptoms. A doctor first inserts a catheter (a slender, flexible tube) into the body through a small hole near the groin and performs an angiogram (see page 184). Injecting a special dye through the catheter helps locate blockages in the leg arteries with an X-ray. The doctor then positions the catheter near serious blockages and inflates a balloonlike device at the tip. As the balloon expands, it pushes aside the clogged-up cholesterol, calcium, and other artery waste in order to increase blood flow.

The problem is, angioplasty is only a temporary solution, since the artery is bound to reclog. So after clearing an artery, doctors often insert a stent, a tiny mesh tube made of metal that holds open a blood vessel. Sounds good in theory, but stents frequently fail because they become grown over with scar tissue and other gunk, a phenomenon known as restenosis. However, newer drug-coated stents may prevent restenosis.

As an alternative to balloon angioplasty, your doctor may recommend an endarterectomy, in which artery plaque is carved away with a blade on the tip of a catheter.

Surgery

If blockages in a leg's blood vessels are large and severe or simply don't respond to conservative treatments, your doctor may attempt to reroute blood flow with bypass surgery. Again, the procedure is similar to the life-saving surgery performed on heart patients with damaged coronary arteries. To replace a blocked blood vessel, a surgeon will first "harvest" a healthy vein from elsewhere in your body. (Don't worry; you have plenty of spare veins.) As an alternative, a synthetic vein may be used. The new vessel is then grafted to healthy arteries and vessels to restore blood flow to the lower limb.

BEYOND FOOT ULCERS: GANGRENE, AMPUTATIONS, AND PROSTHESES

We've been warning throughout this chapter that diabetes can produce very serious foot disease. Now here are the grimmest details of all. The situation is officially desperate when you have these three symptoms:

Pain at rest. Unlike intermittent claudication, which produces achiness while walking, critical limb ischemia results in pain all the time. The only measure that seems to help is suspending the foot in what doctors call the dependent position; the classic example is lying on one's back in bed and dangling the foot over the side, which many people with critical limb ischemia do instinctively to relieve pain.

Wounds that won't heal. If a foot ulcer or other sore does not respond to conservative treatments (antibiotics, regular cleaning and dressing, and other measures) after a 4- to 12-week period, it may not be capable of healing.

Gangrene. This is one word you do not want to hear your doctor utter. Gangrene is the death of tissue, which occurs due to ischemia, or loss of blood flow. Gangrene can become infected, too. When severe PAD cuts off circulation to the feet, gangrene can result. It usually starts in the toes but may spread to the entire foot. Gangrene has the following symptoms:

- Pain, as tissue dies, followed by numbness
- Skin discoloration, with the area usually turning black
- Oozing pus from the edges of the diseased flesh
- Foul odor if the skin is infected
- Fever and general feeling of malaise and illness

A doctor may conduct a test or two to diagnose gangrene, but the disease is so distinctive that most know it when they see it. Patients receive antibiotics to prevent infection. If the skin is already infected, the antibiotics are delivered intravenously. At this advanced stage, bypass surgery or medication may still salvage an endangered toe or foot. However, a doctor may determine that an infection is so aggressive that it could spread throughout the body. In that case, removing the limb may be the only remaining alternative.

Amputation is the surgical removal of an external body part. Surgeons attempt to preserve as much healthy tissue as possible, but the primary goal of amputation surgery is to save your life. Therefore, the surgeon may have to start the amputation above the diseased portion of a limb to ensure that all infected tissue has been removed. Following amputation surgery, the remaining limb (called the residual limb) is wrapped tightly, to help it form a shape suitable for an artificial limb, known as a prosthesis.

Patients who have had limbs amputated can usually begin the process of being fitted for a prosthetic limb about a month or two after surgery. Patients fitted with prosthetic limbs need to visit a prosthetic center frequently for refitting and alignment adjustments. Prosthetic limbs typically last three to five years before needing to be replaced.

Your Eyes and Diabetes

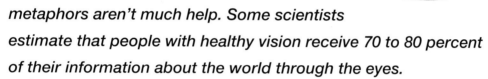

The eyes are the window to the soul, as the old saying goes. And we hold the gift of vision in such high regard that it has become a metaphor for wisdom and prescience. But when your eyesight goes on the blink (pardon the pun), metaphors aren't much help. Some scientists estimate that people with healthy vision receive 70 to 80 percent of their information about the world through the eyes.

When you were diagnosed with diabetes, one of your first thoughts may have been: Does this mean I'll go blind? It's an understandable fear, since diabetes is the number one cause of blindness. However, following the commonsense guidelines in this chapter can help prevent visual impairment.

Keep Looking Sharp: Your Eyes and Diabetes

Within 20 years of being diagnosed with type 1 diabetes, nearly all patients have some evidence of diabetic retinopathy. This common disorder, the result of damage to the retina caused by high glucose levels, is the leading form of eye disease among people with diabetes. It also afflicts type 2 patients, the majority of whom show signs of retinopathy at the time they are diagnosed. Diabetes increases the risk for other common eye diseases, too. While aging causes natural changes to the eyes that can diminish vision—which is why reading glasses have become a baby boomer fashion staple—diabetes can make matters worse. You may only need a stronger prescription or lose some peripheral vision. However, diabetes can also have a devastating impact on eyesight. In one study, 3.6 percent of patients with type 1 diabetes were legally blind, while about half as many type 2 patients had the same degree of vision loss. (See "20/20 Questions," page 198, to learn what it means to be legally blind.)

The Eyes

Like so many body parts, the eyes customarily come in matching pairs. Each eye is roughly one inch in diameter, though only about one-sixth is visible; the rest of the orb is tucked into the eye socket. The portion of the eye seen by the outside world resembles a tiny fried egg, in a way. The white exterior is connective tissue called the sclera, while the colored center, actually a ring of tiny muscle fibers, is known as the iris. The iris contracts and dilates to alter the size of the pupil, a small, dark opening in the middle of the iris that controls how much light enters the eye. (In rare cases, the eyes are not a perfect match; people with a condition called heterochromia have two different-colored irises. For some reason, this phenomenon is more common in some animals, including dogs.)

SEEING THE FUTURE

As with many complications of diabetes, one of the greatest risk factors for developing vision problems caused by high blood sugar is time. That is, the longer you have diabetes, the greater the risk for developing retinopathy. That's especially true if you have type 1 diabetes.

Years After Onset of Type 1 Diabetes	Percentage of Patients with Signs of Retinopathy
3 years	8 percent
5 years	25 percent
10 years	60 percent
15 years	80 percent

The eye is frequently compared to a camera, with good reason. A thin, transparent shell called the cornea protects the outside of the eye and acts as a lens, focusing incoming light, which is directed to a second lens tucked behind the pupil. This interior lens changes shape to adjust the focus, then bounces light to the back of the eye, where a ring of nerve cells called the retina collects light, converting it into electrical messages. These messages are then transferred along the optic nerve to the brain, which interprets the world that our eyes see.

Diabetic Retinopathy

Damage to the retina from high blood sugar interferes with the eye's ability to send information to the brain, a condition called diabetic retinopathy. The condition does not always cause symptoms. Some patients only know they have diabetic retinopathy because doctors discover evidence of the damage in an eye exam. However, the condition can lead to severe vision loss. In fact, diabetic retinopathy is the leading cause of blindness among adults. The National Eye Institute classifies four stages of diabetic retinopathy:

Mild Nonproliferative Retinopathy

The blood vessels in the retina may begin to swell and develop small bulges. Doctors call these bulges microaneurysms, since they resemble the blood vessel abnormalities that cause brain aneurysms. Blood vessels may leak blood or fluid, forming deposits called exudates.

Moderate Nonproliferative Retinopathy

Diabetes causes blockages in blood vessels throughout the body—no exceptions. As retinopathy worsens, the tiny tubes that nourish the retina start to clog.

Severe Nonproliferative Retinopathy

At this stage, so many blood vessels in the retina become blocked that parts of the retina begin to starve. In a panic, the eye signals the brain to build new blood vessels to renourish the deprived parts.

Proliferative Retinopathy

Who does anything well when they're in a panicky rush? The brain triggers the

TROUBLESHOOTING CHECKLIST

Don't dismiss vision problems as the effects of fatigue or advancing middle age, especially if they are persistent or seem to be getting worse. Talk to your physician if you experience any of the following visual disturbances:

- ☐ Blurry vision
- ☐ "Floaters," or spots that dance before your eyes
- ☐ Night blindness
- ☐ Double vision
- ☐ Loss of peripheral vision
- ☐ Difficulty reading
- ☐ A feeling of pressure in the eyes

ROUTINE MAINTENANCE

Damage to the eye's blood supply that leads to vision loss can go on for years before symptoms arise, so regular examinations are critical. Other steps that can prevent eye disease offer additional benefits, such as preventing heart attacks.

- Have your eyes examined at least once a year; your eye doctor should dilate your pupils to check your retinas as part of a thorough examination.
- Maintain tight glucose control.
- Keep your blood pressure down—take blood pressure medication if necessary, eat a healthy diet, and exercise regularly.

growth of new blood vessels, a process called neovascularization. But the new vessels are weak and abnormal.

Nonproliferative retinopathy (sometimes called background retinopathy) may be very mild. A patient may not notice any vision changes and only learn of a problem during an eye exam. However, as blood vessels begin to leak into the retina, vision may blur. Problems become more serious if leaky blood vessels cause the macula, an area in the retina, to swell, interfering with the ability to see fine details. When severe, this problem, called macular edema, can cause blindness. Vision may blur further as the capillaries, or small blood vessels, feeding the macula become blocked.

Proliferative retinopathy gets its name from the way new blood vessels proliferate, or grow rapidly, in the eyes to compensate for blocked or damaged blood vessels. Unfortunately, these frail replacement vessels do far more harm than good. They do a poor job of supplying blood, and these new vessels can break down and leak (or hemorrhage) into the vitreous, a gellike substance in the center of the eye. A minor leak may result only in the appearnace of a few "floaters" (spots that dance before your eyes). If you have floaters, see an eye care professional for treatment as soon as possible to prevent more serious bleeding. A major vitreous hemorrhage can cause significant vision loss and even blindness. The growth of new blood vessels can also produce scarring that may cause the retina to wrinkle or become detached, further damaging eyesight.

Early signs that you may be developing diabetic retinopathy include
- blurry vision
- "floaters"
- night blindness
- double vision
- loss of peripheral vision
- difficulty reading
- a feeling of pressure in the eyes

Other Eye Disorders You Should Know About

Diabetic retinopathy is the most common eye disease that afflicts people with diabetes, and it is the leading cause of blindness in American adults. But people with diabetes are also at greater risk for two other eye diseases: glaucoma and cataracts.

Glaucoma

This disease, which afflicts about three million Americans, accounts for 9 to 12 percent of all cases of blindness in the United States. Glaucoma occurs when fluid fails to drain properly from the eyes, causing pressure to build and damage the optic nerve. There are several types of glaucoma. Diabetes raises the risk for neovascular glaucoma, a rare form of the disease. Diabetic retinopathy may cause the growth of new blood vessels on the iris, shutting off the flow of fluid and increasing pressure inside the eye. People with diabetes may be up to twice as likely to develop glaucoma as the general public.

Cataracts

More than half of Americans older than 80 have a cataract or have had cataract surgery, yet diabetes patients are 60 percent more likely than others to develop this eye disorder. A cataract is a cloudiness caused by changes to fibers in the eye lens. Although a cataract may not cause complete blindness, it can block enough light to obscure visual details and clarity.

Preventing Diabetic Retinopathy

If you're reading this book, then there's some good news: It's not too late to take important steps to save your sight. Here are three things you can do that will help you keep reading for many years. (One step that may not be an option for you is to avoid becoming a mother, since having a baby increases the risk of retinopathy in women with type 1 diabetes. You can read more about the link between pregnancy and retinopathy in Chapter 17.)

Maintain Tight Glucose Control

The Diabetes Control and Complications Trial showed that aggressive insulin therapy dramatically reduces the risk of vision loss. In that study, researchers compared type 1 diabetes patients who gave themselves three or more insulin injections per day (or had an insulin pump) with another group of patients who received one or two insulin injections daily. At the start of the study, none of the patients had signs of retinopathy. After an average of 6.5 years, patients in the aggressive-treatment group were 76 percent less likely to have developed retinopathy. (In an accompanying trial, patients who started with mild signs of retina damage cut in half their risk of further vision loss if they received aggressive insulin treatment.)

OPTOMETRIST OR OPHTHALMOLOGIST: WHAT'S THE DIFFERENCE?

There are two types of eye-care professionals who are qualified to examine your peepers for problems. Understanding the differences in their education and training can help you decide which professional to see.

An optometrist, or doctor of optometry, has an O.D. after his or her name. If you wear eyeglasses or contact lenses, you probably had your eyes examined and received the prescription for your lenses from an optometrist. (However, you probably purchased your glasses from an optician; in some states, opticians dispense contact lenses, too.) Optometrists are not medical doctors but must have an undergraduate degree, then complete a four-year program at an accredited optometry school. Although they do not perform surgery, optometrists treat patients before and after eye operations. They can also prescribe eye medications.

An ophthalmologist, on the other hand, is a medical doctor (M.D.) or doctor of osteopathy (or D.O., who receives similar education as a medical doctor, with additional training in "manual medicine," or manipulation of the muscles and bones). In addition to a bachelor's degree, an ophthalmologist attends four years of medical school, followed by a one-year internship and three-year residency. Ophthalmologists conduct eye exams, treat diseases and injuries (including performing surgery), and prescribe drugs.

You can receive excellent care and treatment from either an optometrist or ophthalmologist. Your physician or diabetes educator may be able to help you locate an eye doctor who specializes in working with diabetes patients.

Lower Your Blood Pressure

There are plenty of good reasons to keep blood pressure under control, such as lowering the risk for cardiovascular disease. However, high blood pressure also damages blood vessels in the retina, setting the stage for retinopathy. People with high blood pressure seem to have a higher risk for macular edema, as well. A large British study of more than 1,100 type 2 diabetes patients found that lowering high blood pressure reduced the risk of retinopathy by 34 percent over an eight-year period. Patients who maintained healthy blood pressure had sharper vision, too. (Not surprisingly, they also had fewer heart attacks and strokes.)

Don't Smoke

And not just because all those clouds of smoke produced by puffing can obscure your vision; tobacco users have a higher risk for diabetic retinopathy.

Diagnosing Diabetic Retinopathy

The American Diabetes Association recommends that all patients with type 1 disease undergo comprehensive screening for retinopathy within five years of being diagnosed with diabetes. Type 2 patients should have their eyes thoroughly examined soon after they are

diagnosed with diabetes. After the initial screening, all diabetes patients should have an annual eye exam unless your doctor feels that less-frequent check-ups (every two or three years, instead) are adequate.

If you need inspiration to consult your calendar right now and make an appointment with an eye doctor, consider the following:

- In its early stages, diabetic retinopathy may not cause any symptoms, such as blurred vision or floaters. Even so, the blood vessels in your eyes may already be seriously injured.
- Damage to blood vessels in the eyes is often irreversible. That's what makes early detection of eye disease so important. Your doctor has effective treatments that can stop the progression of diabetic retinopathy, but there is no cure for the condition.

Eye exams are performed by an optometrist or ophthalmologist. Try to find one who has experience in diagnosing and treating people with diabetes. (See page 196 for an explanation of the difference between an optometrist and an ophthalmologist.)

An eye doctor starts by checking your visual acuity—that is, how well you can see—by asking you to read tiny letters on a wall across the room. Your doctor will also ask you to follow a moving light with your eyes to see whether their

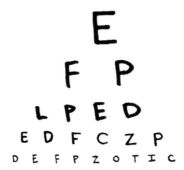

muscles work properly. And the doctor will determine how well your pupils respond to light by shining a beam into your eyes.

Next, your doctor will check for signs of eye disease. Tests may include the following:

Ophthalmoscopic exam. An ophthalmoscope is basically a strong flashlight with a magnifier. Doctors use an ophthalmoscope to examine the internal parts of the eye, especially the retina, its blood vessels, and the optic disc, which is the point where the optic nerve meets the retina. To get a better view, the doctor may put special drops in the eyes that dilate the pupils.

Fundus photography. The term fundus refers to the deepest part of a structure; in this case it means the back of the eye. Your doctor may use a special camera to scan and photograph the backs of your eyes to detect signs of retinopathy.

Glaucoma tests. Doctors use several different devices called tonometers to measure pressure inside the eyes, which can indicate the presence of glaucoma. One of the most widely used methods is called air-puff tonometry. To perform the test, your doctor will stabilize your head by having you rest your chin on a padded stand. Then, while you stare at a bright light, the tonometer emits a soft puff of air at your eye. The instrument measures how the air puff changes the light reflected off the cornea. Other types of tonometer are available. Some use pencil- or wandlike devices that are touched to the eye to measure internal pressure.

Fluorescein angiography. If your doctor suspects diabetic retinopathy, this test may be used to "map" the blood vessels of the eye to determine which ones are leaking or blocked. The doctor first injects a dye into a vein in the arm,

20/20 QUESTIONS

Ever wonder what 20/20 vision is? If your eye doctor says you have it, that means you can read random letters that are ⅜ inch tall from a distance of 20 feet. (Try this at home: Type a few letters in 30-point characters on a computer screen and stand 20 feet away. If you can read them, you have what's considered normal vision.) Although sometimes referred to as "perfect" vision, 20/20 only measures the ability of your eye to see at a distance. There are many other factors to consider before you would be considered to have perfect vision. Some people have exceptional vision, measured as 20/10: They can see at 20 feet what people with "normal" vision can see at 10 feet. People who are legally blind can't read letters ⅜ inch high beyond a distance of two feet.

which allows a special camera to photograph the vessels in the retina and other structures in the eye.

Treating Diabetic Retinopathy

Your eye doctor doesn't insist on seeing you at least once a year because he or she admires your charm and sparkling wit. Early intervention can save your sight or at least prevent it from getting worse if it's already failing. If you have diabetic retinopathy, one of these two procedures may be in your future:

Laser photocoagulation surgery
One way to treat diabetic retinopathy is with a device that performs light amplification by the stimulated emission of radiation—better known as a "laser." ("Photo-" means "light" and "coagulate"

LASER SHARP

Thanks to advances in medicine and technology, many former "four-eyes" have tossed out their spectacles and chosen to have laser surgery to fix lens defects that cause near- and farsightedness. The best known surgical procedure is called LASIK (an acronym for "laser in situ keratomileusis"). Most doctors agree that some diabetes patients can undergo laser surgery to sharpen vision, while others are not good candidates. One major problem: Rising glucose can blur vision, which improves on its own as blood sugar drops. If your glucose is unstable, the results of LASIK surgery are bound to be disappointing. Some doctors also worry that the corneas of some patients with diabetes may not heal properly or that the procedure may further damage the retinas of a patient with retinopathy.

A 2002 study found that diabetes patients who undergo LASIK have higher-than-average rates of post-surgical complications. What's more, compared to patients with normal blood sugar, diabetes patients had poorer results, as measured by how well the procedure improved vision. However, a 2005 study of 24 diabetes patients (7 had type 1, while the remainder had type 2) determined that 43 out of 48 eyes were successfully treated, resulting in significantly improved vision. What was the key? The patients had well-controlled glucose. If you have poor eyesight and are considering laser eye surgery, ask your doctor if you are a good candidate.

In one study, researchers compared a group of patients who underwent laser photocoagulation to treat neovascularization (growth of weak blood vessels in the eyes) or bleeding in the vitreous with a group of similar patients who did not receive the treatment. Just 11 percent of the treated patients progressed to severe vision loss versus 26 percent of the untreated patients.

Vitrectomy

Doctors use this procedure when blood has leaked into the vitreous, causing severe proliferative diabetic retinopathy. As you may know, "-ectomy" means "removal by surgery." If blood has filled the vitreous, blurring vision, it may eventually be reabsorbed by the body. If not, a surgeon may remove the vitreous, along with the abnormal blood vessels causing the problem in the first place. The vitreous is replaced with a clear solution.

refers to clotting.) These light-emitting tools can be used to treat proliferative retinopathy, macular edema, and neo-vascular glaucoma. By zapping trouble-making blood vessels growing out of control in the retina, a laser can slow or stop the progression of proliferative retinopathy, though the treatments do not cure the disease. The same is usually true of laser treatments for macular edema, though some patients may experience small improvements.

Your Skin and Diabetes

If you are tempted to flip past this chapter because you think skin care is for sissies, think again, buster. Skin damage is a major complication of diabetes, with the potential to produce everything from barely noticeable blemishes to disfiguring scars. What's more, maintaining healthy skin is crucial for warding off disease and protecting your innards from the perils of the outside world.

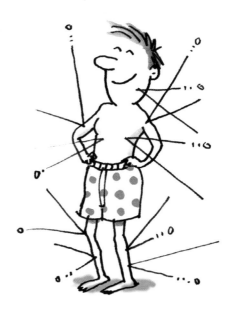

As the following pages will persuade you, every diabetes patient should get to know his or her skin better. By examining yourself every day, from head to toe, you may be able to spot small problems before they turn into serious ones. And, as you'll learn, the skin problems described in this chapter can serve as a caution that greater health concerns may lie beneath the surface.

The Bare Facts:
Your Skin and Diabetes

Diabetes patients do not have a monopoly on skin problems. Hardly! Walk into any pharmacy or supermarket and you will find aisles overflowing with emollients, creams, astringents, and salves—evidence that damaged skin is a consuming cosmetic and medical concern for the general population. However, having diabetes appears to increase the risk for rashes, sores, and other conditions that affect your facade. According to the American Diabetes Association, about one-third of patients will develop a skin disorder at some point.

The skin on your lower extremities is particularly vulnerable to problems; see Chapter 10, which—like a good pair of shoes—covers your feet.

THE SKIN

As every child learns in school, the skin is the largest organ *in* the body. Your hide has a surface area of about two square yards and weighs about 10 pounds. Technically, you could say that the skin is the largest organ on the body, since it acts as a protective covering for your bones, muscles, and organs. However, the skin is more than mere armor, with many of its critical roles performed below the exterior.

The body's outer shell, called the epidermis, is made up of a top layer of skin cells that are dead. That's just as well, since they are constantly flaking and peeling off anyway. Fortunately, the body replaces these so-called horny cells just as quickly with new ones, as cells in the lower layer of the epidermis divide. Some cells in the epidermis produce melanin, the pigment that provides skin color.

Beneath the epidermis lies the dermis. Hidden from sight, this layer is packed with vital equipment that keeps the skin healthy and performs various functions. In the health-and-beauty department, there are hair follicles and sebaceous glands, which produce oil called sebum that moistens the skin. The dermis also contains nerve endings, which detect pain and pressure and govern the sense of touch. They also sense temperature, advising the brain when it's time to slip on a sweater or change into shorts. Furthermore, the dermis is home to sweat glands, which help regulate body temperature by producing cooling perspiration. Blood vessels constrict to conserve body heat when you're cold,

TROUBLESHOOTING CHECKLIST

If you have always wanted to splurge on a full-length mirror, now would be the time. A good handheld mirror would help, too. Using these tools to examine every inch of your skin daily can help detect small problems before they turn really ugly. Talk to your doctor if any of the following skin changes occur and persist:

☐ Itchiness

☐ Redness, inflammation

☐ Scaliness

☐ Lumps, especially if they leak discharge (which is a nicer word than "pus")

☐ Pain

☐ Discoloration, blotches, or any other changes in appearance

☐ Blisters

☐ Shininess, hair loss

☐ "Thick" skin

along with their usual duties of providing nourishment to all of the skin and its various structures.

The third and innermost tier of the skin is called the subcutaneous layer. Mostly made up of fat, it provides insulation and protects bones and organs from bumps and bangs.

HOW DIABETES AFFECTS YOUR SKIN

High blood sugar can rough up smooth skin in several ways. Elevated glucose results in high levels of compounds called advanced glycosylation end products (AGEs), which damage nerves and blood vessels that are necessary to keep skin healthy. However, your body's defense against high blood sugar may cause collateral damage to the epidermis, as you'll read in a moment. The first two major conditions we'll discuss, dry skin and skin infections, are common medical problems that can affect anyone, whether they have diabetes or not. However, people who have the disease are far more likely to develop these skin conditions. Many of the lesser-known skin problems discussed later primarily afflict diabetes patients.

Dry Skin

If you spend all day scratching and your skin would make an iguana blush, chances are you're going to flunk your next blood-sugar test. When glucose levels rise too high, the body tries to get rid of the excess sugar through frequent urination. The more you urinate, the more fluid your body loses. If you don't replace that lost fluid by guzzling lots of water, you become dehydrated, which causes (among other symptoms) dry skin.

As skin loses moisture, it becomes itchy. In severe cases, red scales may form. Scratching can cause sores to crack, opening the skin to an invasion of infectious bacteria. (See Skin Infections, page 205.) Damage to blood vessels and nerve endings in the skin from high glucose levels makes matters worse.

Of course, you don't need diabetes to develop dry skin. But people with diabetes need to be particularly wary of the environmental influences that can turn anyone's skin to parchment. In cold climates, winter is a worrisome time, since heating systems sap the air of indoor humidity and cold winds chap the skin. Hot showers or baths with soaps and shampoos strip sebum from the skin any time of year.

To Prevent Dry Skin:

Shorten your showers. Long, hot showers or baths may feel great, but they strip away natural oil that keeps skin soft and moist. Bathe in warm water, use mild soap and shampoo, and don't linger too long. Pat dry with a towel.

DRY SKIN: IS IT YOUR MEDS?

Many commonly prescribed drugs can cause dry skin. Talk to your physician if your skin is parched and you take prescription medications, especially any of these:

- Statin drugs, such as atorvastatin (Lipitor) and simvastatin (Zocor), which lower cholesterol
- Nicotinic acid (niacin), used to increase HDL ("good") cholesterol
- Diuretics, used to lower blood pressure
- Isotretinoin (Accutane), prescribed to treat acne
- Etretinate (Tegison), prescribed to treat psoriasis. Dry skin can also be a side effect of diuretics.

And don't overdo it: Cleanliness may be next to godliness, but bathing too frequently will dry your skin.

Stay well lubed. Apply skin moisturizer after you bathe. Ask your doctor to recommend a brand. Slather the stuff on liberally everywhere except between the toes, which should be kept dry to avoid the nasty fungal infections you'll read about later.

Drink up. Water, that is, to keep your body well hydrated.

Get misty. Unless you live in a tropical climate, use a humidifier to keep the air in your home and workplace from becoming dry during cold winter months.

SKIN INFECTIONS

Skin infections can afflict anyone, too, though doctors agree that having diabetes greatly increases the risk for an invasion of microscopic meanies. The bacteria called *Staphylococcus aureus* (better known as staph) and the fungus *Candida albicans* cause many of the skin infections that are most common among people with diabetes.

Some of the more common bacterial skin infections to watch out for include these:

Boils. (Warning: The following definition gets pretty icky, fast.) Boils are painful red lumps that usually occur when bacteria infect a hair follicle. As inflammation worsens, the boil fills with pus and forms a yellow head before rupturing and draining. (Told you so.) Any part of the skin can develop a boil, though these ghastly little sores seem to like hairy areas, for obvious reasons, especially where you sweat a lot. (That means that the face, neck, armpits, and other sweat-inducing zones are most likely to get "boiled.")

Treatment: Hot compresses may relieve pain and make a boil heal faster. If a painful boil persists, see a doctor, who may drain the sore and give you a prescription for antibiotics. Above all, don't squeeze or pop a boil, which could worsen an infection.

Carbuncles. When a bunch of boils gang together, they form a carbuncle.

Treatment: Carbuncles are more serious than single boils, so see a doctor.

Sties. A sty is like a boil, only it forms on the edge of or under the eyelids. A sty

205

A Scary Fungus Among Us

Fungal infections usually produce itchy, uncomfortable, and aesthetically displeasing skin rashes. But people with diabetes have a heightened risk for becoming infected with a potentially deadly fungus that causes a condition called mucormycosis (sometimes called zygomycosis). The problem starts with a common fungus from the class known as phycomycetes, which is found in soil and dying plants. Most people encounter this fungus every day without worry. But anyone whose immune system isn't working at full power—including patients with poorly controlled diabetes—may be vulnerable to these germs. Mucormycosis usually begins as a sinus infection, but inflammation may spread to the brain, lungs, or heart, resulting in blood clots or pneumonia. Mucormycosis can afflict the gastrointestinal tract, skin, and kidneys, too. Symptoms may include

- sinusitis (nasal discharge, with pain, pressure, or tenderness in the sinus region)
- fever
- swollen or protruding eyes
- scabs in the nasal passage
- red skin around the nose
- coughing or vomiting, especially if it produces blood
- shortness of breath
- abdominal pain
- pain in the flank, or lower back beneath the rib cage

Mucormycosis is a serious condition that requires immediate medical attention. Contact your physician if these symptoms develop and persist.

may be painful or grow large enough to block vision.

Treatment: Warm compresses may relieve pain and encourage a sty to shrink, but see a doctor if the problem persists. Antibiotic creams can help heal a sty and prevent recurrence. Never squeeze or pierce a sty.

Some of the more common fungal infections (also known as *tinea corporis*) to afflict people with diabetes include these related conditions:

Athlete's foot. You don't have to be a super-jock to get this itchy, scaly menace; you can read about it in Chapter 10, which is devoted to the various and all-too-common forms of diabetic foot disease.

Jock itch. Likewise, you don't have to wear an athletic supporter to develop this uncomfortable condition, though those snug-fitting protective garments can contribute to the problem (which explains why jock itch usually afflicts males). Also known as *tinea cruris,* the problem begins as an itchy red rash around the genitals, which can spread to the inner thigh.

Ringworm. As the name suggests, this fungal infection forms ring-shape scales on the skin that may itch. (Fortunately, it doesn't mean you have worms, though having an infectious fungus is nothing to brag about.) Ringworm often develops on the scalp, though it can turn up on other parts of the body. Ringworm of the toenails and fingernails, called onychomycosis, is a common problem. The nails turn thick and discolored, and there's not much your manicurist can do about it.

Fungal infections can turn up on other parts of the body. Over-the-counter medications may help, but your physician can prescribe a more powerful antifungal drug to clear up persistent problems.

To Prevent Skin Infections:

Keep it clean. We know, we know, we just got done telling you that bathing too often can worsen dry skin. But that doesn't mean you should turn into Pigpen. A thorough daily cleaning will keep bacteria at bay.

Keep it dry. Again, isn't dry skin a threat? Yes, but so are dark, damp places on the body, such as between the toes and under your arms, where fungus can grow. Using a little talcum powder on areas where skin rubs against skin isn't a bad idea.

MORE SKIN PROBLEMS

The following conditions are less common than dry skin and skin infections (some are downright rare). Some are merely cosmetic problems, while others produce physical symptoms. Recognizing them can help you get prompt medical attention and prevent needless worry.

Acanthosis nigricans (AN)

This condition produces thick, dark patches on the body; doctors sometimes say the skin appears velvety. The armpits, back, neck, and other regions prone to sweating are most often afflicted. AN may occur because an unknown "trigger" in the body causes skin cells to accumulate. Some doctors believe excess insulin is one potential trigger, which may be why AN appears to be more common in people with type 2 diabetes. In fact, while AN doesn't hurt

ROUTINE MAINTENANCE

Don't dismiss skin care as a mere cosmetic concern. A healthy hide helps guard your body against infections and other serious internal diseases. Taking the following steps will help you avoid minor annoyances, such as itching, as well as major complications.

- Control your blood sugar.
- Avoid long, hot showers and baths.
- Keep your skin clean, but don't bathe too often, especially in cold months.
- Apply moisturizer (except between the toes) after bathing.
- Put a damper on dry air; use a humidifier in your home and workplace.
- Drink plenty of water.

or itch, it's a signal to doctors that a patient may have insulin resistance. (A rare form of AN has been linked to cancerous tumors.) Given its association with type 2 diabetes, it's no surprise that AN is more common in obese people; it also seems to be more prevalent in people with dark skin.

Bumps and Bruises

If you inject insulin, you may develop bruises or swollen lumps of fat (known as lipo-hypertrophy) if you don't rotate injection sites on the skin. Read about this unsightly problem in Chapter 3.

Diabetic Blisters

Sometimes called *bullosis diabeticorum,* this uncommon problem is most likely to afflict someone with diabetic neuropathy, or nerve damage that is caused by elevated blood sugar levels. Blisters, like those you might get from a serious burn, may form on the hands, fingers, arms, legs, feet, or toes. Although they are usually painless, diabetic blisters may be alarming. If you get one, though, don't worry; they will usually heal on their own, especially if you get your blood sugar under control.

Diabetic Dermopathy

This common diabetes-related skin problem is also known as "shin spots," since it usually appears on the front of the lower legs. The shiny round or oval brown spots develop as tiny blood vessels in the legs narrow and thicken. Shin spots are usually harmless other than mild itching or burning, so they don't require treatment.

Diabetic Thick Skin

No one likes being called "thin skinned," but your doctor isn't paying you a compliment if he or she says your skin is thick. It's not clear why, but diabetes patients tend to have thicker-than-average hides. The problem can take one of several forms. In digital sclerosis, the digits in question are the fingers and toes, but this term includes the back of the hands, too. The skin not only thickens; it turns waxy-looking and feels tight. The joints may stiffen, too. When the skin on the back of the neck or upper back thickens, doctors call the problem *scleroderma diabeticorum*. Lotions or moisturizers may help soften the skin.

Disseminated Granuloma Annulare

Similar in appearance to *necrobiosis lipoidica diabeticorum* (see opposite page), this condition causes a ring-shape rash that is red, brown, or sometimes simply a slightly different shade than one's skin. It can spring up on the trunk, neck, arms, legs, and even the ears. If the rash is hidden from sight, you may not require any treatment, since it doesn't ache or itch. To treat the condition for cosmetic purposes, doctors usually prescribe steroids.

Eruptive Xanthomatosis (EX)

As the name suggests, eruptive xanthomatosis creates bulging deposits of yellowish fat in the skin. The thinner the skin, the more noticeable the eruption, which is why the eyelids are so commonly affected (a problem doctors call xanthelasma). However, EX can pop up in other parts of the body, particularly the buttocks. In addition to itching, the lumpy skin is usually rimmed in red. This is not many people's idea of an attractive look, but EX is more than a cosmetic concern. These skin eruptions form when unhealthy levels of fats called triglycerides build up in the blood because your body has become resistant to insulin and cannot get rid of them. In other words, lumpy skin may be the least of your worries. Treatment consists of eating a healthy diet and taking medication to control glucose and blood fats.

Necrobiosis Lipoidica Diabeticorum (NLD)

This rare condition produces blotches on the skin, too, in the form of large, reddish-brown, scarlike sores. Over

GUM DISEASE: IT'S NOTHING TO SMILE ABOUT

You may not think of the moist tissue that lines the inside of your mouth as skin, but it is. And, like your external covering, the skin inside your pie hole can become infected. In fact, having diabetes is one of the leading risk factors for gum disease, also known as periodontal disease. Bacteria in the mouth can infect the gums, causing inflammation known as gingivitis. Left untreated, the problem can deteriorate to periodontitis, or the breakdown of bone and tissue that hold your choppers in place, resulting in lost teeth. Studies show that diabetes patients who don't maintain tight glucose control have an especially high risk for periodontal disease. In addition to keeping blood sugar under control, regular brushing and flossing are the keys to keeping your smile intact.

time, the sores may turn yellow. NLD can be itchy and painful. (Patients without diabetes may develop the condition, in which case doctors just call it *necrobiosis lipoidica*.) NLD is three times more common in women than in men. No one knows why or what causes the condition. However, it appears to occur as collagen (fiber that holds cells together) breaks down beneath the skin. There is no treatment for NLD, but if a sore breaks open, it requires prompt medical attention.

Vitiligo

Certain diseases, including type 1 diabetes, seem to predispose people to developing this harmless but cosmetically bothersome skin condition. Like type 1 diabetes, vitiligo is an autoimmune disorder, meaning it occurs when the body's immune system mistakenly attacks healthy cells. In this case, the victims are melanocytes, cells that make skin pigment. Vitiligo produces pale patches of discolored skin. The hands, arms, and other parts of the body that receive a lot of sun exposure are most commonly affected, though any portion of your epidermis is vulnerable.

Yellow Skin

No one is certain why, but people with diabetes occasionally develop a yellowish hue to their skin and nails. According to one theory, the problem occurs because some varieties of those irksome advanced glycosylation end products (AGEs) we talked about earlier are yellow in color. If your glucose isn't under control, AGEs accumulate in the blood, which may tint the skin. Although having jaundiced skin is no fun, there is no treatment other than regaining control over blood sugar.

Diet, Exercise, and Diabetes

Discussing diet and exercise at the same time may seem impractical, like trying to jog while eating a turkey sandwich. But when you have diabetes, food and physical activity must be part of the same conversation. The types of fuel you choose for your body, when you add them to your tank, and how much you burn will all influence your blood sugar control and risk for diabetes-related complications.

If you have type 1 diabetes, it's essential to balance what you eat—and when—with how active you plan to be on a given day. If you have type 2 diabetes, choosing the right foods and doing some serious huffing and puffing could slow the progression of your symptoms, reducing—even eliminating—the need for medication. This chapter offers some guidance on what to do after you slip on the bib or lace up your running shoes.

Diet and Diabetes: Shaking Off Sugar Myths

Before the discovery of insulin in 1921, the primary treatment for diabetes was diet therapy. Doctors put patients with diabetes on a very low-carb and very low-calorie diet—basically a starvation diet. The diagnosis of diabetes in those days was a death sentence; patients died within two years either from starvation or ketoacidosis, a buildup of toxic acids in the blood.

The availability of insulin changed everything—but not right away. In theory, diabetes patients who injected the critical hormone could now eat a potato, a slice of bread, or any other carbohydrate-rich food without fear that their blood sugar would soar. Still, doctors remained cautious about carbs for many years. In the early 1960s, however, scientists showed that a high-carbohydrate, low-fat diet was not only safe for people with diabetes, it also helped lower cholesterol.

Even then, most doctors still assumed that diabetes patients had to avoid so-called "simple" carbohydrates such as table sugar and honey, believing that these sweeteners broke down too rapidly, causing blood glucose to spike. Doctors counseled patients to get their fix of carbs from starchy foods, assum-

ing that the body took longer to take apart these so-called "complex" carbohydrates, meaning they would enter the bloodstream more gradually.

By the 1990s, researchers had demonstrated that such sugar-phobia was unfounded. Studies showed that the *type* of carbohydrates a diabetes patient consumes is less important than the *amount* of carbohydrates he or she eats in a given day. Yet, many people with high blood sugar still assume that cherished foods containing a lot of sugar, such as candy, cakes, and ice cream, are strictly off limits.

What's more, newly diagnosed patients often think that they have to go on a "diabetic diet" and are surprised to hear that there is no such thing. In fact, the

ideal diet for a diabetes patient looks a lot like the ideal diet for anyone who wants to stay healthy and reduce disease risk. However, to be sure you're eating foods that keep your blood sugar in the healthy range and minimize your risk for diabetes complications, it's likely that your physician will refer you to a diabetes educator or registered dietitian who can help you devise a personalized meal plan.

When recommending the types and quantities of foods you should eat, a diet and nutrition expert will take into account

- your age
- your weight, and whether you need to lose some (or a lot)
- your height
- how often and how hard you exercise
- whether or not you inject insulin or use insulin-promoting medications
- other drugs you may be taking
- your personal tastes
- your cultural and religious heritage

Determining a safe and healthy amount of carbohydrates for you to consume each day is the bedrock of a comprehensive meal plan. However, it is only the beginning. A well-designed diet for a diabetes patient should

- reduce the risk of hypoglycemia
- reduce the risk for diabetes compli-

WHAT IS A REGISTERED DIETITIAN?

Registered dietitians are nutrition experts who work in a variety of settings, including hospitals, clinics, and private practice. A registered dietitian has to earn a bachelor's degree from an accredited university or college (some attain advanced degrees) and participate in a 6- to 12-month professional training program at a health care facility, community agency, or food-service corporation. The candidate must then pass an exam administered by the Commission on Dietetic Registration. Some registered dietitians specialize in diabetes education. Your doctor or diabetes educator can recommend a registered dietitian to help you design a healthy meal plan. If you go shopping for a nutritionist to work with on your own, look for an "R.D." after his or her name. A great place to start is the American Dietetic Association Web site, www.eatright.org.

cations and conditions that often accompany blood-sugar problems, including heart disease, stroke, high cholesterol, high blood pressure, and kidney disease
- provide all the vitamins, minerals, and nutrients you need to keep your body running in top form
- control weight
- instruct patients who use insulin or take diabetes drugs how to adjust

ARTIFICIAL SWEETENERS: SHOULD YOU SHIRK SUGAR?

Sure, if you're looking for a way to lower your carbohydrate and calorie intake. Also called sugar substitutes, these man-made products add sweetness to foods and drinks. But because they are so intensely sweet, only tiny amounts are needed, meaning they add few or no calories and carbs to foods. That means they won't make you fat or raise blood sugar.

Although some studies have raised questions about the safety of certain artificial sweeteners over the years, there is no conclusive evidence that any of the four approved by the U.S. Food and Drug Administration pose a health threat. Here they are, with their sweetness relative to sugar:

- Saccharin (Sweet'N Low) is 300 times sweeter than sugar.
- Aspartame (NutraSweet and Equal) is 180 times sweeter than sugar.
- Acesulfame potassium (Sunett) is 200 times sweeter than sugar.
- Sucralose (Splenda) is 600 times sweeter than sugar.

There are a few precautions to consider before using artificial sweeteners: Pregnant and breast-feeding women should not use saccharin, while people with a hereditary condition called phenylketonuria should not consume aspartame.

medication levels to accommodate changes in a meal routine

This chapter offers some general concepts and basic rules that will help you to understand and follow a meal plan designed to control blood sugar and prevent the array of medical problems high blood sugar can cause. (Children and pregnant or lactating women with diabetes have special dietary needs, which will be discussed in later chapters.)

NUTRIENTS 101: SOME STUFF YOU SHOULD KNOW ABOUT WHAT YOU STUFF IN YOUR MOUTH

Here's a brief primer on the three basic nutrients you require: carbohydrates, protein, and fat.

What Are Carbohydrates?

Potatoes and pinto beans. Carrots and cauliflower. Rye bread and rock candy. These foods have one thing in common: They're all sources of carbohydrates, which are the body's favorite source of

energy. Although they are made up of only carbon, hydrogen, and oxygen, carbohydrates come in all shapes and sizes. They are found in fruits, vegetables, grains, beans, dairy foods, and just about everything you eat other than meat, fish, or fat. Broadly speaking, carbohydrates fall into three categories:

Sugars. The word "sugar" may make you think of the white granules you spoon into coffee or add to baked goods, but the sweet stuff comes in many varieties. Made up of relatively simple combinations of molecules, the sugars include sucrose (found in table sugar and some fruits and vegetables), fructose (found in fruit and honey), and lactose (found in milk), among others.

Starches. Although they consist of sugar units, the complex structure of starches makes them a distinct type of carbohydrate. (In fact, nutritionists used to call starches "complex carbohydrates," though the term has fallen out of favor with many of them.) The large size of starch molecules also sets them apart from sugars; they're too big for taste bud receptors on the tongue, which is why starches usually don't taste sweet. Starchy foods include potatoes, bread, pasta, and rice.

Fiber. Your grandma called it "roughage." Your gut calls it "indigestible." Like starch, fiber is made up of an intricate array of sugar molecules. But the sugar molecules in fiber aren't absorbed into the bloodstream as fiber passes through the gastrointestinal tract; that's because the body lacks enzymes to break it down. But even though fiber isn't a nutrient, per se, it does plenty of good, as you'll read later. Only plant foods naturally contain fiber; some rich sources include wheat bran and oat bran.

While all foods cause glucose levels to rise, carbohydrates have the swiftest impact, producing an increase in blood sugar within two hours of a meal. However, several factors—such as how much fiber or fat the meal includes—can affect speed of digestion. About half of your calories (from 45 to 65 percent) should come from carbohydrates.

Protein

The bricks and mortar of every inch of tissue in your body, protein comes primarily from animal foods, including meat, fish, eggs, and dairy foods. However, beans are an

excellent, if underappreciated, source. The body breaks down protein into smaller amino acids. The main role of amino acids is to construct and repair muscles, organs, and other body tissue, although these little protein-ettes can be converted to glucose for use as energy when carbohydrates are in short supply.

Fat

Until carb-bashing became fashionable in the 1990s, fat endured many years as the number-one nutritional villain. Neither rogue nor hero, fat is an essential nutrient that just happens to make many decadent foods taste delicious. During digestion, fats break down into fatty acids, which serve several roles. Your body uses fatty acids as a backup source of energy, though it also deploys fat to build cell membranes, insulate and pad organs, and dissolve certain vitamins (which allows them to enter the bloodstream). There are four basic types of fat:

Saturated fat. Fat molecules are made up of chains of carbon atoms with attached pairs of hydrogen atoms. Scientists say this form of fat is "saturated" because each molecule is packed to the rafters with hydrogen. For complex chemical, biological, and anthropological reasons, many human beings (especially in the western hemisphere) find the taste of saturated fat to be exceptionally yummy. Whole milk, ice cream, butter, and juicy steaks are all rich sources of saturated fat. Need we say more? Yes: Saturated fat also causes a rise in LDL cholesterol, the bad kind that lodges in arteries and increases the risk of cardiovascular disease.

Monounsaturated fat. These fat molecules are missing one chain of hydrogen atoms ("mono-" means "one"). Foods that are very high in monounsaturated fat are liquid at room temperature and include olive, nut, and canola oils. Avocados and most nuts are good sources, too. Unlike the saturated variety, monounsaturated fats are good for you, since they lower LDL cholesterol.

Polyunsaturated fat. Margarine, many kinds of vegetable oil (including corn oil), and fish are all sources of polyunsaturated fats, which are made up of molecules missing more than one pair of hydrogen atoms. While polyunsaturated fats don't get the bad press saturated fat receives, one type—known as omega-6 fatty acids—has been linked to health problems, including high blood pressure, an elevated risk for blood clotting, and low levels of HDL ("good") cholesterol. On the other hand, the omega-3 fatty acids in fish oil appear to be good for the heart. Evidence suggests that they reduce the risk of sudden cardiac death (which is caused by erratic heart rhythm), in addition to lowering cholesterol and triglycerides.

Trans *fat.* This form of unsaturated fat has been chemically altered to prolong its shelf life. And shelves—in your local supermarket—are just where you'll find these fats, which are used heavily in commercial baking. Many cookies, cakes, chips, crackers, and pastries contain *trans* fats, and that's just the start. *Trans* fats are often used in frying, so many fast foods are laden with the stuff. They also turn up in vegetable shortening and some margarines (especially the stick variety). You may appreciate a long shelf life when you discover an unopened bag of chips you left in the cupboard six months ago. But the convenience *trans* fats offer comes with a cost. *Trans* fat is chemically similar to saturated fat; not surprisingly, it, too, raises LDL cholesterol.

THE MEAL DEAL: GETTING THE MOST FROM FOOD

The science of nutrition leaves little question that food choices influence overall health. That's especially true for diabetes patients. Although there is no diabetic diet, adhering to some of the basic tenets of healthy nutrition can improve glucose control and reduce the

THE ABCS OF EATING WELL FOR INSULIN USERS

- Adjust when necessary. Eating the same portions at the same time every day makes it easier to maintain blood sugar control. But now and then, you may decide in advance that you want to splurge on dessert. If you take insulin, knowing how to adjust your dose can prevent unwanted spikes in blood sugar.
- Balance your diet. It's okay to enjoy desserts and other favorite foods, as long as you eat a balanced diet that includes plenty of fruits, vegetables, beans, and whole grains.
- Consistency is key. Experts encourage patients who inject insulin or take insulin-promoting medications to eat at the same time every day, which makes it easier to time the medicine's onset with the rise of glucose levels in the blood. Also, patients should avoid skipping meals and eat the same amount of food. However, if you're taking a long-acting background insulin (Lantus, Levemir) and then a rapid-acting insulin (Humalog, Novolog, Apidra) to manage carbohydrates, it's not necessary to follow these three rules of thumb.

risk of complications. Here's a four-course lesson on making better food choices whether you're in a French café or your own kitchen.

Eat Healthy Portions of Healthy Carbohydrates

Read that headline again carefully and please take note that it does not say *Sugar is the Devil's Candy and Must Never Again Touch Your Lips*. There is nothing wrong with enjoying an occasional candy bar, can of cola, or ice-cream cone. But to make sure your diet doesn't disrupt your blood glucose levels, it's important to work with a diabetes educator or dietitian to determine a safe amount of carbohydrates for you to consume each day. Since your diet guru can't be at your side at each meal to ensure that you don't exceed your carb limit, he or she may teach you to use one of the following techniques to help decide which and how many carbs to eat each day:

Carbohydrate counting. If you are taking insulin, carbohydrate counting is actually the most flexible eating plan. Carbo-hydrate counting allows you to more accurately estimate how much insulin you'll need to inject before eating in order to accommodate the ensuing rise in blood sugar. Your doctor or dietitian will recommend a number of insulin units per grams of carbohydrates in a meal. Chances are, at first you may need to experiment a little to find the right proportion. Carbohydrate counting can also help you eat roughly the same amount of carbs at each meal, which will help to maintain even, healthy blood sugar during the day.

If you're not taking insulin, the strategy of counting carbohydrates is kind of like living on a fixed income. You will get a set daily limit of how many carbohydrates you can eat, as measured in grams, but it's up to you to decide how you want to "spend" them at each meal. A slice of wheat bread has 13 grams of carbohydrates, and a medium-size apple packs about 20. Meanwhile, a small slice of chocolate cake will set you back 32 grams. Slurp down a McDonald's strawberry milk shake at lunch and you just blew 67 grams from your daily carb account.

Carbohydrate counting is not difficult; it just takes a little practice and access to two pieces of nutritional information: the number of carbohydrates in each food that makes up a meal and the amount of each food (or serving size) you will be eating. With packaged foods, this information is printed on the Nutrition Facts panel. For nonpackaged foods, books and Web sites for carbohydrate counters are available. Some restaurants provide the information.

Exchange lists. To make it simple to add variety to meals, the American Dietetic Association and the American Diabetes Association publish these easy-to-use lists. Foods are grouped by categories, such as starches, vegetables, fruits, meats, and so on, with predetermined portion sizes. All food exchanges within a category have roughly equivalent nutritional value and impact on blood sugar levels. For instance, if you wake up some morning and decide you want a bowl of cereal or oatmeal instead of your usual toast, an exchange list can tell you how much cereal or oatmeal you can eat and still keep your blood sugar level in the target range. Ask your diabetes educator or dietitian about exchange lists.

Remember, there are no "bad" carbohydrates. But favoring some over others will improve your glucose control and give your overall health a boost. Here are some good rules to follow:

Go with the (whole) grain. If you think 7-grain bread, brown rice, and whole-wheat pasta are just for people who wear Birkenstocks and beads, it's time to get hip to the benefits of whole grains. Most Americans grew up eating white bread and white pasta. Wheat is the grain most commonly used to make these starchy foods. Picture a wheat field. Notice something that doesn't quite fit? *Wheat isn't white.* Millers produce white flour by grinding wheat to remove the sturdy outer layers of the grain, known as the bran and germ. Unfortunately, the process known as refining not only strips away the bran and germ, but it also removes lots of fiber (see pages 222–224 for why that matters), vitamins (especially vitamins B and E), and minerals, too. The same thing happens when rice is processed to make it pearly white.

The U.S. government requires commercial bakers to restore some of those nutrients; the process is known as enrichment. But some nutritionists believe that the body is better able to absorb and use naturally occurring vitamins and minerals. What's more, enrichment does not return to the finished product the countless micronutrients in grains, whose role in health scientists are only now beginning to understand.

Whole-grain breads, pasta, and rice are made with the entire grain, preserving all of those valuable nutrients. Whole grains have a bolder taste and chewier texture than most of their paler cousins. Add them to your diet, and over time, you may find that white bread and other refined grains taste bland. Beware of imitators: Some commercial bakeries sell "wheat" bread that is simply white bread that has been dyed brown. Pasta makers sometimes dye pasta brown,

SHOULD YOU USE THE GLYCEMIC INDEX?

Ready for a little controversy? Earlier in this book, we told you that your body can't tell one carb from another, that they all raise blood sugar pretty much the same. Strictly speaking, the story is slightly more complex. Scientists have shown that some carbohydrates cause a greater increase in blood sugar following a meal than others. The glycemic index is a method for measuring whether an individual food causes an immediate surge in blood sugar (high glycemic foods) or a gradual rise in blood sugar (low glycemic foods). The glycemic index rates a food's capacity to raise blood sugar by comparing it to a standard—either white bread or glucose—that is given a rating of 100. If a food raises blood sugar faster than white bread, its rating is higher than 100. If it raises blood sugar more slowly than white bread, its rating will be lower. The idea behind the glycemic index is to allow you to compare the effect of various foods on your blood sugar and to make choices that help you maintain a more constant blood sugar.

If you're confused, don't worry. Plenty of people with advanced degrees scratch their heads when trying to figure out how to use the glycemic index, which is actually even more complicated to use than it seems. That's because you rarely eat just carbohydrates. Meals, even individual foods, may be prepared with or contain fat and fiber, both of which slow the breakdown of carbohydrate into glucose. A baked potato is a good example: Eat a plain one, and your blood sugar may soar. But if you add a pat of butter, it will rise more gradually. But how much? Hard to say. Cooking method, too, can affect how you metabolize a carbohydrate. For instance, pasta cooked al dente (firm) is absorbed more slowly than pasta that is cooked longer.

Furthermore, if you're sticking with healthy carbohydrate choices—that is, lots of fruits, vegetables, and whole grains—you're probably eating at the low end of the glycemic index scale anyway. The American Diabetes Association has stated that while the glycemic index may be a useful tool in meal planning, the total amount of carbohydrates you consume is the most important factor in controlling blood sugar.

too, to make it appear healthier. Look for the words *whole grain* or *whole wheat* on package labels.

Don't peel out. Paring off the skin of apples or other fruits strips away fiber and nutrients, so leave it on. Corn and beans have edible skin, too. Foods with edible seeds, such as berries, are fiber filled, too.

Get colorful. Nutritionists believe that the same chemicals that give certain kinds of fruits and vegetables a brilliant hue may also promote health and fight disease. Tomatoes and watermelon, for instance, get their red color from an antioxidant called lycopene, which may prevent some cancers. You may want to see green on your plate, in particular. Some researchers believe that the antioxidants lutein and zeaxanthin, which are found in spinach, collards, kale, and broccoli, may strengthen the retina, the ring of nerve cells in the eyes that are vulnerable to blinding damage from high blood sugar.

Know your beans. They aren't as glamorous as prime rib or lobster, but lowly legumes are among the healthiest foods on the planet. Packed with fiber, protein, B vitamins, and other nutrients, beans and lentils belong on any healthy menu. There is an astonishing array of beans, from garbanzos to great northerns, each with a distinct taste. Beans go well in salads, stews, and soups, as well as curries, casseroles, and an endless list of ethnic dishes.

Eat Less Fat

Diabetes increases the risk of heart attacks and strokes, so it's essential to cut back on saturated fat, which raises levels of artery-clogging LDL ("bad") cholesterol. But reducing fat can offer an added health bonus for diabetes patients, thanks to two things that happen inside your body when you consume the gooey stuff. First, fat loiters in the stomach for a long time. While you process carbohydrates in just a few hours, it can take six to eight hours for the fat in a cheese pizza or milk shake to empty out of the stomach and into the intestines. Furthermore, fatty acids interfere with the work of insulin. Consuming large amounts of fat, then, can lead to insulin resistance and rising blood glucose levels.

These twin phenomena explain why bingeing on high-fat snacks is doubly dangerous when you indulge at bedtime. If you scarf down a pint of cookie-dough ice cream, then check your blood sugar before brushing your teeth, the numbers probably won't alarm you. But overnight, after all that fat has had

221

time to ooze into your bloodstream and block insulin from storing glucose, your blood-sugar reading will likely be off the chart.

Fat has an important role in your diet, but use it wisely by following a few rules:

Embrace mono-tony. "Good fats" is not an oxymoron. Monounsaturated fats have a number of health benefits. Eat an avocado salad for lunch and a handful of nuts as a midday snack. Cook with olive, canola, and nut oils.

Become an omega man (or woman). Omega-3 fatty acids are another healthy fat, so replace some of your meat entrées with fish, especially salmon, mackerel, white albacore tuna, bluefish, and other oily sea critters.

Make the switch. Experiment with fat-free and reduced-fat foods, and switch the ones you like for full-fat versions in your diet. Don't drink whole milk; even two percent contains a lot of fat. Stick with skim or one percent.

Master marinades. You don't need to drown a steak in béarnaise sauce to make it taste great. Experiment with different meat marinades, which can be as simple as a cup of soy sauce (low sodium, of course).

Go lean. Avoid fatty meats, such as porterhouse and rib-eye steaks. Instead, choose top round or sirloin cuts, which you can marinate in advance. Trim off as much fat as possible before you cook a steak.

Get "tubby." If you must have a spread for your toast or dinner rolls, use tub margarine. Stick margarine contains too much *trans* fat. It's okay to use a bit of butter now and then, but due to its high saturated fat content, better make it a rare event.

Eat More Fiber

Remember back in the 1980s, when oat bran bread became the toast of the town? Research suggested that eating oats and other high-fiber foods could fight heart disease and some cancers, making consumers weaned on white bread switch to dark loaves. Boring bran cereal became hip. Bakeries added oat muffins and bagels to their menus.

Food trends come and go, of course, so fiber's reputation as a health savior has faded slightly. However, fiber should never go out of fashion in your diet.

There are two kinds of fiber in food:

- Insoluble fiber. As the name suggests, this is fibrous stuff in plants that doesn't dissolve as it passes through the gastrointestinal system, so you can't digest it. Instead, insoluble fiber absorbs water and helps move waste through the colon. Whole-wheat bread is a good source of insoluble fiber, as are many vegetables.
- Soluble fiber. This isn't digested, but it does get gummy in your gut. That allows it to grab fat molecules before *they* can be absorbed into the blood, whisking them out of the body through the intestines. Along with oat bran, dried peas and beans, barley, apples, oranges, carrots, and other fruits and vegetables are rich in soluble fiber.

Although fiber is a type of carbohydrate, your body can't digest it, so you can't burn it as energy. However, fiber has a long slate of benefits. Health authorities recommend eating 25 to 30 grams of fiber per day, yet Americans only consume about 14 or 15 grams daily, on average. Which is too bad, since

- Fiber helps control blood sugar. Fiber in a meal slows other carbohydrates from entering the bloodstream, which prevents glucose spikes. It's as though sugar and starch molecules keep bumping into all that roughage while trying to get out of your gut. A 2004 scientific review in the *Journal of the American College of Nutrition* found that eating high-fiber foods consistently lowers postmeal glucose levels in people with diabetes.
- Fiber lowers cholesterol and other blood fats. The same review found solid evidence for the theory that daily doses of dietary fiber reduce cholesterol and triglycerides, another form of artery-clogging fat. That seems to be true of soluble fiber in particular; it sops up cholesterol and fat in the diet before it can enter the bloodstream.
- Fiber fills you up. So does fat—but fat has almost twice as many calories per gram as high-fiber foods. Eating plenty of low-calorie foods that provide satiety—that belly-pleasing sense of fullness that persuades you to set down your fork and push away

CLEARING THE AIR ABOUT FIBER

If you are planning to add fiber to your diet, start slowly to avoid developing flatulence. While insoluble fiber passes through the gut with little fanfare, soluble fiber is attacked by enzymes in the large intestine. The process produces a variety of gases, which can cause abdominal discomfort and social embarrassment. Doctors recommend increasing fiber intake by a small amount each week to allow your body time to adjust to your new diet. Over-the-counter products such as Beano may help reduce gassiness. Drinking plenty of fluids will help prevent constipation.

from the dinner table—can help control weight.

- Fiber is a freebie. Since you don't digest fiber, it has no calories. In fact, if you count carbs and consume a meal that includes more than five grams of fiber, you can subtract them from the overall gram count for the meal.

Fiber has lost a tiny bit of its miracle-food image in recent years. That's because studies suggest that roughage may not reduce the risk of colon cancer, as doctors once believed. Furthermore, if you develop gastroparesis or certain other gastrointestinal complications of diabetes, your doctor may recommend cutting back on fiber-rich foods, at least temporarily.

A final caveat: While fiber supplements can offer a convenient and effective way to add bulk to your diet, try to get your fill from foods. High-fiber pills, powders, and snacks contain natural substances such as psyllium seed husks (which come from a type of plantain). But fiber-dense foods are also excellent sources of vitamins, minerals, and other salubrious stuff. What's more, it's worth noting that fiber supplements are commonly used as laxatives, so it's important to use them as—and only when—prescribed.

Eat Less Salt

As you learned in Chapter 8, diabetes and hypertension have an unsavory association. You can develop hypertension, or high blood pressure, whether or not you have diabetes. But high glucose levels damage the kidneys, interfering with the organs' ability to filter blood. That allows too much junk to pass back into circulation, which increases your blood's volume, raising blood pressure.

What does this have to do with salt? Most of the sodium you eat comes from sodium chloride—common table salt. And sodium can cause blood pressure to rise in some people. There's no way of knowing whether your blood pressure will go through the roof if you consume too much sodium, so the smart move is to consume less of this mineral.

Depending on your current diet, that may mean you need to take some dramatic steps. The human body only requires 400 milligrams of sodium to maintain fluid balance. Yet, the typical American consumes more than 3,000 milligrams each day. The government recommends limiting sodium intake to 2,400 milligrams per day. Sound like a lot? That's only equivalent to the sodium in about one teaspoon of table salt.

Yet, the saltshaker on the dining room table is only a small part of the problem. Sodium is a stealth mineral. Start reading package labels, and you will find that many processed foods derive much of their flavor from sodium. In fact, according to one estimate Americans get 77 percent of their sodium from prepared or processed foods.

Where does all the salt come from? Salty-tasting foods like deli meat and hot dogs are obvious sources. But others are a surprise. Did you know that a fast-food cherry pie can contain twice as much sodium as a small order of French fries? Some other sources of sodium to watch out for (some obvious, some not) include

- fast-food meals
- canned soups and vegetables (unless marked low- or no-sodium)
- frozen foods
- breakfast cereal and instant oatmeal
- condiments
- pickles
- seasonings
- antacids

Nutritionists say that the human taste for salt can be unlearned. Cut back on high-sodium foods for a few weeks, and eventually your palate can adapt. Here are some strategies that will help:

- Look for the words "reduced sodium" or "no salt" on packages (you can always add a small sprinkle).
- If you buy canned foods that are swimming in salt, rinse them to remove some sodium.
- Eat fresh produce when possible and cut back on processed or fast foods.
- Get creative with herbs and spices to add some zing to food that might otherwise taste bland without salt.
- Don't automatically add salt to a dish; taste it first—you may be pleasantly surprised. Do the same before adding salty condiments.
- Tell restaurant servers you want your meals prepared without monosodium glutamate (MSG) or high-sodium ingredients.

Girth Control: Maintaining a Healthy Weight

Rates of type 2 diabetes are rising in this country. American waistlines are bulging. If you think the simultaneous occurrence of these two trends is a coincidence, then you may need a quick review of the link between blubber and blood sugar: People with excess flab tend to develop insulin

HOW DO YOU MEASURE UP?

Here is an example of how the body mass index works, using a person who is 5 feet 9 inches tall.

Height	Weight Range	BMI	Considered
5 feet 9 inches	124 lbs or less	Below 18.5	Underweight
	125 lbs to 168 lbs.	18.5 to 24.9	Normal
	169 lbs to 202 lbs.	25.0 to 29.9	Overweight
	203 lbs or more	30 or higher	Obese

resistance. The fatter you get, the more stubbornly your cells resist insulin, causing blood sugar to rise. If you lose weight, insulin resistance decreases, improving blood glucose levels and reducing the risk for heart disease.

If you have a weight problem, you may kid yourself that your love handles are "cute" and that the extra baggage you've been lugging around is harmless. But your doctor knows better. Scientists developed a measurement known as the body mass index (BMI) that helps physicians determine when a patient's poundage threatens his or her health. The higher your BMI, the greater your risk for heart disease and other killers.

Unlike the reading on your bathroom scale, the BMI expresses whether your weight is proportionate to your height. The Centers for Disease Control and Prevention uses the following guidelines to interpret BMI results for adults older than 20:

You are overweight if
• your BMI is between 25 and 29.9.

You are obese if
• your BMI is 30 or higher.

To figure out your body mass index, first you need to weigh yourself. Then get out a calculator and use this formula: Divide your weight in pounds by your height in inches. Divide the number you get by your height in inches (yes, again). Then multiply the result by 703. The number you get is your BMI. A person who weighs 190 pounds and is 5 feet 9 inches tall would have a BMI of 28. Here's how the calculations look:

1. 190 pounds ÷ 69 inches = 2.75

2. 2.75 ÷ 69 = 0.0399

3. 0.0399 x 703 = 28

See "How Do You Measure Up?" on the opposite page for examples of how changes in weight affect your BMI status.

The BMI does an accurate job of identifying people whose weight poses a health risk, with some exceptions. Highly trained athletes, for example, often have a high BMI, because muscle is heavy and can throw off results. However, if you have type 2 diabetes and you have a high BMI, chances are this caveat does not apply to you.

THAT HOT NEW DIET— SHOULD YOU TRY IT?

What's the hot, new weight-loss fad this year? Low-carb, high-protein, no-fat? Cabbage soup? Martinis and whipped cream? (If you think we're joking about that last one, chew on this: A diet book with that very title was popular in the 1960s.)

Although these books usually portray losing weight as a complicated process

that requires following carefully pre-scribed steps, there is nothing mysteri-ous about weight loss. You simply have to burn more calories than you eat. But have you ever wondered what the heck a calorie is? Food is fuel for the body. As your cells burn fuel they create energy, which allows you to walk, talk, think, blink, and do everything else you need to do in the course of daily living. Scientists use calories to measure the amount of energy contained in a food or beverage.

So does that mean a can of soda (150 calories) is a better source of energy than a celery stalk (6 calories)? Not exactly. The amount of energy your body burns is measured in calories, too. Unless you're very active, consuming a lot of high-calorie foods causes the body to store the unused fuel in the form of fat, usually on your hips, thighs,

227

and buttocks. To lose love handles and other unsightly fat deposits, you have to create a calorie deficit—that is, consume fewer than you burn. To drop one pound, you have to create a deficit of 3,500 calories.

However, as anyone who has ever gone on a weight-loss diet knows, while shedding pounds can be a challenge, it's keeping them off that is really hard. You will have a greater chance of success if you work with your diabetes educator or dietitian to come up with a weight-loss plan that identifies which foods to eat, how many calories to consume each day, and a reasonable target weight.

A healthy weight-loss goal is one to two pounds per week until you reach the target weight. Although a carefully designed diet is essential, it's just one-half of a weight-loss plan. Getting plenty of exercise is the other. The rest of this chapter looks at the science of sweat therapy.

Exercise and Diabetes: How to Get Physical

Your current relationship with physical activity may be intimately linked with the form of diabetes you have. According to *The Physician and Sportsmedicine,* a respected medical journal, those

with type 1 diabetes often want to exercise but sometimes should not, while those with type 2 diabetes almost always should exercise but often don't want to.

In other words, people with type 1 diabetes need to overcome certain obstacles to ensure that exercising doesn't cause more harm than good. Meanwhile, lack of physical activity may prevent people with type 2 diabetes from controlling the condition more effectively. But the two groups have this in common: There's little question that regular physical activity can benefit anyone who has diabetes.

Exercise may have the most immediate benefits for patients with type 2 diabetes. While working the muscles can make anyone use insulin more efficiently, studies suggest that exercise leads to sustained improvements in glucose control primarily in type 2 patients. However, making a daily commitment to physical fitness—whether that means a trip to the gym, a long bike ride, or simply parking way out in section Z when you go to the shopping mall—produces many other bonuses. Regular exercise can

- add years to your life.
- lower the risk of cardiovascular disease.
- improve symptoms of certain diabetes complications, such as intermittent claudication (pain in the lower limbs while walking).
- increase coordination and prevent falls in the elderly.
- improve mood.

A fitness trainer or your doctor can help you create an exercise program that suits your needs, based on the form of diabetes you have, whether you have

any complications that may affect your choice of physical activity, and whether weight loss is a goal.

EXERCISE AND TYPE 1 DIABETES

As with hitting a baseball, timing is everything when it comes to exercise for people with type 1 diabetes. You may want to jump on your bicycle right away when you feel the urge to go for a long spin, but you do so at your own peril. Physical activity lowers blood sugar—the longer and more vigorous the workout, the lower it can drop—so taking steps to make sure the time is right for your body to exercise will help you avoid hypoglycemia and its unpleasant effects.

Mind you, this doesn't mean that those with type 1 can't enjoy an active lifestyle. As long as your blood sugar is under control and you don't have complications that limit your mobility or tolerance for exercise, there is no reason to fear the treadmill. Just be sure to follow a few simple rules.

1. Don't exercise if your fasting glucose is higher than 250 mg/dl and you test positive for ketones.

2. Exercise with caution if your fasting glucose is higher than 300 mg/dl in the absence of ketosis.

RUN FOR YOUR LIFE

Researchers at the Cooper Institute in Dallas, Texas, rated the activity level and fitness of more than 1,200 men with type 2 diabetes. A dozen years later, they showed that men who were physically active on a regular basis and were moderately fit had a 60 percent lower death rate than unfit men who didn't exercise.

3. Consume carbohydrates before exercising if your glucose level is below 100 mg/dl, based on your health care professional's advice.

4. Monitor blood sugar before, during, and after exercise. Obviously, the only way you'll know whether your glucose level is too high or low is if you use your meter. But checking during a workout (if it lasts longer than 30 minutes) and when you're finished will provide important information about how exercise affects your insulin use. Based on how your blood sugar changes after a workout, your doctor or diabetes educator will recommend necessary changes to your insulin dose and provide advice about whether you need to consume carbohydrates before exercising. Since you will probably respond differently to a 30-minute swim than a 60-minute walk, be sure to do before-and-after testing for all the different activities you participate in.

5. Keep glucose tablets or some other carbohydrate source handy.

Your caregiver may recommend consuming some carbohydrates during extended exercise, perhaps every 30 minutes or so. Regardless, keep an emergency source of glucose on hand in case you become hypoglycemic.

EXERCISE AND TYPE 2 DIABETES

Imagine you were just voted off the TV show *Survivor*. "The tribe has spoken," says the grim-faced host, dousing your torch. You walk away, bitter toward the backstabbers who sent you packing, but you're humored by a thought: They're going to be eating ants and tree bark tonight, but you're about to fill your groaning belly with some real food. Then a producer delivers some more bad news: It's a three-hour drive to the hotel and all he has to offer you in the meantime is a pimento-loaf sandwich—and you hate pimento loaf. *What are you going to do?*

You're probably going to eat the pimento loaf. That's sort of like what happens in your body during exercise if you have insulin resistance. Hardworking muscle cells that normally refuse to use glucose suddenly can't get enough of the stuff. Desperate to produce energy to keep your limbs moving, the hungry cells greedily lap up glucose. As a result, there's less excess sugar floating around in the blood and causing problems. And the effect lingers: A single bout of exercise can improve insulin sensitivity for a day or more. (But the effect wears off soon after, a good reason not to skip more than a day between workouts.)

A scientific review of more than a dozen studies, published in the *Journal of the American Medical Association* in 2001, found that the average type 2 patient who exercises regularly has an A1c (the standard measure of blood glucose levels) of 7.65 percent—close to 7 percent, which doctors consider healthy. Type 2 patients who don't exercise, meanwhile, have an average A1c of 8.31 percent. While an 0.66 percent difference between the groups might not sound like much, other studies suggest that such a reduction in A1c significantly reduces the risk for diabetes complications.

Exercise does more for type 2 patients than improve blood sugar, of course. Sweat therapy can also

- help to control weight.
- lower cholesterol and other blood fats.
- lower blood pressure.
- improve other risk factors for heart disease.

Some type 2 patients have something in common with people who have type 1

diabetes. Even if you don't inject insulin, you may need to adjust your medication dose if you take certain diabetes drugs. Sulfonylureas or meglitinides coax the pancreas into making more insulin to compensate for the body's resistance to the hormone. Over time, however, your newly toned muscle cells will become less resistant, so in order to avoid hypoglycemia, you may need to lower your dose of the drugs.

WORKING OUT: THE BASICS

If you're starting a new workout regimen, following these guidelines will help you get the best results, avoid injuries, and stick with the program.

Talk to Your Doc

See your physician for a complete medical exam before adopting a new workout regimen. A health evaluation will give your doctor some idea of what level of exercise you can handle and what, if any, complications you may have that could be exacerbated by the wrong type of physical activity.

Don't Skimp

Good-quality exercise equipment pays for itself in the form of better protection against injuries. That's especially true for footwear—take note in particular if you have evidence of intermittent claudication or other evidence of peripheral

WEIGHTING GAME: SHOULD YOU PUMP IRON?

There was a time when the only people hanging around the weight room at the gym were no-necked guys named Gus and Vito who could bench-press Volkswagens and cared more about sculpting their pecs and abs than slashing their disease risk. Move over, boys. Medical researchers have shown that resistance training—the most common form is lifting weights—has myriad health benefits, especially for diabetes patients. Along with improving coordination and preventing falls, muscle building can improve insulin sensitivity, especially in people with type 2 diabetes. In fact, research suggests that pumping iron lowers insulin resistance just as well as aerobic exercise.

The basic unit of resistance training is the repetition—that is, the act of lifting a weight and setting it back down once. Although serious weight lifters often bulk up by doing just a few repetitions with very heavy weights, the American Diabetes Association recommends doing many repetitions with light weights. Start with one set of 10 to 15 repetitions of a given exercise 2 or 3 times per week at first. Over time, try to progress to 3 sets of 8 to 10 repetitions. How much should you lift? Your muscle should be completely fatigued by the time you finish the third set. A fitness trainer can instruct you on proper resistance-training technique.

Weight lifting may not be appropriate for patients with certain complications; see A Few Words of Caution, page 235.

neuropathy (loss of sensation in the lower limbs). When exercising, wear shoes with air or gel midsoles (the shock-absorbing pads between the soles and feet) and a generous toe box. Always wear socks to keep your feet dry.

Warm Up and Chill Down

Giving your muscles and joints a little time to get warm and loose before exercising may prevent injuries. Start with some running in place or brisk walking for a few minutes, then spend a few more minutes stretching your muscles. Don't stretch cold muscles, as that can cause tears. And if you can only stretch once during your routine, stretch *after* exercising when it's most beneficial, rather than before. Don't bounce when you stretch, as that, too, can cause tears.

Start Slow

Many new workout regimens come to a screeching halt the day after they start. The reason? An overenthusiastic newbie spends four hours at the gym going full throttle on every one of the cardio and weight machines, trying to make up for years of sloth in one session. The next day, the newbie wakes up with stiff, throbbing joints and limbs. Exercise physiologists even have a name for this familiar woe: delayed onset muscle soreness, or DOMS. Fitness trainers say that this day-after misery is often enough to sour good intentions and send someone back to the sofa instead of the stair-climber.

There is an easy way to minimize or avoid this pitfall: Start slow. If you are out of shape and haven't exercised in years, you may want to begin by walking at an easy pace for five minutes per session, gradually adding minutes and increasing your pace. If you begin a resistance-training program (and that may not be a bad idea; see "Weighting Game: Should You Pump Iron?" on the opposite page), start by lifting light weights, just a few times. If you're worried about sore muscles, talk to your trainer. If he or she gives you the "no pain, no gain" speech, find another trainer.

How Much Should I Exercise?

Studies show that it takes at least 150 minutes of aerobic exercise per week to attain significant health benefits, including better blood sugar control, reduction of heart disease risk, and weight maintenance. How you accrue your minimum of 150 minutes is up to you, but the American Diabetes Association recommends spreading your weekly workout quota over at least three days, while not going more than two consecutive days without exercise.

If you have lost a large amount of weight—more than say, 30 pounds—exercising on all or most days will help you keep the flab from returning. In fact, one study of people who successfully maintained long-term weight loss found that they had one important quality in common: They exercised for about one hour per day.

How Hard?

Think like Goldilocks: Not too hard, not too soft. Maintaining moderate intensity while exercising will help you get the most out of a workout without pooping out too early. Your goal should be to get your heart beating at 50 to 70 percent of its maximal rate (as measured by beats per minute). Don't worry, attaining a productive but safe target heart-rate range while exercising isn't as hard as it sounds.

First, determine your target heart-rate range by using the following formula:

1. Subtract your age from 220.

2. Multiply the result by 0.5 to determine the low end of your target heart-rate range.

3. Multiply the result from step one by 0.7. This is the high end of your target heart-rate range.

For example, a person who is 45 who wants to exercise at 50 to 70 percent of maximal heart rate would have a target heart-rate range between 88 and 123 beats per minute. Here's how that computation looks:

$$220 - 45 = 175$$

$$175 \times 0.5 = 87.5$$

$$175 \times 0.7 = 122.5$$

Once you have determined your target heart-rate range, you can put it to use the next time you're exercising. Follow these steps:

1. Wait until you have reached what feels like moderately intense exertion, then stop and quickly take your pulse.

2. Using the index and third fingers of one hand, gently touch the radial artery on the thumb side of your other wrist. The radial artery is located just below the wrist. It may take some practice to find it.

3. Starting at zero, count the number of pulses you feel for ten seconds.

4. Multiply the result by 6. (Alternatively, you may count pulses for six seconds and multiply by 10.)

Does the number fall within your target heart-rate range? If so, keep it up. If it's too low, pick up the pace. If your heart is racing too fast, ease up. After checking your pulse a few times, you will get to know what a moderately intense workout feels like.

And if all that sounds too complicated, try the talk test instead:

- If you're breathing hard but can keep up a casual conversation while exercising, you're probably doing fine.
- If you can sing "The Surrey with the Fringe on Top," from *Oklahoma!*—or any other song—during a workout, you probably need to push yourself harder.
- If the only words you can manage are "call" and "911," you're overdoing it.

Identify Yourself
Just to be on the safe side, always wear a bracelet or shoe tag identifying yourself as a person with diabetes when you work out.

Stay Well Lubed
Drink plenty of water before, during, and after exercise. Dehydration can spoil a good workout.

Travel in Pairs
You may want to find a fitness buddy to exercise with; this is one case where

peer pressure may actually be a good thing, since you're less likely to blow off a workout if it means letting down a friend.

Have Fun

Across the nation, there are untold numbers of stationary cycles and elliptical trainers sitting in basements and spare bedrooms, draped with drying laundry, their original purpose abandoned due to boredom or because someone hated using the machine. Choose an activity you enjoy and you'll be more likely to stick with it.

A FEW WORDS OF CAUTION

Although all diabetes patients should strive to be physically active, some forms of exercise require extra precautions (or may be too risky, period) for people who have the following complications.

Autonomic Neuropathy

Patients who have this form of nerve damage may not be able to detect symptoms such as sweating and rapid heart rate that signal the onset of exercise-induced hypoglycemia. They also have a high risk for orthostatic hypoten-

sion during exercise performed while upright, so cycling or swimming may be better choices than walking or running. Beware of exercising in very hot or cold climates, and be sure to drink plenty of water.

Retinopathy

Some types of physical activity increase the risk of a hemorrhage in the eye or a detached retina. Avoid activities that involve a lot of jarring or straining, such as jogging or weight lifting.

Peripheral Neuropathy

If you can't feel your feet, how will you know if you're pounding the pavement too hard? People with serious loss of sensation in the lower limbs should not overdo weight-bearing exercise. Repetitive, intense pressure on the feet can cause ulcers. You may also fail to realize that you have broken a foot bone, then exacerbate the damage through continued use. If you have nerve damage that limits feeling in your feet, low-impact exercise, such as swimming, cycling, or rowing, may be the best choice.

Sex and Diabetes

If you can't remember the last time you did anything in your sleeping quarters besides sleep...

If your idea of a romantic evening has become a cup of herbal tea and whatever is on Lifetime...

If you haven't heard the sound humorist S. J. Perelman called "the triumphant twang of a bedspring" in far too long...

...then diabetes may be spoiling your love life. Happy, healthy sex requires a delicate interplay between the central nervous, circulatory, and endocrine systems—and high blood sugar can foul up any step along the way. But don't dismiss sexual difficulties as a "quality of life" issue. Problems in the bedroom may be the first signs that more serious trouble is brewing. Fortunately, as this chapter shows, there's no need to take sexual dysfunction lying down.

Love Affairs: Sex and Diabetes

According to an oft-quoted statistic, 50 percent of male diabetes patients and 30 percent of female diabetes patients experience sexual problems. However, many experts feel that the prevalence figure for women is probably too low. In other words, diabetes-induced sexual dysfunction does not discriminate—and, either way, it is a serious health issue.

Although the result can be serious physical and psychological distress, diabetes-related sexual problems too often go unmentioned because patients are reluctant to talk about sensitive issues with doctors. Increasingly, though, physicians include questions about patients' sex lives as part of routine health screening. And not because they like pillow talk, either. The same medical problems that lead to sexual difficulties can offer early evidence of diabetic neuropathy, cardiovascular disease, and other serious medical conditions. For instance, a 2005 study published in the *Journal of the American Medical Association* found that men with erectile dysfunction have a 45 percent increased risk for heart disease.

The single best thing you can do to keep passion alive is to maintain healthy blood sugar levels. But when problems occur, help is available. This chapter looks at how diabetes affects sexual health in men and women, with advice on how to rekindle the flames.

Male Sexual Health and Diabetes

Men with diabetes don't necessarily lack sexual desire; their problem most often takes the form of a power outage. Smoking, heart disease, lack of exercise, and plenty of other conditions or habits can lead to difficulty achieving an erection. But diabetes packs a double whammy below the belt, as you'll see.

ERECTILE DYSFUNCTION

Once rarely discussed in public, this common male health problem has come out of the bedroom in recent years, thanks to the introduction of several effective new treatments. Sometimes called impotence, erectile dysfunction (ED) affects about 5 percent of American men in their 40s and up to 25 percent of men by the age of 65. However, doctors agree that men with diabetes have

FERTILITY AND YOUR PLUMBING

Overcoming erectile dysfunction may not be the end of sexual difficulties for a small number of men with diabetes. During normal ejaculation, muscle contractions force semen out of the penis through the urethra. However, damage to nerves controlling muscles called sphincters can impair their ability to contract and close the bladder, allowing some or all of the semen to enter. This is called retrograde ejaculation. Although the condition is uncommon, men with diabetes have an increased risk. Semen does not damage the bladder and simply flushes out of the body with urine. But retrograde ejaculation may interfere with fertility, a concern for men trying to become fathers. Furthermore, a male who develops the condition may not produce any semen when he ejaculates, which some men find disturbing.

an even greater risk. Estimates vary, but surveys suggest that male diabetes patients are two to three times more likely to have ED than men who don't have diabetes. Some studies also suggest that male diabetes patients develop more serious, harder-to-treat cases of ED, too.

To understand erectile dysfunction better, it helps to brush up on a bit of male reproductive biology. The penis has two cylindrical chambers on either side, known as corpora cavernosa, and a third, called the corpora spongiosum,

underneath. A membrane called the tunica albuginea surrounds these chambers, which are filled with blood vessels and other tissue. Urine and ejaculate pass out of the body through a tube called the urethra.

An erection occurs when some stimulus (use your imagination) triggers sexual desire in a male. Nerve signals from the brain or genitals (depending on the source of stimulation) cause blood vessels in the penis to dilate, or widen, and fill with blood. Normally, blood flows in and out of the penis, as it does in other parts of the body with healthy circulation. But during an erection, the tunica albuginea helps to trap blood in the penis. The resulting pressure causes the penis to expand and become firm.

Given the balance of psychology and physiology required for an erection, it's hardly surprising that the process goes awry now and then. That is, most men, regardless of what they say, experience failure below the belt at some time in their adult lives. ED is diagnosed in men who are frequently unable to obtain an erection adequate for intercourse.

Unless you skipped all the way ahead to this chapter, you can probably guess how the physiology of an erection creates several potential trouble spots for a man with diabetes. First, as Chapter 6 explains, diabetes patients often develop clogged arteries. Among other health problems, blockages in these vessels may slow blood flow to the penis to a trickle too weak to produce an erection. Diabetes can also cause scarring in smaller arteries in the penis, which could prevent tissue from expanding. Meanwhile, high blood sugar may damage the nerves that initiate and control erections. Finally, certain bad habits that have been linked to diabetes, including smoking, alcohol abuse, and lack of exercise, seem to interfere with healthy erections, too.

Diagnosing Erectile Dysfunction

A physical exam and patient history may provide a doctor with all he or she needs to diagnose ED. The doctor will check if the patient's penis has any abnormalities that might interfere with attaining an erection. A weak pulse at the wrist or ankle may be signs of poor circulation. A doctor will also look for evidence of neuropathy. A blood test may reveal deficiencies, such as low

testosterone. (Normal levels of the hormone are necessary for a male to be potent.)

A physician will ask a lot of questions, too, about your sexual history and recent experiences, your partners, drug use (both prescription and recreational), diet, emotional state of mind, and other matters that may affect your ability to have and maintain an erection.

Treating Erectile Dysfunction

While there is no cure for ED, there are plenty of ways to overcome its frustrating symptoms.

Oral medication. ED drugs are among the best-selling and most heavily promoted prescription pills on the planet. You rarely watch a baseball game or NASCAR event without having to sit through one of those wink-wink commercials with some middle-aged guy prattling on in suggestive language about how some medication helped him get his mojo back. The revolution began in 1998 with the introduction of sildenafil, better known by its brand name, Viagra, the first oral drug approved by the Food and Drug Administration for treating ED. Since then, several others have followed. As a group, they have been credited or blamed, depending on whom you ask, for producing a new generation of gray-haired Lotharios and diaper-changers. But despite all the jokes told by late-night talk show hosts, these drugs have allowed millions of men to enjoy healthy sex lives, with little inconvenience or risk of side effects. They are

- sildenafil (Viagra)
- vardenafil (Levitra)
- tadalafil (Cialis)

Technically, these drugs are called phosphodiesterase (PDE) inhibitors. They work by boosting the level of a chemical needed to form an erection. PDE inhibitors allow a man to have an erection if he receives the proper stimulus, whether it's a sight, scent, sound, or caress. In other words, they do not increase sexual desire; that part is still up to you.

Men take these drugs about an hour before they plan to have sex. Doctors say sildenafil and vardenafil begin to work within an hour, and their benefits last at least four hours. The makers of tadalafil claim that its effects last up to 36 hours. Although the drugs haven't been compared in formal trials, individual studies suggest that they are equally effective, producing improved erections about 75 percent of the time.

PDE inhibitors are considered reasonably safe to use; mild headaches, skin flushing, and stuffy nose are the most common side effects. Shortly after the introduction of sildenafil, concerns arose that these drugs increase the risk of heart attacks. However, it appears that not all users are at risk. Only certain groups of men cannot take PDE inhibitors or must use them with care. For example, PDE inhibitors can cause a dangerous drop in blood pressure when combined with nitrates, which are drugs used to relieve angina (chest pain), and alpha blockers, used to treat prostate problems or high blood pressure. Your doctor may decide you're not a good candidate for PDE inhibitors if you have had certain other conditions. Finally, a small number of men who use these drugs have lost vision in one eye; the risk appears to be greatest in users who have various health problems, including diabetes.

If PDE inhibitors don't help, your doctor may recommend that you try other medications that have reputed benefits for men with ED. They include certain antidepressants, as well as the drug yohimbine. A dietary supplement called yohimbe (derived from tree bark) that contains the main chemical in yohimbine is sold without a prescription, but it should be avoided. The purity of dietary supplements sold as "aphrodisiacs" is notoriously unpredictable. Besides, if you're taking medicine for a health problem such as ED, you should be monitored for side effects by a physician.

Other medications. Effective as the new ED pills may be, they don't work for all men. If that's the case, your doctor may prescribe medicine that increases blood flow to the penis in a more direct manner. Alprostadil (Caverject, Muse, and other brand names) is a vasodilator drug, meaning that it increases circulation by expanding blood vessels. But instead of popping a pill, you either inject alprostadil into the penis with a needle or insert a suppository containing the drug into the urethra. Alprostadil can produce an erection within minutes.

Even a type 1 diabetes patient who has been injecting insulin since childhood may hesitate at the thought of putting a needle in his penis. But injected alprostadil produces an erection about 85 percent of the time, according to the American Urological Association, making it more than twice as effective as the suppository method. Injecting alprostadil may cause scarring on the penis, and some men who use the drug complain of aches or a burning sensation. Another potential problem: priapism, or a prolonged and sometimes painful erection that is a medical emergency.

Although low testosterone is a relatively rare cause of ED, men who need a boost of the hormone can get it through periodic injections in a doctor's office or by wearing a skin patch.

Vacuum devices. For a drug- and needle-free alternative for overcoming ED, some men opt for a vacuum erection device. The user places a plastic cylinder over the penis, then uses a hand or battery-operated pump to draw out the air inside. The drop in air pressure increases blood flow to the penis, causing it to expand. To maintain the erection, an elastic band is placed around the base of the penis to prevent blood from flowing out.

Penile implants For the patient who is willing to undergo surgery (performed

241

SEX AND BLOOD SUGAR

Although fumbling around for your glucose meter probably won't enhance the romantic mood, doctors say insulin users should check their blood sugar before engaging in sexual activity to avoid hypoglycemia. Apply the same rules as you would if you were heading out for a jog: If glucose is too low, eat a carbohydrate before *l'amore* or right after. You may also want to treat yourself to a small snack afterward to prevent delayed hypoglycemia.

on an outpatient basis), penile implants are another option. There are two basic types of implants, also called penile prostheses. Inflatable implants consist of cylinders inserted into the corpora caver-nosa (the twin shafts that run the length of the penis) and a pump implanted in the scrotum. The versions most widely used today, three-part implants, include a reservoir placed in the abdomen, too. To achieve an erection, the pump is squeezed, which inflates the cylinders with a saline solution. At the end of sexual activity, the cylinders are emptied by returning the saline solution to the reservoir, either by pressing a "deflate" button on the pump or by bending the penis several times.

So-called malleable penile implants are simply a steel or plastic rod coated in silicone. The man bends the implant into the desired position when he's ready to have sex, then returns it to the "down" position afterward.

Penile implants require a bit of manual dexterity to operate. They can lead to infections in one to five percent of cases and occasionally malfunction. In fact, three-part implants fail 10 to 15 percent of the time within the first five years.

Other types of surgery. In some cases, surgeons are able to repair blocked arteries that have reduced blood flow to the penis, as well as tie up leaky veins that cause blood to drain too quickly from the penis. But the former procedure is usually reserved for younger men who have suffered a physical trauma that has caused artery damage, while the latter has only a modest success rate.

Psychological counseling. In the pre-Viagra era, men with ED often heard that the problem was all in their heads. Doctors now believe that most problems with erections are due to physical problems. Still, psychological causes can't be ruled out, as experts say they may be at the root of 10 to 20 percent of ED cases. Stress, guilt, anxiety, and grief can all be culprits. If your doctor suspects that your mind is interfering with your love life, he or she may refer you to a psychotherapist or psychiatrist for counseling.

Female Sexual Health and Diabetes

For women, sexual dysfunction linked to diabetes is more varied and complex than in men, but it's no less troubling. The disease can take the steam out of intimacy in a number of ways. Complicating matters, the onset of menopause in middle age can produce symptoms similar to those caused by poorly controlled glucose, creating challenges to finding the right treatment. Unfortunately, as in many other areas of medicine, women have received less attention than men from scientists studying the way blood sugar problems affect sexuality. However, the situation is slowly changing.

LACK OF LUBRICATION

Nerve damage, one of the most common complications caused by poorly controlled glucose, can reduce or block the production of slippery fluids that moisten the vagina to make sexual intercourse easier and more pleasurable. Poor circulation caused by blocked arteries can dry up natural lubricants, too. Vaginal dryness can lead to dyspareunia, or pain during intercourse. A 2002 survey of women with type 1 diabetes found that poor vaginal lubrication was the most common sexual difficulty.

Treatment

Stock your nightstand with a "personal lubricant," such as K-Y Jelly, and use it to moisten the vagina before intercourse, reducing friction and the pain it causes. If vaginal dryness causes general discomfort all the time, consider a longer-lasting vaginal moisturizer, such as Replens or Lubrin. The latter products may reduce the risk of infections, too.

LACK OF AROUSAL

Up to one-third of women with diabetes may experience a loss of sex drive at one time or another. Obviously, painful intercourse will cause a woman to lose interest in sex in a hurry. But having diabetes can douse the flames of passion for women in other ways, too. Nerve damage may reduce sensitivity in the genitalia, limiting sensation and making it difficult to achieve orgasm. Some prescription drugs may lower libido. Having high blood sugar can leave you feeling blah and unsexy. Depression is common in diabetes patients, while women with type 2 disease who struggle with weight

problems may feel anxiety about their attractiveness. Conditions such as gynecologic infections (see below) can disrupt the joy of sex, too.

Treatment

To begin with, don't be shy. A frank conversation about the problem with your physician is the best first step. Treating vaginal dryness or infections will help make sex more appealing. Medication or psychotherapy may relieve underlying depression or anxiety. Your physician may refer you to a sex therapist, a specialist trained to help couples overcome physical and emotional barriers to intimacy.

GYNECOLOGIC INFECTIONS

As we mentioned in Chapter 8, diabetes patients have a high risk for urinary tract infections. The same is true for vaginal yeast infections, which are often caused by a fungus called *Candida albicans*. It's perfectly normal to have small amounts of yeast on your skin, in the mouth and digestive tract, and inside the vagina. However, under normal circumstances, the vagina produces acids that keep the population of yeast low. High blood sugar (among other influences) can lower acidity in the vagina, allowing yeast to flourish there and cause infections.

The symptoms of a yeast infection may include

- pain during intercourse or urination
- vaginal discharge that may be watery or resemble cottage cheese
- itching and burning about the vagina and labia
- red and irritated skin on the vagina and surrounding skin

If you develop a yeast infection, you may not be the only one suffering; men who have sex with an infected partner have a 12 to 15 percent chance of developing itching and a rash on their penis. About three-quarters of women have yeast infections at one time or another. But women with diabetes may develop recurrent vulvovaginal candidiasis (RVVC), which doctors define as four or more vaginal yeast infections per year.

Treatment

If you develop a yeast infection, get evaluated by a physician, at least the first time it happens. Over-the-counter products are available, but your doctor may offer special instructions about proper use to treat your condition. He or she will likely recommend one of the following antifungal medicines:

- Clotrimazole (Gyne-Lotrimin and other brands), which comes in a

BLOOD SUGAR AND M & M (MENSTRUATION AND MENOPAUSE)

Changes in hormone levels that occur during menstruation and menopause influence blood sugar, a fact women with diabetes must consider as part of their glucose management plan. For starters, blood glucose may rise just before a woman has her period, as high levels of progesterone and related hormones appear to cause temporary insulin resistance. However, estrogen rises immediately before a period, too, and in other women that increase seems to improve insulin's effect— sometimes too well, resulting in hypoglycemia. As a woman enters menopause, her body gradually makes less estrogen and progesterone until levels are very low, which may also cause blood sugar to fluctuate.

The link between hormones and blood sugar makes a strong argument for keeping a daily logbook to detect patterns in how glucose levels change. You and your doctor or diabetes educator can use this information to adjust insulin or drug doses.

variety of forms, including cream, lotion, and solution, that are applied to the skin; lozenges known as "troches" that dissolve in the mouth; and tablets and creams that are inserted into the vagina. These products are sold over the counter.

- Miconazole (Monistat and others), sold in various forms, including spray, cream, lotion, or powder. Also sold without a prescription.

- Fluconazole (Diflucan), sold by prescription as a pill or liquid.

Some research suggests that one popular folk remedy, inserting into the vagina plain yogurt that contains active *lactobacillus* cultures, may help; adding it to your diet may prevent yeast infections, too. See Chapter 8 for more tips on avoiding genitourinary tract infections.

Psychological Issues and Diabetes

Having a chronic, lifelong illness can leave you feeling sad, angry, frustrated, and generally out of sorts. While diabetes patients have always known that dealing with the disease can be emotionally draining, in recent years the medical establishment has recognized the role psychological problems play in managing diabetes.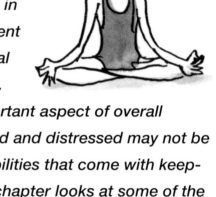

Not only is a healthy psyche an important aspect of overall health, but a patient who is distracted and distressed may not be able to attend to the many responsibilities that come with keeping blood sugar under control. This chapter looks at some of the major psychological complications that can accompany diabetes and offers some ideas on how to handle them.

Your Mind Matters

Not long ago, if a doctor included any form of psychological evaluation as part of routine patient care, it consisted of one question: How are you feeling? Today, many doctors make detailed inquiries about psychological issues during annual checkups and office visits. Questions once thought to be too touchy-feely for physicians trained to treat diseases of the body are now considered important screening tools. Science has shown, time and again, that a sound, serene mind is essential for robust physical well-being.

That's particularly true for diabetes patients, who must be clear-headed enough to manage much of their own care, even as they may be grappling with anger, grief, guilt, denial, frustration, disappointment, or all of the above. Too often, patients with psychological problems fly under the radar, so to speak, even though these problems affect their quality of life and diabetes management. According to one estimate, only about one-third of diabetes patients with depression have been diagnosed.

With that in mind, the American Diabetes Association recommends that physicians start asking patients questions about mental health at the time

they are diagnosed—before trouble arises—and continue to monitor the patient for signs of psychological problems as a way to reduce the risk of diabetes complications.

So don't be surprised if your doctor asks you

- how you feel about having diabetes.
- how the disease is affecting your mood and daily quality of life.
- what you expect from treatment.
- what kind of support you have—social, emotional, and financial.
- how well you are handling glucose monitoring, medications, diet, and other aspects of daily care.
- if you have any preexisting psychiatric conditions that may be affecting your ability to manage diabetes.

If you feel burdened by your emotions, however, don't wait for your doctor to inquire about your state of mind. The best time to raise concerns about psychological problems is today. Your psyche may be suffering needlessly, and you may spare your body from the ravages of chronically elevated glucose. Consider this: A 2004 scientific analysis published in *The Lancet,* a British medical journal, found that intensive psychological therapy can help diabetes patients cope with the emotional aspects of the condition *and* decrease A1c by as much as one percent—a drop in blood sugar that would make you and your doctor very happy.

THE PSYCHE

You can't see or touch your psyche. Doctors, psychologists, and philosophers don't agree on what the psyche is or if it even exists. Some people use the term as a synonym for "mind," "spirit," "self," or "soul." (In Greek mythology, Psyche is the personification of the soul.) Sigmund Freud thought that the psyche consists of two parts, the conscious and subconscious. The former includes the thoughts and ideas you are aware of, while the latter is a massive reserve of feelings, memories, impressions, and other information that exist beneath our awareness yet influence our behavior. For example, you might have the conscious thought, "I think I'll jog down Oak Street instead of Elm. It's much prettier." Meanwhile, at the unconscious level, your psyche is silently reminding you that the movie *A Nightmare on Elm Street* scared the daylights out of you.

It could be that conflicts in the subconscious mind cause problems for the psyche, though the causes of psychological disorders remain mysterious. However, most patients respond to mental health counseling, relaxation techniques, medication, or some combination of the three.

Researchers Richard R. Rubin and Mark Peyrot have identified three common psychological problems of particular concern for diabetes patients: depression, anxiety and stress, and eating disorders. We'll discuss each of them in turn.

Depression

Having any chronic disease increases the risk for depression. Diabetes is no exception. According to some estimates, about one in five diabetes patients experiences persistent bouts of the blues. That means depression is three times more common among people with diabetes than it is in the general population.

Studies show that depressed diabetes patients tend to have worse glucose control than their more-optimistic counterparts, possibly because persistent despair and gloominess make it harder to deal with the many responsibilities of managing diabetes. So it's not surprising that they also tend to have more complications. For instance, a 2005 study in *Diabetes Care* found high rates of depression among patients with diabetic neuropathy. Some researchers believe that a common hormonal imbalance may be linked to both mood problems and difficulty controlling blood sugar.

Symptoms of depression can include
- disturbed sleep patterns (either insomnia or oversleeping)
- loss of interest in hobbies and favorite pastimes
- a change in appetite
- lack of energy
- feelings of worthlessness, hopelessness, or helplessness
- self-loathing
- feeling guilty for no reason
- difficulty concentrating
- irritability

- low self-esteem
- suicidal thoughts

If you have several of these symptoms for an extended period, your doctor may diagnose depression. There are two primary methods of treatment: counseling and medication. These can be used on their own or in combination, depending on the severity of the depression and its source.

Mental health counseling. If all you know about psychotherapy comes from TV and movies, you may think psychotherapy involves lying on a couch and talking endlessly about your tortured childhood to a bearded man who is taking notes. But talk therapy needn't be long-term (though there is certainly a place for that, too). Short-term, focused psychotherapy can help you address your diabetes-related problem head-on. In fact, some research suggests that a form of counseling known as cognitive-behavioral therapy (CBT) may be particularly beneficial. In CBT, a therapist helps the patient identify and replace negative, inaccurate, and destructive thoughts and behaviors with healthier, more constructive thoughts and actions.

Medication. When you have depression, brain chemistry is out of balance. Modern antidepressant medication simply adjusts levels of neurotransmitters, the chemical messengers that deliver signals from one neuron (brain cell) to another. These are not "happy pills," as ill-informed skeptics sometimes suggest. There are several categories of antidepressant drugs, but the most commonly prescribed today are known as selective serotonin reuptake inhibitors, or SSRIs. Serotonin is a neurotransmitter believed to help regulate mood. SSRIs appear to work by keeping serotonin at work longer. Fluox-etine, better known by the brand name Prozac, is one of the most widely prescribed SSRIs. Others include paroxetine (Paxil), sertraline (Zoloft), and citalopram (Celexa).

Anxiety and Stress

Everyone feels a bit nervous or on edge now and then, but people with anxiety disorders worry so much that their fretting interferes with daily life. Studies suggest that people with diabetes often struggle with anxiety; the condition is probably about as common among diabetes patients as depression. Patients may feel a general sense of anxiety about having the disease or cite specific concerns, such as fear of hypoglycemia, needles, sexual difficulties, or weight gain. Doctors say that diabetes patients who feel anxious and stressed out are less likely to carefully manage blood sugar, increasing the risk for complications. Like depression, anxiety disorders often go undiagnosed.

DOES STRESS CAUSE DIABETES?

Patients sometimes ask their doctors if living a chaotic, overscheduled lifestyle caused them to develop diabetes. While there is no proof that stress causes the disease, it sure doesn't help those who have it. Stress hormones allow the body to respond to a crisis or threat—real or imagined—by preparing it to fight or flee. One critical role of stress hormones is to release glucose so that muscle cells have a ready source of energy. An occasional spike in blood sugar is no big deal for most people, but chronic stress caused by financial problems, a failing marriage, or other ongoing woes could lead to persistent elevated glucose levels. What's more, stress can distract you from important priorities, such as monitoring blood sugar and exercising, and encourage unhealthy behaviors, like overeating high-calorie comfort foods. The message is clear: High levels of stress can increase your risk for diabetes complications, so find a way to chill out when life boils over.

Many symptoms of anxiety overlap with those of depression. They may include

- feeling "stressed out"
- restlessness and irritability
- lack of energy
- difficulty concentrating
- muscle tension
- the jitters
- headaches
- poor sleep
- excessive sweating
- palpitations or shortness of breath
- upset stomach

The treatment choices for anxiety, like those for depression, fall into two main categories: behavioral treatments and medication.

Relaxation therapy. A little stress is good for us; the "oh-my-gosh!" reflex allows us to meet deadlines and sprint through airports to catch connecting flights. However, when the so-called "fight or flight" instinct works overtime, anxiety and stress result. Fortunately, you can learn to turn off or tone down the panicky voice in your head through various relaxation techniques. There are countless relaxation methods; the key is to find one that works for you and stick with it, whether you choose meditation, yoga, prayer, needlepoint, or Three Stooges movies.

FINDING HELP AND SUPPORT

In the cast of characters you turn to for help managing diabetes, a psychotherapist can play an important role. "Psychotherapist" is a catchall term for any kind of mental health counselor, which includes psychologists, social workers, and psychiatrists. If you are interested in seeing a therapist for treatment, your physician or diabetes educator may be able to refer you to a counselor. If not, asking friends and family members or checking the Yellow Pages or Internet may be your next best options. After meeting with a therapist for the first time, the critical question to ask yourself is: Can I talk about my problems with this person? Be sure to discuss the therapist's methods and fee policy. Some experts recommend "trying out" two or three therapists for one session before settling on one whom you trust and who makes you feel at ease.

Joining a support group allows you to share your fears and anxieties with people who truly understand them: other diabetes patients. To find a support group, ask your diabetes educator, call your local hospital or chapter of the American Diabetes Association, or search the ADA Web site. If you would rather type than talk, countless groups "gather" on the Internet.

Studies have shown that one technique in particular, biofeedback, may be able to help type 2 patients keep glucose levels under control. In biofeedback, a therapist asks the patient to think about relaxing his or her body. Meanwhile, sensors attached to the skin deliver information to a computer monitor or

251

other medium in the form of data about a biological function that increases or intensifies when we're stressed out, such as circulation, skin temperature, or muscle tension. Receiving this "feed-back" reinforces a patient's innate ability to slow the pulse or reduce muscle tension, which has a relaxing effect.

Medication. In some cases, doctors may prescribe medications called benzodiazepines, such as alprazolam (Xanax), to control anxiety. Benzodi-azepines work fast and cause few side effects, other than drowsiness. How-ever, they can be highly addictive, so these pills are typically used for short periods and may be a poor choice for patients with alcohol or drug abuse problems.

One alternative to benzodiazepines is the drug buspirone (BuSpar), which belongs to a newer class of drugs called azipirones. Buspirone takes longer to produce benefits and may have side effects such as dizziness, headaches, and nausea, but it is less addictive than alprazolam (Xanax). In addition, some doctors claim success in treating anxiety with antidepressants, especially SSRIs.

Eating Disorders

Given the central role diet plays in controlling blood sugar, it's not surpris-ing that many diabetes patients be-come preoccupied with food. However, that preoccupation can morph into unhealthy practices. Studies suggest, for instance, that young women with type 1 diabetes have a heightened risk for food bingeing and bulimia (vomiting or using laxatives to avoid weight gain). Furthermore, one-third to one-half of young women with type 1 disease may engage in a practice known as "insulin purging." Because injected insulin allows the body to burn glucose as fuel and store the leftovers as fat, these women reduce their usual insulin dose to avoid gaining weight. Reducing the dose causes the body to get rid of excess glucose in the urine instead of storing it as fat. It also allows blood sugar to rise because there isn't enough insulin, increasing the risk of complications.

Treatment options for eating disorders also include therapeutic intervention and medication.

Counseling. Experts say that treating eating disorders requires a team approach. A psychotherapist can help the patient cope with underlying emo-tional problems that contribute to self-destructive eating habits. A dietitian can offer education and counseling about healthy nutrition. And, of course, the patient's physician treats and controls the effects of elevated glucose.

Medications. Doctors sometimes prescribe antidepressants to treat eating disorders.

PSYCHOLOGICAL INSULIN RESISTANCE

When a patient with type 2 diabetes can no longer control blood sugar with diet, exercise, and oral medication, the next obvious step is to begin insulin therapy. However, doctors say that many patients have an emotional response to this news and resist the idea of taking insulin. When a patient is hesitant or flat-out refuses to take insulin, physicians sometimes say he or she has psychological insulin resistance (PIR).

Several studies reflect the prevalence of PIR. In one large trial, more than one-quarter of type 2 patients who were prescribed insulin refused to take the drug, at least initially. In another, up to three-quarters of patients said they were reluctant to take insulin. The longer you put off taking insulin, though, the more damage high blood sugar has a chance to do. Two experts on diabetes and behavior—William H. Polonsky, Ph.D., of the University of California, San Diego, and Richard A. Jackson, M.D., of Boston's Joslin Diabetes Center—have identified six

attitudes and beliefs that can cause PIR. Here they are, followed by a healthy dose of reality:

1. Patients view taking insulin as a loss of control. In one survey, half of patients interviewed said they believed that insulin therapy would restrict or disrupt their lives. Some patients worry that taking insulin will rob their lives of spon-

DOES YOUR DOCTOR HAVE PIR?

If you believe that insulin therapy is unpleasant and a hassle—even though you don't use it—you may have gotten that impression from your physician. Experts say patients aren't the only ones who can develop psychological insulin resistance. Occasionally, doctors may also be reluctant to put a patient on insulin therapy, whether or not they are conscious of their bias.

There are several reasons a doctor may delay prescribing insulin to patients who need it, according to William H. Polonsky, Ph.D., and Richard A. Jackson, M.D., two leading authorities on PIR. A doctor may
- anticipate a patient's negative reaction to hearing he or she needs insulin.
- fear the patient will experience frequent bouts of hypoglycemia.
- worry that treating a patient who takes insulin will require more of his or her time.

PIR can be contagious, so your doctor's bias and reluctance may rub off on you. If you have repeatedly failed to meet blood sugar goals, yet your physician has not discussed insulin therapy, ask why.

taneity, make travel and dining out difficult, and create other hassles. Others worry about the threat of hypoglycemia and weight gain.

ROUTINE MAINTENANCE

Psychological problems can create a vicious cycle for diabetes patients. For example, patients may become depressed because their efforts to lower blood sugar aren't working. Out of frustration, they quit monitoring their glucose, skip insulin therapy, and ignore their diets, resulting in even worse blood sugar.

- Don't let your psyche suffer; include your emotional well-being as part of your overall health-maintenance plan.
- Discuss your psychological health with your physician on a regular basis. Don't wait for the doctor to raise the issue.
- Engage in relaxation techniques daily, whether you have a diagnosed psychological condition or not. Finding a way to calm your mind has many benefits, which may include lower blood sugar.
- Consider creating an entry for emotional health in your logbook. For instance, you might score your stress level each day on a scale from 1 (calm, easygoing) to 10 (gut-roiling, head-splitting, come-in-off-that-ledge stressed-out). Look for trends in how emotions affect your blood sugar by comparing a month of stress notations with your glucose readings.
- Take prescribed medication for depression or other psychological conditions.

The facts: The wide variety of insulin available can accommodate most lifestyles and allow for spur-of-the-moment changes in plans. Hypoglycemia is a concern, but once a patient learns to manage insulin therapy and oral medications, it is a less common occurrence. Weight gain caused by insulin, if any, is usually modest.

2. Patients lack confidence in their ability. Giving yourself insulin injections is definitely trickier than popping a pill once or twice a day. Not surprisingly, nearly half of patients prescribed insulin worry that they will make mistakes by messing up the timing or delivering the wrong dosage. Unfortunately, self-doubt can turn into a self-fulfilling prophesy, as patients who lack confidence often do a poor job managing insulin treatments.

The facts: Worries about proper technique can be overcome by working closely with your diabetes educator and—as the old saying goes about getting to Carnegie Hall—practice, practice,

practice. Using an insulin pen instead of a needle may be less intimidating.

3. Patients feel a sense of failure. Patients often say that needing insulin is proof that they did a poor job of taking care of their diabetes. As Polonsky and Jackson explain, "insulin is viewed as a well-deserved punishment for one's own gluttony, sloth, or negligence..."

The facts: Diabetes is a chronic disease and many patients eventually require additional forms of treatment. As many as one-third of type 2 patients need insulin therapy at some point. Accepting that possibility early on can eliminate the shock factor if the need arises.

4. Patients have misconceptions about insulin. A patient will often see a prescription for insulin as proof that his or her condition is worsening. Moreover, some patients worry that insulin itself makes you sick. That may be especially true if an older relative lost eyesight or required amputation soon after beginning insulin treatments.

The facts: While taking insulin slightly increases the risk of hypoglycemia, there is no truth to myths such as "insulin makes you go blind." When a patient's condition worsens soon after commencing insulin therapy, it's likely that years of poorly controlled blood sugar were the culprit.

5. Some patients have needle phobia. Many patients complain that they don't want to jab themselves with a sharp object several times a day for the rest of their lives.

The facts: A mental health counselor can help patients overcome fear of needles. Genuine needle phobia is relatively uncommon. In many cases, patients discover that their anxiety about injecting themselves comes from their frustration with having diabetes.

6. Patients often have the "What's In It for Me?" syndrome. A patient overcome with doubts and fears about insulin may have a hard time believing the drug's benefits outweigh perceived potential harm. One study found that only one in ten type 2 diabetes patients believed that insulin therapy would improve their health.

The facts: Attaining better glucose control through insulin therapy not only reduces the risk for long-term complications, it can also improve mood, energy level, and sleep quality.

Children and Diabetes

Want to invest in your child's future? You can sock away money in a trust fund, in a savings account, or under the mattress to help pay for higher education or a first home. But if your child has diabetes, the care and attention you devote to managing the disease today will pay even greater dividends. You will reduce the risk of long-term complications by keeping the child's blood sugar in check, of course. However, you will also instill lifelong values—such as the importance of frequent glucose testing, scrupulous administration of medication, and healthy lifestyle choices—that will serve him or her well for many years to come.

Kid Talk: Children and Diabetes

Once upon a time, there was "juvenile diabetes" and "adult diabetes." Doctors now use the terms "type 1 diabetes" and "type 2 diabetes" to reflect new understandings about the disease. After all, adults can develop the former (though about three-quarters of new type 1 diabetes patients are under 18), while legions of young people in this country have turned up in doctors' offices in recent years with type 2 diabetes.

However, that doesn't mean children with diabetes can be treated like miniature versions of adult patients. Because their bodies are still developing, children require a treatment plan of their own. There is no substitute for working closely with your child's diabetes-management team to create a strategy

tailored to his or her specific needs. This chapter provides essential background on critical topics including medication, diet, exercise, health screening, and other aspects of managing a child's diabetes—such as school-related issues—until he or she can take over that role.

Medication

The goal of diabetes management is to keep blood glucose levels as close to normal as possible. For children with diabetes, that often means using some form of medication.

INSULIN

A child with type 1 diabetes must inject insulin several times a day to control his or her blood glucose levels. A growing number of children with type 2 diabetes use insulin, too. At first, you may find the nuances of insulin bewildering. What's the difference between rapid-acting and short-acting insulin? Why doesn't a daily injection of long-acting insulin do the trick? What do all these terms—onset, peak, duration—mean?

> ### CHILDREN AND DIABETES BY THE NUMBERS
>
> - Americans under age 18 who have diabetes: more than 229,000
> - Children diagnosed with type 1 diabetes annually: about 13,000
> - Children with diabetes diagnosed with type 2 before 1994: 5 percent
> - Children with diabetes diagnosed with type 2 today: up to 45 percent

You can refer to Chapter 3 for an overview of insulin, but your child's diabetes-management team will help you plan precisely how to replace this critical hormone. Together, you will determine

- how much insulin your child requires every day, based on body weight and age.
- which type of insulin, or what combination of insulin types, best suits your child.
- which delivery system—syringe, insulin pen, or pump—makes the most sense.
- which injection sites will work best and how to rotate them.

Diabetes requires an extraordinary amount of self-management, which is way beyond the ability of young children. How, you may wonder, will you ever trust your child, who can't tie her own shoes or make his own bed, with a needle and vial of insulin? Although you will likely be involved in your child's daily diabetes maintenance until he or she leaves the nest, you'll be relieved to know that children gradually assume greater responsibility for controlling blood sugar as they get older. Your role in their diabetes management and your major concerns will change over time. A typical progression might look something like this:

Infancy

Although rare, type 1 diabetes occasionally emerges in babies.

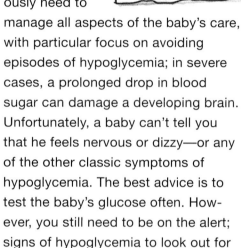

Parents obviously need to manage all aspects of the baby's care, with particular focus on avoiding episodes of hypoglycemia; in severe cases, a prolonged drop in blood sugar can damage a developing brain. Unfortunately, a baby can't tell you that he feels nervous or dizzy—or any of the other classic symptoms of hypoglycemia. The best advice is to test the baby's glucose often. However, you still need to be on the alert; signs of hypoglycemia to look out for may include

- jitteriness
- irritability
- lethargy
- seizures
- bluish skin
- breathing problems
- feeding problems

Toddlers (1 to 3 years)

It is a fact of early childhood: Kids sometimes scream, kick, and fuss. Tempting as it may be to disregard a child's temper tantrum, that's

not an option when the child has diabetes. That's because it may be difficult to tell the difference between "normal developmental opposition" (the term psychologists use for everyday wailing and throwing of toys) and a bout of hypoglycemia. A child may act cranky and difficult if his or her blood sugar has dropped, so doctors encourage parents to check glucose levels just to be sure.

On the other hand, parents must guard against becoming overly protective and treating the child as though he or she belongs in a bubble, which could hinder natural development.

Preschool and Early School-Aged Children (3 to 7 years)

At this age, a child still lacks the physical coordination, mental development, and maturity to manage daily care. However, this is the time to get the child involved by having him or her take part in testing glucose levels, keeping records, and learning how to count carbohydrates. Doing so not only

serves as an introduction to the skills he or she will need but will also build confidence.

Keep in mind, though, that even if your child is a little chatterbox, he or she may still not be able to articulate, or even recognize, the symptoms of low blood sugar. You may need to learn to decipher certain phrases, such as "I'm hungry" or "I feel funny," which could be a child's code language for "I think my blood sugar is low."

School-Aged Children (8 to 11 years)

By this age, children can start to inject insulin and test their glucose, but only with adult supervision. Studies show that relying on a child to manage diabetes on his or her own at this age often results in poor glucose control. The insulin pump is an increasingly popular option for kids at this age, and even younger, though it also requires adult oversight.

TROUBLESHOOTING CHECKLIST

A child may not be able to recognize, or even describe, the onset of symptoms when blood sugar is out of balance. So you have to do it for him or her. What's more, beware of mood problems a child may develop, as they may interfere with successful blood sugar control. Watch out for the following:

- ☐ Jitteriness, lethargy, and any unusual changes in behavior or appearance in infants

- ☐ Apparent temper tantrum (which may mask hypoglycemic episodes) in older children

- ☐ "Code" phrases, such as "I feel funny" or "I'm hungry," which your child may use when he or she feels the symptoms of low blood sugar

- ☐ Extended periods of anxiety or depression

259

Depression and anxiety are normal responses among kids diagnosed with diabetes in this age range, though those problems often fade after six months or so. Still, preadolescent children begin to develop a sense of their place in society and may feel that having diabetes makes them "weird" or "different." It's important to encourage kids to participate in school activities, make friends, and have normal, healthy relationships.

Adolescents

By teen-hood, a child has developed considerable manual dexterity, mental ability, and—hard as it may be to believe at times—maturity. That means he or she can assume much of the responsibility for diabetes management. In fact, the growing streak of rebellion and independence many teens display (often in unfortunate haircuts and unfathomable fashions) may lead the adolescent with diabetes one day to blurt out, *I don't need your help, I can do this myself*. However, your son or daughter does still need help, especially with the finer points, such as when and how much to adjust insulin doses. Research shows that teens who continue to work with their parents maintain better glucose control.

It's important to keep in mind, however, that butting in too much—when it comes to the teen's diabetes management or anything else—can lead to sour relations. Studies suggest that glucose control suffers when teens and parents squabble.

As children grow and age, their insulin requirements change. That's especially true during puberty, when hormonal havoc causes a phase of insulin resistance, dramatically increasing the required dosage. This lasts until they develop a stable health pattern, which is earlier for women than for men. Lifestyle behaviors, such as excessive consumption of carbohydrates or excessive exercise, also play a role.

ORAL DIABETES MEDICATIONS

Metformin (Glucophage) is the only oral diabetes medicine approved by the Food and Drug Administration for use in children. Metformin does not increase insulin levels; it works by causing the liver to release less glucose into the blood and making cells more sensitive to the actions of insulin. Metformin can cause side effects, including vomiting, constipation, and heartburn, as well as a "full" feeling in the belly. If your child finds the side effects unbearable, talk to his or her physician. However, metformin's side effects often fade over time.

Although other oral diabetes medications are not approved for children, they can be prescribed "off label" if a physician feels that a child with type 2 diabetes will benefit.

Diet and Exercise

Children with diabetes should eat a nutritious, balanced diet that promotes good health—the same kind of diet all kids should eat. If possible, work with a dietitian to ensure that your child's meal plan accommodates his or her individual needs, which vary depending on the type of diabetes. Likewise, all children with diabetes benefit from getting plenty of exercise, which helps control blood sugar, especially in type 2 diabetes patients. Aiming for 60 minutes of physical activity each day is a good goal. If your child uses insulin, gym teachers and sports coaches need to know.

TYPE 1 DIABETES

A child with type 1 diabetes needs adequate calories and nutrients to encourage healthy growth. The timing and size of meals are critical factors, since a premeal dose of insulin is necessary to keep blood sugar levels after eating. Parents often find that it's easier to keep a child's glucose in the healthy range if the family eats breakfast, lunch, and dinner at the same times every day.

Since exercise can cause hypoglycemia, monitoring glucose levels is essential both before and after any kind of physical activity. That includes gym class, soccer practice, or an extended game of tag with friends in the backyard. To prevent low blood sugar, a child may need to eat a carbohydrate snack before, during, and after exercising, depending on how long he or she romps around. Your diabetes educator can recommend how much food a child should eat to maintain healthy glucose levels during exercise.

TYPE 2 DIABETES

There is growing evidence that parents can pass along a genetic tendency to acquire type 2 diabetes to their children. But heredity is not destiny, so you can't blame genes alone when a kid develops the disease. Scientists know that excess body fat is linked to insulin resistance, which sets the stage for diabetes. And the formula for obesity is simple: eat too much, exercise too little.

261

No one is sure how many American children have type 2 diabetes, but their ranks are on the rise. In this country, the age of the average patient who is diagnosed with the disease has dropped six years since the late 1970s. Disturbing as this unwelcome trend may be, it seems less shocking when you consider these eye-popping numbers:

- The amount of soda pop Americans consume has increased 500 percent over the past 50 years. The average adolescent gets more than 10 percent of his or her calories from the sugary, fizzy drinks.
- The typical child in the United States eats 650 percent more fast food today, as measured by calories, than in the 1970s. That's an increase from 2 percent of total calories to 15 percent.
- A study by the Centers for Disease Control and Prevention found that nearly two-thirds of American children between the ages of 9 and 13 engaged in no physical activity during school hours, while more than one in five didn't exercise outside school, either.
- More than one-third of American children watch at least three hours of television on an average school day.

You don't need to read medical journals to know that these trends help explain the super-sizing of the American child that has occurred in recent years. But if you did, you would find plenty of studies, such as a 2003 report in *Archives of Pediatric and Adolescent Medicine,* which showed that children who watch more than two hours of television per evening have a 50 percent increased risk of being overweight, while drinking three or more soft drinks a day ups the risk to 61 percent. Another study found that the likelihood of being obese increases 12 percent for every hour of television a child watches each week.

First-line therapy for most children who are diagnosed with type 2 diabetes consists of strict orders to eat smaller portions, avoid junk food, put down the remote control or video-game joystick, come out of the Internet chat rooms, and get moving. Although many will eventually require medication to control blood sugar, some kids may be able to forestall or avoid glucose-lowering medication through improvements in diet and exercise alone.

What's more, eating healthier foods and exercising can reduce the risk of another threat for children with type 2 diabetes: cardiovascular disease. Although heart attacks are rare in children, studies show that damage to arteries begins early. That's particularly true in kids with type 2 diabetes, who often have elevated cholesterol, triglycerides, and blood pressure, in addition to insulin resistance.

Chapter 13 gives an overview of healthy nutrition for diabetes patients, but a dietitian or diabetes educator can help you determine your child's specific dietary needs and design a meal plan tailored to your family's lifestyle and cultural preferences.

HEALTH SCREENING FOR CHILDREN WITH DIABETES

After a child has been diagnosed with diabetes, the American Diabetes Association recommends the following schedule for health screening:

Every Three Months
- A1c, a measurement of average blood glucose control
- Height and weight
- Body mass index
- Blood pressure
- Examination of injection sites
- Review of self-testing blood glucose records
- Testing for psychological problems

Annually
- Evaluation of nutrition therapy
- Microalbuminuria test for signs of kidney disease after a child turns

GENERATION EX-TRA LARGE

Years	Obese Children (ages 6 to 11)	Obese Adolescents (ages 12 to 19)
1963 to 1970	4.2 percent	4.6 percent
1971 to 1974	4.0 percent	6.1 percent
1975 to 1980	6.5 percent	5.0 percent
1988 to 1994	11.3 percent	10.5 percent
1999 to 2000	15.3 percent	15.5 percent

GOALS FOR GLUCOSE, KID-STYLE

Doctors sometimes say a healthy goal for children with type 1 diabetes is to achieve "near-normal" glucose levels. While it would be swell if your child maintained an A1c of 7 percent or lower—the same goal as for adult patients—concerns about hypoglycemia must be balanced against the desire to aggressively lower blood sugar in children. Prolonged low glucose can cause brain damage in very young children. As kids get older, their eating and exercise patterns become unpredictable. What's more, parents must rely, in part, on school personnel to help manage a child's glucose. Hormonal changes at puberty add a further challenge to tight control.

While your child's diabetes-management team will establish appropriate goals for glucose levels, the American Diabetes Association (ADA) offers the following guidelines for children with type 1 diabetes. (The ADA has not established guidelines for children with type 2 diabetes; however, the National Diabetes Education Program suggests that parents of type 2 patients use the glucose goals detailed below.) Remember, these are only guidelines. Your doctor may recommend higher goals if your child has frequent hypoglycemia or hypoglycemia unawareness.

Age	Blood glucose before meals (mg/dl)	Blood glucose bedtime/overnight (mg/dl)	A1c (%)
Under 6 years	100 to 180	110 to 200	7.5 to 8.5
6 to 12 years	90 to 180	100 to 180	Less than 8
13 to 19 years	90 to 130	90 to 150	Less than 7.5

ten and has had diabetes for at least five years

- Ophthalmologic exam, for signs of retinopathy, starting at around age ten and after the child has had diabetes for three to five years
- Thyroid function test (for children with type 1 diabetes)
- Foot exam

Other Tests

- Blood lipids, such as cholesterol and triglycerides, as recommended by your child's physician
- Your child's eye doctor may decide that less-frequent exams are permissible
- Screen for celiac disease, an autoimmune disease that's more common in children with type 1 diabetes

COPING WITH SCHOOL DAYS

You have mastered the art of monitoring your child's glucose and giving insulin injections. Now you have to trust total strangers to do it for you? Parents of children who require insulin often worry as they send Junior off to school with his insulin kit and glucose meter. But knowing your child's rights and upholding your responsibilities can help alleviate the stress and strain. You'll be relieved once you make a plan and go over it during a visit with the school nurse.

Your Child's Rights

Federal law designates diabetes as a disability, making it illegal for schools and day care centers to discriminate against anyone who has the disease. What's more, schools that receive funds from the U.S. government have to make reasonable efforts to accommodate children with diabetes and the steps they need to take to maintain glucose control. That means the child can expect

- to be assisted in blood sugar monitoring and insulin injection by school personnel
- to be allowed to have snacks as necessary
- to participate in all programs available to other children

In addition, there is a long list of other rights that, in sum, strive to ensure that a child with diabetes has the same access to a complete education and extracurricular activities as any other kid. You can look up the laws and read them for yourself. They are

- Section 504 of the Rehabilitation Act of 1973
- The Individuals with Disabilities Education Act of 1991
- The Americans with Disabilities Act

Your Responsibilities

Introducing yourself to the nurse at your child's school, as well as his or her teach-

ers and principal, would be a good start. But don't show up empty-handed: Arrive with a diabetes medical-management plan, which your son or daughter's health care team will prepare. (You can find a sample on the ADA Web site, www.diabetes.org.) This document provides school officials with everything they need to know about your child and his or her condition, including

- how often and when to check glucose levels
- how much insulin to administer for given glucose values
- when and what the child should eat
- symptoms of hypoglycemia and how to treat it
- anything else adults supervising your child need to know in order to help him or her manage diabetes

Naturally, you are also responsible for providing all medical equipment and supplies, snacks, emergency telephone numbers, and any other essential items.

ROUTINE MAINTENANCE

Until your child can assume all of the responsibilities of managing diabetes, you must assume the role of in-house health care worker, diabetes educator, and cheerleader. Maintaining tight glucose control will spare your child long-term complications, as will instilling the principles of good diabetes self-care.

- Test glucose levels often; experts recommend four to eight times per day.
- Take all diabetes medications on schedule.
- Maintain glucose meters and insulin-delivery equipment (syringes, pens, and pumps).
- Bring your child for quarterly and annual medical checkups.
- Update your child's diabetes medical management plan. Be sure the nurse and officials at his or her school have a copy of the latest version.
- Ensure that your child is getting plenty of exercise and eating a healthy, balanced diet.

Pregnancy and Diabetes

Before picking out names, choosing paint colors for the nursery, and deciding whether the little genius should attend Harvard or Yale, expectant mothers with diabetes should consider how the disease will affect their pregnancy. That may be obvious enough to prospective mothers who already have type 1 or type 2 diabetes. However, each year thousands of preg-nant women who never gave the disease a

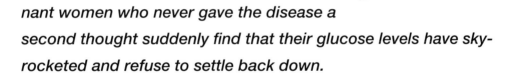

second thought suddenly find that their glucose levels have sky-rocketed and refuse to settle back down.

If you're concerned about controlling diabetes during your preg-nancy, that's good. Turn that concern into action. Put away the baby-name book, paint samples, and college brochures, and begin taking steps to protect yourself and your developing child. Reading this final chapter is a good start.

Special Delivery: Pregnancy and Diabetes

Pregnant women with diabetes come in two varieties. Some have type 1 or type 2 diabetes before conceiving; this is called pregestational diabetes. Others develop blood sugar problems during pregnancy; this is known as gestational diabetes and is the most common variety after type 1 and type 2 diabetes. About 200,000 women in the United States develop gestational diabetes each year.

As this chapter makes all too clear, pregnancy can be full of risks for a woman with diabetes and her developing child. Yet doctors insist that one simple measure—keeping blood sugar in check—can greatly reduce, and even eliminate, those risks. For example, statistics show that birth defects are two to three times more likely in children of mothers who have diabetes. But a closer look at the research reveals that women with diabetes who maintain tight glucose control bear children with birth defects at the same rate as in the general population—about one to two percent of pregnancies.

GESTATIONAL DIABETES

You thought it was going to be just another routine office visit. You're seven months into your pregnancy, and everything seems to be going fine. Then your doctor delivers news that hits you like a lightning bolt: You have gestational diabetes.

In fact, although the diagnosis may have been a shock, it probably wasn't a complete surprise. Early in your pregnancy, or perhaps before, your physician may have cautioned you about your risk for gestational diabetes. Any woman can develop the condition, but as we explained in Chapter 1, certain attributes increase the odds. Here's a quick refresher on the risk factors:

- Age: being older than 25
- Family history: having a parent or sibling with diabetes
- Ethnicity: being of African, American Indian, Asian, Hispanic, or Pacific Islander descent
- Weight: being significantly overweight
- Previous history: having already had gestational diabetes or given birth to an infant who weighed more than nine pounds

- Higher than normal blood sugar levels: having ever been told that you have prediabetes, impaired glucose tolerance, or impaired fasting glucose
- Previous difficult pregnancy

So how does this version of the disease differ from type 1 and type 2 diabetes? Gestational diabetes occurs when a woman develops insulin resistance while she's pregnant. About seven percent of pregnancies produce gestational diabetes. Scientists suspect that the wave of hormones a woman manufactures to support the health of a developing child interferes with the action of insulin, causing an increase in blood sugar. Expectant mothers with gestational diabetes rarely have the traditional symptoms of the disease, such as constant thirst, because their degree of hyperglycemia is slight.

Gestational diabetes poses many of the same risks that occur when women with type 1 or type 2 diabetes become pregnant. You may develop hypertension or need to have a cesarean section. And the baby may be overweight or have hypoglycemia on delivery. You will read more about these risks and others later in Complications and Conception: 7 Good Reasons to Control Blood Sugar During Pregnancy, page 271.

DOES THIS MEAN MY BABY WILL HAVE DIABETES?

It's the first question many diabetes patients ask when they begin to ponder parenthood. Chapter 1 spells out the odds for type 1 patients; less is known about whether type 2 diabetes is inherited, though scientists strongly suspect that parents pass along an increased risk for the disease. If you're a concerned parent-to-be, your best bet is to consult a genetic counselor. These health professionals can explain and interpret inheritance patterns and how your (or your partner's) diabetes affects the risk of bearing a child with the disease. Most major medical centers have a genetic counselor on staff. You may also contact the National Society of Genetic Counselors (www.nsgc.org).

Gestational diabetes usually disappears when a pregnancy ends. However, a small number of women continue to have elevated blood sugar, and the condition morphs into type 1 or 2 diabetes. Furthermore, one bout with gestational diabetes makes you more likely to develop the condition if you become pregnant again. Finally, your risk for developing type 2 diabetes sometime in the next decade or so soars by up to 50 percent.

Screening for Gestational Diabetes

If your physician suspects you may be at risk for gestational diabetes, he or she will order glucose testing at your first prenatal office visit. Chapter 1 explains in detail how glucose testing works, but here's a brief overview. Your physician may use a fasting blood glucose test (blood is drawn after fasting overnight) or a random blood glucose test (sometimes called a casual blood glucose test; no fasting required). The following test values suggest you may have diabetes:

- Fasting blood glucose: 126 mg/dl or higher
- Random blood glucose: 200 mg/dl or higher

A retest may be necessary to confirm the diagnosis unless you have obvious symptoms of high blood sugar, such as those listed above. If your glucose readings fall below these levels, you're in the clear—at least for now. If you fall into a high- or medium-risk group, your doctor will test for gestational diabetes again between the 24th and 28th week of pregnancy. This time, you will be given an oral one-hour random glucose tolerance test. A test result of 140 mg/dl or higher will trigger additional testing, in which your blood glucose levels will be tested before you consume a

heavy dose of carbohydrates (100 grams, or the amount in 2½ cans of Dr Pepper) and then every 60 minutes for 3 hours after. If you exceed two or more of the glucose levels in the following chart, you have gestational diabetes:

Fasting	95 mg/dl or higher
1 hour	180 mg/dl or higher
2 hours	155 mg/dl or higher
3 hours	140 mg/dl or higher

After delivering your baby, there is one more round of tests to go. Gestational diabetes usually goes away after a pregnancy ends, but a small number of women continue to have blood sugar problems. Within 6 to 12 weeks of delivery, your doctor will conduct a follow-up test to determine whether your glucose levels have returned to normal.

Pregestational Diabetes

Managing diabetes is hard enough as it is. Managing diabetes while trying to nurture a growing life in the womb is even harder still—and even more important. However, women with preexisting diabetes can greatly increase their chances for an uncomplicated—or, at least, less-complicated—pregnancy by taking several critical steps in the months before they start trying to get pregnant.

Plan Ahead

About two-thirds of pregnancies in women with diabetes aren't planned. But if you have diabetes, planning ahead is extremely important to ensure your health and that of your baby. Meet with your diabetes healthcare team to discuss all the necessary steps to take before you attempt to get pregnant.

Get Control of Your Blood Sugar

If you have allowed your glucose levels to creep up (or, worse, you have no idea what they are), now is the time to regain control. Try to get your A1c within one percent of the upper limits of normal (usually defined as seven percent). Even lower would be better (but watch out for hypoglycemia). Keep in mind that women don't usually know they're pregnant for several weeks after conception, yet during this time a fetus's developing organs may be exposed to toxic levels of glucose. Waiting until you become pregnant to lower blood sugar puts a fetus at increased risk for birth defects.

Have a Complete Health Evaluation

Your physician needs to assess your risk for diabetes complications that may worsen during pregnancy, including retinopathy, nephropathy, neuropathy, and heart disease.

Talk to a Physician About Your Medications

If you currently take oral diabetes drugs, your physician will probably switch you to insulin therapy, due to concerns that these medications may harm a fetus. Other drugs often used to treat conditions common in diabetes patients may pose concerns, too, including ACE inhibitors and ARBs (used to lower blood pressure) and statins (which lower cholesterol).

Quit Smoking and Abstain from Alcohol

Good advice whether you have diabetes or not. Your body needs to be in tip-top shape for a healthy pregnancy.

COMPLICATIONS AND CONCEPTION: 7 GOOD REASONS TO CONTROL BLOOD SUGAR DURING PREGNANCY

Women with poorly controlled diabetes, and their infants, have an increased

THE PILL TO TAKE AFTER YOU CONCEIVE

Diabetes is the leading cause of birth defects. Studies show that maintaining good glucose control reduces the risk, but a 2003 study in the journal *Pediatrics* suggests that another step may help. A large study of more than 6,000 babies by researchers at the Centers for Disease Control and Prevention found that women with diabetes were four times more likely than women without the disease to have infants with birth defects. But that increased risk was limited to women who did *not* take a daily multivitamin. Meanwhile, diabetes patients who took multivitamins before and after getting pregnant had no increased risk for bearing children with birth defects. It's possible that multivitamin users have other good health habits that protected their developing babies. But popping a multivitamin every day has no downside and may offer some protection against potentially devastating harm to a fetus.

risk for the following conditions during pregnancy and childbirth:

Birth defects. Women who have high glucose levels during the first six to eight weeks of pregnancy are most likely to bear children with birth defects. During that time, a baby's major organs are forming. High glucose levels can interfere with healthy development and damage the fetus's heart and spinal cord, as well as bones, kidneys, and gastrointestinal system. One study found that women who failed to attain good glucose control before getting pregnant were ten times more likely to bear a child with a birth defect.

Jaundice. For some reason, babies born to women with diabetes sometimes have this yellow discoloration of the skin and eyes. Jaundice occurs when the blood contains too much bilirubin, a by-product made when red blood cells break down. Although jaundice is usually harmless and fades after a few days, a physician must monitor the condition.

Macrosomia. This condition is also known as gigantism and large-for-gestational-age infant, but you can just think of it as Really Big Baby Syndrome. Plainly stated, women with poorly controlled glucose during pregnancy often give birth to immense infants. How big?

By one definition, a baby is considered abnormally large if it weighs more than 9 or 10 pounds or tips the scales at a weight higher than 90 percent of other newborns. Apart from the fact that a large newborn can't squeeze into the darling little outfit you knitted for him (and boys are more likely to be plus size than girls), what's the big deal? Plenty.

- The risk of stillbirth (death of a fetus in the late stages of pregnancy) increases dramatically when an infant is very heavy (10 to 12 pounds). The risk is even higher in mothers with uncontrolled diabetes.
- Fat infants often grow up to be fat adults, with an increased risk for type 2 diabetes. (Interestingly, children with low birth weight appear to have a high risk for developing diabetes, too.)
- During delivery, big babies have a heightened risk for a scary situation called shoulder dystocia, in which the infant's head emerges but the shoulders get stuck. Shoulder dystocia can result in serious harm to both the infant and mother.
- Women who have large infants are twice as likely to require cesarean delivery; they also experience more birth canal injuries.
- Moms are also more likely to experience hemorrhaging and need a blood transfusion.

- Lugging around a heavyweight fetus can make the last months of pregnancy a backbreaking experience.

Preeclampsia. About eight percent of all expectant mothers develop high blood pressure, edema (fluid retention), and elevated levels of protein in the urine sometime after the 20th week of pregnancy. Having diabetes is one of several factors that seems to increase the risk for preeclampsia, though its exact cause is not known. Symptoms include

- swollen hands and face (especially upon rising)
- weight gain
- headaches
- low output of urine
- nausea, vomiting, and abdominal pain
- visual disturbances, such as bright flashes in the eyes

A doctor confirms a diagnosis of preeclampsia with blood, urine, and liver tests. The only known cure for the condition is for the expectant mother to deliver the baby. In serious cases, labor may be induced. Hospitalization is usually necessary.

Polyhydramnios. A fancy way of saying excess amniotic fluid around the baby, which can lead to several complications, including preterm delivery (see page 274).

Postnatal hypoglycemia. A fetus receives oxygen from the mother's blood, which passes through the placenta, an organ attached to the lining of the uterus. Nutrients, including glucose, pass through the placenta, too. If a mother's blood sugar is high, the fetus' will be, too. That explains why babies born to women with high glucose get so fat. But it also means that the developing infant's pancreas will produce lots of insulin to process all that sugar. If the baby's pancreas fails to slow down insulin

TROUBLESHOOTING CHECKLIST

If you have gestational diabetes or if you have preexisting diabetes, review the symptoms of hypo- and hyperglycemia in Chapter 5. However, you should also be on alert for preeclampsia, which causes dangerously high blood pressure. Although preeclampsia is sometimes called a "silent" threat, it may tip its hand with certain symptoms, including

- ☐ swollen hands and face (especially upon rising)
- ☐ weight gain
- ☐ headaches
- ☐ low output of urine
- ☐ nausea, vomiting, and abdominal pain
- ☐ visual disturbances, such as bright flashes in the eyes

ROUTINE MAINTENANCE

Diabetes patients must tend to an extraordinary amount of their own medical care, and becoming pregnant increases your patient caseload. That makes the following routine steps even more important:

- Make all scheduled office visits and check in regularly with your diabetes health care team.
- Eat a balanced, nutritious diet.
- Get some exercise every day.
- Check your blood glucose levels frequently.
- Take all prescribed medicine.
- Be vigilant about hypo- and hyperglycemia. Know the symptoms and how to respond.

production after birth, hypoglycemia is a risk.

Preterm delivery. Some complications from elevated glucose during pregnancy can induce early delivery. Premature babies have a higher risk for breathing and heart problems, brain hemorrhages, gastrointestinal difficulties, and poor vision.

COPING WITH DIABETES DURING PREGNANCY

The following measures can help safeguard your health—that means both of you—from conception to delivery.

Eat Right

Meet with a dietitian as part of your preconception planning if possible. Eating a balanced, nutritious diet is an essential part of maintaining good glucose control—for you and your baby.

Exercise

Some pregnant women run marathons. You don't have to be quite so ambi-

tious, but keeping up an active lifestyle will help control glucose. Get started before you become pregnant, even if it's just a brisk walk every day.

Monitor

Keeping your blood sugar in the healthy range is a challenge when you're pregnant, so keep your glucose meter handy. You may want to check your glucose up to eight times a day. Some emotional symptoms of hypoglycemia mimic mood swings that occur naturally during pregnancy or after giving birth. To be safe, check your blood sugar when you're feeling cranky or down.

Take Your Medicine

If your doctor has prescribed insulin during your pregnancy, take all doses as needed, based on your meal schedule and glucose readings.

Watch Out for the Low-Down

The cost of striving for tight glucose control can be occasional bouts of hypoglycemia. Keep carb snacks or glucose tablets close by. Make sure your family and friends know the symptoms of severe hypoglycemia and what to do if you develop them.

Customer Support

Got a question we didn't answer? The following sources can help. (Fair warning: Web sites, and Web site addresses, may come and go. If the URLs listed here don't work, you can try locating these organizations online with a search engine.)

General Information About Diabetes

The American Diabetes Association

WEB SITE: www.diabetes.org
E-MAIL: Ask ADA@diabetes.org
TELEPHONE: (800) DIABETES (342-2383)
MAILING ADDRESS: ATTN: National Call Center
1701 North Beauregard Street
Alexandria, VA 22311

The ADA's massive Web site offers basic facts about diabetes and information about all aspects of living with it, from legal matters to what to eat for dinner. There's a valuable resource guide, which is updated annually, to help you shop for equipment. For a diabetes-related question or to request an information packet, use the e-mail address above.

The Centers for Disease Control and Prevention

WEB SITE: www.cdc.gov/diabetes
E-MAIL: cdcinfo@cdc.gov
TELEPHONE: (800) CDC-INFO (232-4636)
MAILING ADDRESS: 1600 Clifton Road
Atlanta, GA 30333

Another good source for general information about diabetes, this site features a special section for kids and is also available in Spanish.

Joslin Diabetes Center

WEB SITE: www.joslin.org
TELEPHONE: (800) JOSLIN-1 (567-5461)
MAILING ADDRESS: One Joslin Place
Boston, MA 02215

This hospital has spun off clinics all across the United States. You'll find a list of them, with lots of other diabetes information, on the Web site.

National Diabetes Information Clearinghouse

WEB SITE: www.diabetes.niddk.nih.gov
E-MAIL: ndic@info.niddk.nih.gov
TELEPHONE: (800) 860-8747
MAILING ADDRESS: 1 Information Way
Bethesda, MD 20892–3560

Run by the National Institute of Diabetes & Digestive & Kidney Diseases, this site offers a wealth of educational materials about diabetes. You can order information by mail, too.

MedlinePlus

WEB SITE: http://medlineplus.gov

A joint venture of the National Library of Medicine and the National Institutes of Health, this site is a great source of general health information. However, if you plug "diabetes" into the site's search engine, you'll find news about research, basic information, and lots of links to other Web sites.

David Mendosa's Diabetes Directory

WEB SITE: www.mendosa.com/diabetes

David Mendosa is a guy with diabetes who seems to have made it his mission to know everything about the disease—and to share it. There are loads of valuable links and more here.

Diabetes Monitor

WEB SITE: www.diabetesmonitor.com

This Web site is operated by a doctor and nurse who want to help educate people with diabetes.

Children

Juvenile Diabetes Research Foundation

WEB SITE: www.jdrf.org
E-MAIL: info@jdrf.org
TELEPHONE: (800) 533-CURE (2873)
MAILING ADDRESS: 120 Wall Street
New York, NY 10005-4001

Look here for research on type 1 diabetes.

Children with Diabetes

WEB SITE: www.childrenwithdiabetes.com

Billing itself as "the online community for kids, families, and adults with diabetes," this Web site offers one-stop browsing for anyone looking for information about caring for a child with the disease.

Research

The Diabetes Action Research and Education Foundation

WEB SITE: www.diabetesaction.org
E-MAIL: info@diabetesaction.org
TELEPHONE: (202) 333-4520
MAILING ADDRESS: Diabetes Action Research and
Education Foundation
426 "C" Street, NE
Washington, DC 20002

This group funds research on diabetes treatment and prevention, including alternative and nutritional therapies. The Web site's coolest feature: The "Ask the Diabetes Educator" page.

Type 1 Diabetes TrialNet

WEB SITE: www.diabetestrialnet.org
TELEPHONE: (800) HALT-DM1 (425-8361)

Scientists at 18 diabetes research centers have formed this network to learn more about how to prevent and treat type 1 diabetes. The network is studying people with type 1 diabetes, as well as their family members; volunteers are needed.

Complications

The following Web sites are good starting points for getting more information about many of the complications diabetes may cause.

American Amputee Foundation

WEB SITE: www.americanamputee.org

National Amputation Foundation

WEB SITE: www.nationalamputation.org

American Foundation for the Blind

WEB SITE: www.afb.org

National Kidney Foundation

WEB SITE: www.kidney.org

International Foundation for Functional Gastrointestinal Disorders

WEB SITE: www.iffgd.org

American Heart Association

WEB SITE: www.americanheart.org

American Psychological Association

WEB SITE: www.apa.org

American Urological Association Foundation

WEB SITE: www.urologyhealth.org

American Podiatric Medical Association

WEB SITE: www.apma.org

Diabetes Educators
American Association of Diabetes Educators

WEB SITE: www.aadenet.org/
E-MAIL: aade@aadenet.org
TELEPHONE: (800) 338-3633
MAILING ADDRESS: 100 W. Monroe
Suite 400
Chicago, IL 60603

The AADE Web site features a "Find an Educator" search tool.

Exercise
Diabetes Exercise and Sports Association

WEB SITE: www.diabetes-exercise.org

DESA promotes the importance of physical fitness for people with diabetes. Their Web site has information about exercise and nutrition, as well as a forum for members to swap ideas.

Magazines and Journals
Diabetes Forecast
Published by the American Diabetes Association

WEB SITE: www.diabetes.org/diabetes-forecast.jsp
TELEPHONE: (800) 806-7801

This monthly magazine features the latest news about diabetes research, inspirational stories, exercise tips, recipes, and more.

Diabetes Care
Published by the American Diabetes Association

WEB SITE: http://care.diabetesjournals.org

This is the journal your doctor reads—or should read. Look for it in the library at your local hospital. (The online version charges a fee if you want to view recently published articles.)

Diabetic Gourmet Magazine

WEB SITE: www.diabeticgourmet.com

A site that will allow you to explore your inner gourmand. It features a large archive of recipes, cookbook reviews, and lots of other tasty stuff.

Diabetic Cooking
Bimonthly magazine that addresses food management and diet for diabetes control. Each issue has about 50 recipes plus health tips, info specifically for insulin users, and a recipe make-over. Its Web site, www.diabeticcooking.com/index.html, features a searchable database of recipes. You can search by food type, ethnic cuisine, main ingredient, or recipe classification (i.e. casseroles).

Nutrition
American Dietetic Association

WEB SITE: www.eatright.org
E-MAIL: knowledge@eatright.org
TELEPHONE: (800) 877-1600
MAILING ADDRESS: 120 South Riverside Plaza
Suite 2000
Chicago, IL 60606–6995

The "other" ADA is the organization that, among other things, certifies registered dietitians. Its Web site can help you find an R.D. who specializes in diabetes nutrition.

277

Maintenance Schedule

SERVICE	EVERY OFFICE VISIT	EVERY SIX MONTHS	ANNUALLY	DATES OF SERVICE						COMMENT
Blood Pressure	✔									
Cholesterol and Other Blood Fats			✔							
A1c Test		✔								Also required before and after starting a new medication.
Microalbumin Test			✔							
Foot Exam	✔		✔							Frequent exams if you have neuropathy or other risky conditions. Thorough exam at least once a year, including monofilament test.
Eye Exam			✔							Should include pupil dilation.
General Screening for Diabetic Neuropathy			✔							
Psychological Issues	✔									Discuss stress and other problems as necessary.

Index